The New
AMERICAN IMPERIALISM

The New
AMERICAN IMPERIALISM

Bush's War on Terror and Blood for Oil

Vassilis K. Fouskas and Bülent Gökay

Foreword by Peter Gowan

PRAEGER SECURITY INTERNATIONAL
Westport, Connecticut • London

Library of Congress Cataloging-in-Publication Data

Fouskas, Vassilis.
  The new American imperialism : Bush's war on terror and blood for oil /
Vassilis K. Fouskas and Bülent Gökay ; foreword by Peter Gowan.
    p. cm.
  Includes bibliographical references and index.
  ISBN 0–275–98476–1 (alk. paper)
    1. United States—Foreign relations—2001– 2. United States—Foreign
economic relations. 3. United States—Military policy. 4. War on
Terrorism, 2001– 5. Imperialism. I. Gökay, Bülent. II. Title.
JZ1480.F68 2005
327.73'009'0511—dc22   2005017487

British Library Cataloguing in Publication Data is available.

Library of Congress Catalog Card Number: 2005017487
ISBN: 0–275–98476–1

First published in 2005

Praeger Security International, 88 Post Road West, Westport, CT 06881
An imprint of Greenwood Publishing Group, Inc.
www.praeger.com

Printed in the United States of America

The paper used in this book complies with the
Permanent Paper Standard issued by the National
Information Standards Organization (Z39.48–1984).

10 9 8 7 6 5 4 3 2 1

To our daughters, Ada, Leyla, and Helen

Contents

Foreword

The Bush administration's strategic turn after 9/11 has produced a profound intellectual and ethical shock for liberal opinion—the American state's main popular constituency—throughout the world. The enormous and wildly exaggerated liberal hopes of the 1990s that somehow the collapse of the Soviet bloc would produce an end to power politics lie in intellectual ruin. All over the world, one question dominates serious discussion of international relations, a question that would have seemed unthinkable to most commentators five years ago: the nature and dynamics of the new American imperialism.

As Vassilis Fouskas and Bulent Gokay note, American expansionism during the twentieth century has had a qualitatively different character than that of the earlier European empires: it has always been a project for global dominance, not just in the sense of making America the dominant world power but in the much more ambitious sense of reconstructing the world to produce an American global order, one in which states as social systems are brought into harmony with or at least made compatible with the structural characteristics of American capitalism as a social system. This extraordinarily ambitious impulse is masked by an effort on the part of American leaders to equate American capitalist imperatives for the world with those of capitalism in general, an equation belied by the obvious fact that capitalism as a social system can take an extraordinary variety of political and economic forms, as the history of the twentieth century has illustrated.

This central impulse in American imperialism then generates a paradoxical secret: that the most serious threat to American global ascendancy lies in the capacity of other centers to generate alternative ways of organizing international capitalism, ways that could fatally undermine America's capacity to manage and lead the global political and economic order. Such other centers have been America's allies in the capitalist core, the advanced capitalist countries at each end of Eurasia. The failure of these centers to organize the world in the middle of the twentieth century produced American ascendancy after 1945. Washington then turned these centers into protectorates through a militarized confrontation with the Soviet bloc. But the collapse of that bloc at the start of the 1990s presented Washington with the challenge of reconfiguring relations with the other main centers in ways that can rebuild an American-centered capitalist world order. This is an enormous challenge.

The challenge is recognized in the strategic documents of the American state since 1991, most notably in the famous Defense Policy Guidelines leaked in 1992, which spells out the governing priority for the United States to rebuild its mechanisms of control over the main centers of Eurasian capitalism. While American neoconservatives seek to persuade us that this challenge is easily accomplished because of America's overwhelming military dominance in sea, air, and space, the task is a good deal more complicated than that. Military capacity is a necessary condition for American global ascendancy. But it is far from sufficient to produce a positive capitalist international order that works: one that can reproduce itself in a viable and expansive way.

Vassilis Fouskas and Bülent Gökay explore central features of the American project since the mid-twentieth century and draw out both many of the central instruments and mechanisms of the expansionist drive and many of the problems and contradictions that beset it today. Two particularly important dimensions of their study are notable. First, they emphasize the distinctive political and institutional forms of American ascendancy over the capitalist world—notably the hub-and-spoke arrangement in the political-military field. Second, they explore the neuralgic political-economic issues—in the monetary and financial as well as industrial fields—that lurk beneath the smooth skin of American military-strategic capacities.

Their book is also notable for tackling another central, neuralgic issue: the relationship between Washington and Israel. As they shrewdly point out, this link, really cemented in the 1960s, in many ways contradicted the Achesonian principles of American grand strategy. It has become in many ways a great albatross around the neck of those attempting to craft a viable American grand strategy in the post–Cold War era. The relationship is thus a fascinating case study of what Charles Kupchan calls "the vulnerability of Empire."[1]

Unconditional American support for Israel became part of American strategic culture during the Cold War at a time of Soviet-American rivalry in the Middle East along with the American struggle to block the emergency of powerful, autonomous states in the Arab world. There followed a whole series of accretions strengthening the relationship. A central image in American strategic culture is that of America (rather than the Soviet Union) liberating Europe from Nazism—an image underpinning the equation, American military power projection equals freedom and democracy for the targets of American power. Israeli leaders could tap into that image to legitimate their Zionist project in Palestine. The issue of the right of Soviet Jews to emigrate to Israel became another potent link between Tel Aviv and Washington in the Cold War. The militarism-for-democracy theme in American foreign policy also played to Israeli strengths with the claim that Israel was the only democracy in the Middle East. And the persistence of the Israeli-Palestinian and Israeli-Arab conflicts both diverted attention from America's crucial relationship with the oil sheikhdoms and gave Washington a posture as a broker in endless, American-sponsored "peace processes."

Nevertheless, the costs of the U.S.-Israeli alliance for American grand strategy have tended to rise substantially, particularly since the end of the Cold War. These costs are most obvious in the Arab and Islamic worlds, but not only there. The political isolation of Washington on the issue of Israel is truly global. The typical vote at the UN general assembly on the Israel-Palestine issue is four against the rest of the world, the four being the Solomon Islands, Micronesia, Israel, and the United States. The source of this is the nature of the Zionist project as a settler colonization movement. Such settler colonization was, of course, fully acceptable in the Atlantic world in the eighteenth and nineteenth centuries, but it flatly contradicts core international ethical principles of the second half of the twentieth century. In endorsing this Zionist dimension of Israel, Washington has been prepared to flout both the UN Charter and UN resolutions and its own nuclear nonproliferation regimes.

The strategic costs of this continuing U.S. commitment to Israel in the 1990s included the erosion of the U.S. political base in the Arab and Islamic worlds. But the 9/11 challenge had the effect of recommitting the United States to Israel in an even stronger form than before, embedding the Israeli alliance in American strategic culture more deeply than ever—not only by turning the concept of terrorism essentially into a label for Palestinian resistance movements and for pro-Palestinian regimes and movements in the Arab and Islamic worlds, but also through encouraging within the United States the idea that America and Israel are in some sense twins: settler immigration states with religious ideologies in an embattled relationship with the world, facing hostility not only from Arabs and Muslims but also from Europeans and just about everyone else.

Here, then, is a classic case of the mechanisms of imperial vulnerability: To combat threats to the U.S. position in the Middle East and to justify its push for global dominance, Washington's policy elites promoted a new twist to American strategic culture that endorsed the Sharon-Likud variety of Zionism at its center. The result has been, as both Brent Scowcroft and Zbigniew Brzezinski have put it, that Sharon has had the Bush administration around his little finger. The question now is whether strategic pragmatism can enable the Bush administration and future American leaders to break free from this kind of commitment in order to extricate American military resources from the region and rehabilitate and refocus them elsewhere, or whether the post-9/11 strategic culture traps the Bush administration and the American state in political conflicts, while the main strategic challengers they face, in Europe and East Asia, reconfigure their regional arrangements in ways that structurally weaken American hegemony.

In these circumstances, it is little wonder that the American-Israeli relationship has become such an extraordinarily sensitive issue in American politics. Indeed, it is now more or less taboo for people even to discuss the Zionist dimension of Israel. One of the many merits of this book by Vassilis Fouskas and Bülent Gökay is that they explore it openly and frankly.

NOTE

1. Charles A. Kupchan, *The Vulnerability of Empire* (Ithaca, NY: Cornell University Press, 1994).

Peter Gowan
Professor of International Relations at
London Metropolitan University, London,
and Editor of New Left Review

Acknowledgments

The authors gratefully acknowledge the help of friends and colleagues who directly or indirectly contributed to the completion of this volume. These include Peter Gowan for writing the foreword; Leo Panitch, Cornell West, Donald Sassoon, and Molly Greene, who read all or part of the manuscript in its final stage and provided valuable advice and encouragement. We are particularly grateful to Darrell Whitman, who very kindly read the manuscript and made many useful suggestions. The final text was measurably improved by Karen Fisher's copyediting. We also wish to thank our editor at Praeger, Hilary Claggett, for her encouragement, patience, and guidance. Notwithstanding all the help received as mentioned above, the opinions expressed, and any mistakes or misinterpretations, are the sole responsibility of the authors.

Introduction

The *Merriam-Webster Online Dictionary* defines imperialism as "the policy, practice, or advocacy of extending the power and dominion of a nation especially by direct territorial acquisitions or by gaining indirect control over the political or economic life of other areas; *broadly:* the extension or imposition of power, authority, or influence." The *Cambridge Dictionary* defines the term as "when one country has a lot of power or influence over others, especially in political and economic matters." The *American Heritage Dictionary* describes imperialism as "the policy of extending a nation's authority by territorial acquisition or by the establishment of economic and political hegemony over other nations." The *MSN Encarta Dictionary* provides a similar definition: "the political, military, or economic domination of one country over another." Imperialism then can be summarized as the intention of one nation to militarily and economically conquer another.

Imperialism has often clothed itself in noble rhetorical garb, claiming to pursue its hegemony for the good of the nation or even the good of humanity. This was the credo behind the nineteenth-century British Empire, represented in Rudyard Kipling's 1899 poem "The White Man's Burden." As Kipling opined, it was "the duty of the white man...to conquer and control, probably for a couple of centuries, all the dark people of the world, not for his own good, but for theirs."[1] Of course, we now recognize that this is a racist and condescending perspective that attempted to justify the European domination of a less industrially developed people, which itself was an exercise in privileging particular cultural values. Thus, non-European cultures became childlike or demonic, which obligated their domination by Europeans. In fact, for most of the nineteenth century, from 1815 and the Congress of Vienna to the beginning of World War I in 1914, the imperial system ruled the world. The British Empire controlled a quarter of humanity; the Austro-Hungarian Empire ruled in Central Europe; the Ottoman Empire controlled the Middle East, North Africa, and the Balkans; the French and Belgian empires were penetrating deep into Africa; and the Japanese were extending their imperial reach in East and Southeast Asia.

Because these imperial states exercised control through fear and violence, imperialism itself became associated with several other "isms," including militarism, unilateralism, and interventionism, and with images of invasion, domination, exploitation, and war. In that time, this was the nature of imperial control, and because these empires founded their legitimacy on guns and military strength, they could not allow other states to infringe on the territories that they controlled. Thus, they had to launch wars of aggression to defend their imperial system and their supremacy. They could maintain order and stability for relatively long periods, as the experience of the nineteenth century reveals. However, as circumstances changed, the colonial powers were ultimately to engage in large destructive wars that pitted one empire against another. World War I was such a war, pitting the Austro-Hungarian Empire and the Ottoman Empire against the British and French empires. Following the conclusion of the war, the British and French, along with their new ally, the Americans, determined how the spoils from the defeated empires would be divided. However, the tsarist empire of Russia, which sided with the French and the British, was barred from this postwar realignment because the Bolshevik Revolution of 1917 had removed it from the old imperial contracting system.

U.S. global cultural, economic, and political influence since 1945 is often discussed in terms of neo-imperialism, which implies a less overt but equally pervasive and destructive form of domination of formerly colonized spaces. This can be seen in the way the United States worked to maximize the advantage it gained and the power it assumed between 1943 and 1945 from its victory over Germany and Japan, and as a consequence of mounting Soviet casualties and British debt. The shape that U.S. influence assumed was one that would make the world safe for capitalist development, which required, on one hand, containing the USSR and halting the spread of revolution beyond its borders, and, on the other hand, ensuring uncontested American supremacy within the Western capitalist world. During the Cold War years there was little or no tension between these fundamental objectives. However, with the end of the Soviet Union in 1991, the knot tying the basic objectives of U.S. global strategy together began to come unraveled. Once the Communist danger was off the table, American preeminence ceased to be an automatic requirement of the global capitalist system.

Since September 20, 2002, the U.S. government has abandoned its former multilateral approach to global governance and officially adopted an imperial posture known as the so-called Bush doctrine, which is based on militarist and imperial values with theocratic overtones. This current agenda looks much like what some analysts see in U.S. foreign policy at the end of the nineteenth century and the beginning of the twentieth, when the United States actively sought to dominate the entire Caribbean basin, Central America, and even the western Pacific. Six months after it was announced, the new American imperialism was applied as a justification for an unprovoked war against Iraq by the neoconservative administration of the U.S. government. Toppling Saddam Hussein's regime without the support of the United Nations and in the face of strong opposition from traditional U.S. allies was a clear presentation of a unilateralist American foreign policy. The "regime change" in Baghdad, however, was only an opening salvo in a much broader neoconservative agenda that seeks to reshape American hegemonic practices according to old imperial doctrines, but with new postcolonial political and military tools.

The main proponents of this new U.S. imperialism are a relatively small group of well-connected neoconservative ideologues, who in 1997 launched the policy under the title Project for the New American Century. Their primary objective is to use the surplus American military power that remained after the breakup of the Soviet Union to impose a worldwide "Pax Americana" that, in turn, would promote the political and economic interests of the United States and its allies, such as Israel, worldwide.

"Messianic" imperial control of the world by the United States has been implicit in U.S. foreign policy since at least 1945. In fact, as we shall see, the methods for U.S. domination of the world were laid out in the late 1940s. But they have found an opportunity to express themselves explicitly only in the atmosphere of the post–Cold War world. The tragedy of September 11, 2001, gave the Bush administration an opening to assemble the required authority and public support to subdue the "evil dictators" of the world. Following 9/11, the Bush administration confined its decision-making and intelligence assessments with respect to Iraq to a small group of like-minded individuals who were organized into the Office of Special Plans. Even without a clear threat, the Bush administration claimed the right to use preemptive or preventive military force. In a 2002 graduation address to the U.S. Military Academy at West Point, President Bush succinctly stated his argument for "a military that must be ready to strike at a moment's notice in any dark corner of the world. And our security will require all Americans to be forward-looking and resolute, to be ready for pre-emptive action when necessary to defend our liberty and to defend our lives. . . . All nations that decide for aggression and terror will pay a price."[2] The administration now defends this new doctrine of preemptive military action as a necessary adjustment to more uncertain and shifting threats. However, it is a short-sighted policy that promotes action without evidence, which can easily become hostage to hunches and inferences, leaving the world without clear-cut norms for justifying the use of force.

Today's neoconservative agenda seeks what the U.S. ruling class has always desired, which is to impose a U.S. vision of the "free market and democracy" on the entire world, and in so doing secure economic resources and global markets under the control of U.S. authority. It is an agenda that can be themed as the "new American imperialism" in the era of the New American Century. But it is an agenda that requires the constant threat or use of force, and the holy warrior of this Pax Americana is a post–Cold War Dr. Strangelove—a violent warrior who was convinced that the only good adversary is a dead one, without any interest in why the adversary became an adversary in the first place.[3]

The New American Century and new U.S. imperialism are a consequence of changes in the internal dynamics of the global economic system. The U.S. political and economic elites face declining U.S. power in this emerging system and confront a declining ability to continue as the world's economic hegemon. This book is an attempt to describe the origins and dynamics of the new U.S. imperialism, and it concentrates on

U.S. political, economic, military, and ideological motives, actions, and their consequences in the post–Cold War world. It further explores the heart of the Pax Americana, or, as it is commonly described, the New American Century, and tries to explain why raw military power has become the only vehicle through which the United States can continue to maintain its privileged world position.

Our first contention is that the attacks of 9/11 provided an opportunity for the United States to expand and increase its military and economic grip on the resources of Eurasia, and that this reaction to 9/11 is the product of a general decline of U.S. economic power in the world's political system. The events of September 11 did not cause the United States to initiate this new drive for power, because the erosion of U.S. economic power was well under way before the attack. If history contained no September 11 and the terrible events of that day had not happened, it is very likely that the United States would have gone to war in Afghanistan and Iraq anyway.

Our second contention comes from an understanding of the special geostrategic significance of central Eurasia. It is a region that occupies a strategic position in the general geopolitical landscape, particularly in its concentrations of oil and natural gas reserves. Geographically, this region sits astride extremely important transit routes between southern Asia, central Asia, the Middle East, and Europe. In considering this geostrategic position, we set out the economic and political significance of the international competition for the oil and natural gas reserves of the Caspian basin. Our purpose here is to sketch a general outline of the past, present, and post–Cold War stages of this global geopolitical struggle.

Many view the neoconservative clique as a conspiracy. We, however, believe they are merely part of a larger equation of global economic and political conditions. This view is rooted in an understanding that vested interests representing the energy, electronics, weapons, and influential segments of the media and communications industries are always entrenched in key sectors of government. These interests are concerned with maintaining their privileged position, and key elements of the U.S. economic and political elite are now responding directly to changes in global conditions that have arisen since the end of the Cold War. This is not a conspiracy; it is only business as usual. Many if not most of its key members have been active since the era of Richard Nixon and the

Vietnam War, and their shared views were formed during the early decades of the Cold War, which was a deeply anti-Communist and essentially pro-Zionist time. Some were involved in open hostility directed at the Soviet bloc during the Reagan years and have merely continued as the most aggressive but, at the same time, most openly "pragmatic" voices in the U.S. leadership.

Some of the key questions we try to answer are as follows: What is U.S. neo-imperialism, and what are the objectives of the so-called neo-imperial agenda? Most important, do these objectives represent a radical departure from previous U.S. imperial strategy and, if so, how and why? Is this neo-imperialist rule attributed only to the Bush administration's particular and peculiar behavior?

These questions have no simple answers because they are intimately connected to changes that have taken place since the end of the Cold War in 1989–91, but it may be possible to say that the collapse of the Soviet bloc unleashed the newest phase in the so-called New American Century. As a direct consequence of the end of this balance-of-power construction of world politics, the dynamics of U.S. global hegemony lost their systemic logic, and constraints imposed on the world system by the Cold War collapsed. Before the end of the Cold War, U.S. imperial control was essentially a global process, and its particular strategies were instrumental to its global concerns. In this period, U.S. global hegemony relied on a shared global framework vis-à-vis the whole logic, structure, discourses, and practice of the U.S. system of control, encompassing its socioeconomic, political, ideological, and military aspects. When the war ended, so did the logic of this construction.

In the following chapters, we intend to provide a globalist approach to understanding U.S. power exercised worldwide at the start of the new millennium. The central concern is to untangle the global structure and in particular the world economic system through which the United States has been exercising control within the fast-changing environment of the post–Cold War world. The chapters that follow provide a framework for understanding this system and investigating the forces driving the new American imperialism. The main text is divided into two parts. Part I provides an overall picture of the system through an analysis of the economic, political, military, and ideological dimensions of U.S. power. Part II provides a selected number of case studies through which our main assumptions and central analysis are put to the test.

NOTES

1. Rudyard Kipling, "The White Man's Burden." First published in the United States in *McClure's Magazine* 12 (February 1899). Available at http://www .boondocksnet.com/ai/kipling/kipling.html.

2. "President Bush Delivers Graduation Speech at West Point," press release, June 1, 2002, http://www.whitehouse.gov/news/releases/2002/06/20020601-3.html.

3. The movie *Dr. Strangelove* begins during the height of the Cold War. A crazed American base commander, General Ripper, decides that Communism has to be stopped at all costs and orders nuclear bombers into the air. *Dr. Strangelove* is a World War III parody that illustrates how war protocols can go wrong and how even the best of intentions can lead to the most disastrous of results.

PART I

NEO-IMPERIAL STRATEGIES: ILLUSIONS OF POWER

CHAPTER 1

Money, Oil, and Power

GHOST DANCE: ILLUSIONS OF POWER

In early October 1890, representatives of several Native American nations gathered in the dust of Walker Lake in western Nevada. They had come to hear the words of Wovoka, a Paiute "messiah" who claimed that he had a vision in which Native Americans had been given a victory over their tormentors, the white-skinned European masters. In the four hundred years following the European invasion of the Americas, more than 90 percent of their number had been lost to exotic diseases and the technologically superior weaponry that came from Europe. The scattered remnants of these once-proud people found their free-roaming life destroyed, the buffalo gone, and themselves confined to reservations dependent on Indian agents for their existence.[1] The great wheel of history was closing the American frontier at the end of the nineteenth history, thereby steadily erasing the memory of their traditional life. Wovoka's message that warm October day had a universal appeal that cut across tribal differences to reach their collective identity: The Christ had returned and would renew everything as it used to be, but only if they danced with the ghosts of their ancestors.[2] According to Wovoka's vision, the Native Americans should live in peace, work, not lie or steal, and dance a Ghost Dance that would hasten the return of the old world: The buffalo would again be plentiful and the Europeans would be swept away.[3]

As the news of the gathering at Walker Lake spread, Native Americans everywhere took up the Ghost Dance until it came to dominate tribal life in much of the western United States. But rather than a statement of present power, the Ghost Dance represented only a nostalgic appeal for Native Americans to separate themselves from the whites and their religious doctrines.[4] It took particular hold among the Sioux and Arapaho, who saw in it the possibility of restoring a lost past rather than securing a new future. By November, the spreading Ghost Dance had attracted the attention of the U.S. political and military elite who, sensing a threat to their control, launched a campaign to isolate or eliminate its leaders. In mid-November, troops arrived at the Pine Ridge reservation in the Dakota Territory to suppress an expected uprising, and more troops were dispatched to the northern plains in December to capture the leaders of the Ghost Dance. The battle of Wounded Knee that followed, which was more a slaughter than a battle, put an end to the Ghost Dance and killed its principal leaders, including the great Sioux Chief Sitting Bull. The end of the Ghost Dance closed a long and bloody chapter in the European conquest and foreclosed the Native American dream of returning to their past.

The historian Frederick Jackson Turner argued that the American frontier had closed not because the Ghost Dance had failed but because the modern state had triumphed over the wilderness by building railroads, constructing telegraph networks, and stringing barbed wire fences that split the land into neat divisions and assigned to it rights of ownership from which Native Americans were largely excluded.[5] Perhaps it is possible to say in this case that history triumphed over an illusion of power as represented in the Ghost Dance. Of course, history always triumphs over illusions, whether generated by religious incantation, academic hubris, or political claim: The Ghost Dance could not forestall or deflect events because larger forces of social and political change were calling a different tune. But for a brief time the Ghost Dance managed to obscure the realities that awaited the Native Americans who danced, providing a false sense of security against the gathering storm of military reaction. As an illusion of power, the Ghost Dance also deflected the Native Americans from any alternate course that might have offered a better end. But this too seems to have been ordained by a Native American history that dictated internal and external relationships that ultimately created the conditions for Wovoka's vision and its embrace.

The Ghost Dance of the Native Americans has had counterparts throughout history where symbols and rituals have been used to represent and reinforce a sense of power. It can be seen in Greek heroic sculpture and monumental architecture, in the iconography of the medieval Roman Catholic Church, and in the parades and mass propaganda of Nazi Germany. In modern times, it has appeared in the form of the Berlin Wall, in the arrogant claims of petty dictators, and in the press conferences of Western political leaders. What links them together is the hollowness of their claims when measured against actual surrounding conditions. Asserting a claim to power in itself has no power if circumstances make it plain that such power does not exist. If anything, the unmasking of a claim of power as an illusion contributes to a loss of persuasive power by those making the claim.

THE MAKING OF AN ECONOMIC SUPERPOWER

Throughout the twentieth century, the United States patiently built a world system of control, first in Latin America and the Philippines and then in Europe, Japan, Korea, and the Middle East. Its superior army, weapons systems, and intelligence networks have been an essential part of this system, but an equal if not more important role has been played by its control of the world economy. The principal weapon for this economic control has been the position of the U.S. dollar as the world's reserve currency, which gives it a special and powerful status in the world economy. As Susan Strange noted in her 1971 book *Sterling and British Policy*, a "top currency" becomes "the top favourite for international monetary transactions ... it is the choice of the world market. It derives, therefore, from the issuing state's position of economic leadership which inspires monetary confidence even among political opponents."[6]

Dollar hegemony thus has always been strategic to the future of American global dominance, in many respects more important than America's overwhelming military power. While military power is more visible and useful as a display, it is the dollar's role as a reserve currency that secures the domination of the United States in the global economic marketplace. This situation must be seen not merely as a matter of pure economics but as a linking of the dollar as "deeply rooted in the geopolitical role of the United States."[7] Understanding how the dollar works to secure U.S. hegemony requires some review of the historical circumstances that allowed it to become the world's reserve currency at the close of World War II.

The twin disasters of the Great Depression and the war forced a reconstruction of the world's economy that simultaneously gave new life to capitalism and placed the United States at the center of its own globalization project. The uneven evolution of the structure of this new system was predicated on continuing U.S. political and economic leadership. The war devastated large parts of the world, left much of Europe, Asia, and Africa in ruins, and effectively dismantled the prewar structures of the global economy. In particular, it shattered the economic and financial system in France, put Germany to the torch, and nearly bankrupted England. Japan too was substantially destroyed, and all of the Old World powers were in desperate need of reconstruction if the world economic system was to be restored. Amid this chaos, only the United States remained intact, and the war had radically increased its industrial base and made it a safe haven for much of the capital that had fled Europe. This situation created the preconditions for the United States to dictate how the new world order would be organized.

The U.S. political leadership recognized this opportunity well before the war was concluded. In 1944, it called to order the Bretton Woods Conference as the location where negotiations over this new order would take place. With little leverage to argue another case, the attendants agreed to several arrangements that effectively solidified U.S. control over the postwar economic world. This included pegging the value of gold at $35 per ounce, which at once ordered currency according to the U.S. dollar and established its value as the benchmark for global trade. This action had the twofold effect of creating a demand for the dollar as a reserve currency and placing the dollar at the center of a rapidly expanding system of trade and direct foreign investment.[8] The system was essentially the old prewar gold-exchange system, but with the U.S. dollar replacing the British pound as the key currency.[9] This allowed the United States to pyramid dollars on top of gold, while all other governments had to buy dollars and pyramid their currency on top of dollars, and put the dollar in control of the world trade system by directly or indirectly requiring the pricing of goods and services in dollars.

While the Bretton Woods system formalized the hegemony of the U.S. dollar, it did not cause this change: rather, circumstances of the war brought power to the U.S. dollar and the Bretton Woods system organized and institutionalized this power into a world system. This occurred as a consequence of a great inflow of gold into the United States before, during, and after the war,[10] and the residual strength of U.S. productivity as measured against that of its potential rivals. The first case left the United States holding the bulk of the gold supply, which was seen as the basis for currency value under the long-standing preference for an international gold standard. The second and more important case drew on the confidence that the United States could command from its position as the world's only surviving industrial giant. As U.S. industries formed dense host-country and cross-border networks of suppliers, financiers, and final markets, they built an ever-tighter network of international production. In this form, foreign direct investment pushed the internationalization of the American economy and the American state. Thereafter, U.S. national interests increasingly came to be defined as extending and reproducing the world economic system.

But this was not an entirely stable system, nor one that long remained within the control of U.S. political and economic elites. As the 1950s melted into the 1960s, cracks began to appear. The U.S. currency began to inflate in absolute terms, particularly in relation to the currencies of Europe and Japan. Gold flowed steadily out of Fort Knox and the United States, with gold stocks declining from over $20 billion in the early 1950s to $9 billion by the late 1960s. In the early 1960s, the Kennedy administration grew increasingly uneasy about the shifting international economic fortunes of the United States, and by the early 1970s the U.S. balance of trade went into the red and U.S. corporate profits began to shrink.[11] The dollar began to come under pressure from foreign banks that increasingly returned dollars in exchange for gold. Things got so bad that French President de Gaulle proudly announced that his country was returning dollars for gold at a rate that put the French treasury's gold stocks above those of Fort Knox. There were many structural and political reasons for this flight from the dollar, including massive deficits rung up by U.S. military spending for the war in Vietnam. But the decline itself represented a decline in confidence in the ability of the United States to continue to manage the world's economy under the Bretton Woods system.[12]

The international currency crisis reached its peak in mid-1971, when the U.S. balance of payments suddenly tripled, causing a huge jump in dollar holdings by foreign banks. On August 15, 1971, President Nixon went on television to announce that he was taking a series of economic measures in response. He told the world that the United States would no longer honor its agreement under the Bretton Woods system to exchange dollars for gold, and that in its place the United States was offering a system of "floating" exchange rates so that each country's currency would move up or down depending on international demand and, implicitly, on international confidence in any one country's economy.[13] In broad terms, Nixon's statement said that the United States would not honor its debt nor guarantee international currency stability, that Bretton Woods was dead, and that a quarter of a century of U.S. dollar hegemony appeared to be ending.

In the short run, the Nixon dollar doctrine corrected the U.S. balance of payments and trade deficit and restored the economic autonomy of the American state, but at the price of a collapse of share values on world equity markets and a dramatic increase in global inflation.[14] With this radical shift, the dollar became an irredeemable currency no longer defined or measured in terms of gold, which freed restraints on printing dollars. Yet the demise of the dollar as a reserve currency never materialized. Instead, the reserve role of the dollar actually increased for most of the following quarter century, further strengthening the U.S. hold on the world economy. How the United States managed this feat is also a story of crisis and reconstruction that increased the interdependency of the world's systems of trade, currency, and diplomacy.

PETRODOLLARS AND ECONOMIC HEGEMONY

The currency crisis of the early 1970s was accompanied by an international diplomatic and economic crisis in the Middle East. The headlines that defined it as an Arab-Israeli conflict masked its deeper significance in reshaping economic relationships through oil and a change in the posture of U.S. foreign policy. The crisis represented a test of the fledgling Organization of Petroleum Exporting Countries (OPEC), which was eventually resolved through an agreement that stripped OPEC of any political pretense and rendered it subservient to U.S. economic and political interests. With the United States no longer comfortably at the center of a stable international economic system, U.S. foreign relations began to shift from a classic liberal institutionalism to a more aggressive and competitive neoliberal assertion of interests. What is important to understand is that these shifts have deep roots in the way that the international economic system is organized and operates, and additional shifts have occurred and will occur as a consequence of historical factors unrelated to political will.

If gold was the standard for currency and economic integration for much of the nineteenth and twentieth centuries, it has now been replaced by oil. The ability to set the price of gold against a particular currency, as happened with the postwar dollar, has now been replaced with the ability to set the price of oil against a particular currency. But unlike gold, oil has the added power of being central to the industrial processes of modern economies: It relies not on a perception of value but on its actual instrumental value as an essential commodity. Thus, holding the power of setting oil's value against a currency means that transactions in oil will naturally gravitate toward that currency as the most stable indicator of its value. This logic is fully played out when oil contracts are required to be valued in a particular currency, whose strength is then reinforced by the demand for the currency created by the contracting parties.

In the early 1960s, OPEC was fashioned after the thinking of Argentinean economist Raul Prebisch, who chaired the UN Economic Commission for Latin America and argued that national sovereignty over resources was essential for successful development. In theory, OPEC was organized as a producers' bloc that could collectively bargain for the price of oil and thus enhance oil's value to the producing countries. In practice, several large oil-producing countries, including the Soviet Union and the United States, remained outside of OPEC and actively undermined its efforts to control oil pricing. The resulting free market in oil considerably depressed its actual value as an essential commodity. By the early 1970s, most of the oil producers in the Middle East had become members, and the eruption of the 1973 war between Egypt, Syria, and Israel provided an opportunity for these OPEC members to wield oil as an economic weapon against support for Israel outside the Middle East. An oil embargo ensued, which caused skyrocketing prices and set off a series of politically painful oil conservation efforts in the United States and Europe. Eventually, the oil embargo was relaxed and oil prices declined, but the fears that that the embargo provoked continued to fester among the oil-importing industrial countries.

Petrodollars were born as a result of an agreement between the United States and OPEC, which guaranteed OPEC's functional existence in exchange for the dollars that it collected through petroleum contracting. In June 1974, U.S. Secretary of State Henry Kissinger established the U.S.–Saudi Arabian Joint Commission on Economic Cooperation with the specific purpose of stabilizing oil supplies and prices. After a series of negotiations, principally with Saudi Arabia—OPEC's most powerful member—an agreement was concluded in 1975 that committed OPEC to pricing oil exclusively in dollars.[15] Thereafter, even when oil prices might increase, the additional revenue would be denominated in U.S. dollars, which all importing countries would be required to use for this purpose. This would create a dependable demand for U.S. currency regardless of other economic factors and would act as an interest-free loan to the United States when it was repatriated as investments in dollar securities, such as U.S. Treasury notes, U.S. stocks and mutual funds, and U.S. public and corporate bonds. The circle was neatly drawn, but, like Bretton Woods, it began to exhibit holes as petrodollars accumulated. From then onward, only market forces could determine the value of the dollar.[16]

The arrival of the petrodollar agreement also marked the beginning of a new phase in U.S. international relations marked by confrontation rather than negotiation. The U.S. Congress passed the Trade Act of 1974, which under Section 301 (later amended by the Trade Act of 1988) mandated that the U.S. trade representative take "appropriate action to obtain the removal of any policy or practice of a foreign government that violates a bilateral or multilateral trade agreement, or that is unreasonable, unjustifiable, or discriminatory . . . or burdens or restricts U.S. commerce." The act then authorized the president to retaliate against foreign countries that impose such burdens. These retaliations can take the form of suspending the benefits of trade concessions previously granted, or restrictions or fees on the trade of the offending nation.[17] The 1981 agreement with Japan limiting auto exports, the 1982 GATT (General Agreement on Tariffs and Trade) dispute with Europe in which the United States adopted a bilateral approach to trade, the 1984 Caribbean Basin Initiative, the 1985 bilateral trade pact with Israel, and the 1988 North American Free Trade Agreement (NAFTA) can all be seen as evidence of this post-1971 aggressive U.S. stance on economic relations.[18]

The U.S. shift away from multilateralism and liberal institutionalism in international economic affairs in the early 1970s took place through a

privatization of heretofore public economic policymaking, which deepened and accelerated globalization through the vastly increased role
of multinational corporations and banks. Banks like Citibank, Chase
Manhattan, and Barclays Bank, which had performed the role of central
banks in the old days of the gold standard, reassumed that role with
respect to the new global petrodollar economy but without the gold. The
400 percent rise in the price of petroleum in 1973, which abated only
partially by the mid-1970s, generated huge flows of petrodollars into
these banks, which then were charged with profitably recycling them,
in a process that Henry Kissinger dubbed "recycling petrodollars." The
problem had been discussed in 1971,[19] even before the Nixon doctrine
and the OPEC petrodollar agreement, but advance planning failed to
anticipate the flood of dollars that was produced. The strategy was to loan
these petrodollars to developing countries, but few of them could afford the
debt service, let alone the repayment, and a new economic crisis erupted
in the early 1980s around these debts that eventually reached even a
number of East European socialist regimes.[20]

By August 1982, the circle finally broke when Mexico declared that it
would likely not repay its petrodollar loans. The announcement had
followed a 1979 decision by U.S. Federal Reserve Chairman Paul Volcker
that the United States would unilaterally raise interest rates in an effort
to halt a continuing decline in the dollar. In the following three years,
U.S. interest rates soared to record heights. The dollar was saved, but it
left developing countries with crushing loads of debt at usurious rates of
interest. Fearing an economic domino effect from Mexico's announcement, U.S. and British banks demanded that the International Monetary
Fund (IMF) step in and act as a "debt policeman." Under IMF orders,
country after developing country was forced to slash public spending for
health, education, and welfare in order to meet the demands of debt
service for their petrodollar loans.[21]

AT THE END OF THE COLD WAR

The end of the Cold War and the emergence of a new single European
monetary system presented an entirely new challenge to the New American Century. As Eric Hobsbawm described it, the collapse of Soviet

power in world politics "destroyed the . . . system that had stabilized international relations for some forty years."[22] The dramatic and unprecedented events in Eastern Europe and the Soviet Union in 1989–91 radically transformed the geopolitical and geoeconomic contexts of world politics. The bipolar structure of world politics, with the United States at one end and the Soviet Union at the other, was replaced with an uncertain unipolar world, with only the United States remaining as an acknowledged superpower. The collapse of the Warsaw Pact left a zone of conflicting interests stretching from Germany in central Europe to China in East Asia. The United States found itself in a new world with unassailable dominance, but a world that had no clear boundaries or rules, and no counterpoints for the expressions of U.S. power.

The world that emerged is populated with major regional powers that are preeminent in their area, but none that can match the United States in the key dimensions of military, economic, and technological power, which are required to secure global political domination. This leaves the United States relatively free to deploy its quantitatively greater military power to influence the political and economic contexts of world politics and gives it political leverage over much of the globe's significant natural resources. This circumstance worries both U.S. allies and opponents, who must contend with U.S. power at their borders and in the areas that have traditionally been theirs to exploit.[23] It also has opened up the countries of Eastern Europe and the former Soviet Union to large multinational corporations that flood in to organize and control their natural resources and developing industries, thereby transforming the geoeconomic conditions for capital accumulation since 1991.

The collapse of Soviet control over the natural and human resources of this strategic region has resulted in the emergence of a high-stakes game of money and politics that includes such heavyweight contenders as the United States, Russia, and China, along with the biggest global corporations. Eurasia, that vast land between China and Germany, has emerged as the world's axial supercontinent, which now serves as the decisive geopolitical chessboard for political, military, and economic reasons. It accounts for 75 percent of the world's population, 60 percent of the world's gross national product (GNP), and 75 percent of the world's energy resources. Collectively, its power overshadows even that of the United States.[24] On the level of global economic relations, the lure of enormous oil reserves in the Caspian Sea basin has made the region the focus of fierce competition between multinational companies and the governments of the most powerful states. The geopolitics of the area thus are of serious concern.[25]

THE U.S. RESPONSE

The leading power in this competition is the United States, whose military spending is greater than all the military expenditures of the next thirteen countries combined. However, in the other important markers of power the United States is in decline: Its share of world trade and manufacturing is substantially less than it was just prior to the end of the Cold War, and its relative economic strength measured against the European Union and the East Asian economic group of Japan, China, and Southeast Asia is similarly in retreat. Thus, the persistent use of U.S. military power can be viewed as a reaction to its declining economic power and not merely as a response to the post–Cold War geopolitical picture.[26] As Andre Gunder Frank wrote in June 1999, "Washington sees its military might as a trump card that can be employed to prevail over all its rivals in the coming struggle for resources."[27]

The hegemonic position of the United States internationally rests on its ability to control the sources of and transport routes for crucial energy and other strategic material supplies needed by other leading industrial states. Thus, unimpeded access to affordable energy has always been a paramount strategic interest of the U.S. administration and, thus far, the United States has obtained a dominant position in the control of oil and gas resources in Eurasia. It has been able to do this because of its military positioning in the Middle East and its sea and air dominance in the eastern Mediterranean, the Atlantic, the Pacific, and the Indian Ocean, and it appears to be determined to safeguard this domination by assuming a permanent role in Eurasia. In the short term, this policy is represented by the U.S. description of a "volatile Eurasia" in which it has to act "to ensure that no state or combination of states gains the ability to expel the US or even diminish its decisive role."[28] However, in the longer term, U.S. policy seeks to control the energy resources of Eurasia by breaking Russia's monopoly over oil and gas transport routes, promoting U.S. energy security through diversified supplies, encouraging the construction of multiple pipelines through U.S.-controlled lands, and denying other potential powers dangerous leverage over the central Asian oil and natural gas resources.[29]

The events of 9/11 provided an opportunity to the U.S. administration to initiate strong policies to increase its grip on the region as well as to remind the world of America's capacity for political-military control. The terrorist attacks on 9/11 were not a real surprise, and indeed, 9/11 was similar to what seemed to be wild fantasies developed by American strategic analysts and military and intelligence planners that they needed to justify a new active military role in the post–Cold War world. During the 1990s, great efforts were spent imagining new worst-case scenarios stemming from new post-Soviet threats. U.S. security planners came up with all sorts of "evil" new possible threats, from chemical warfare to biological weapons, and from hijacked vehicles and truck bombs to cyberterrorism that would jam 911 services, shut down electricity or telecommunications, disrupt air traffic control, and so on.[30] It was even claimed that "a CyberTerrorist will attack the next generation of air traffic control systems and collide two large civilian aircraft. This is a realistic scenario, since the CyberTerrorist will also crack the aircraft's in-cockpit sensors."[31]

In these nightmare scenarios, particular importance was given to the idea of "rogue states" with "weapons of mass destruction" that would sponsor terrorism. To defend U.S. interests against all these new and mostly imaginary threats, new high-tech combat techniques were developed and deployed during the 1990s, but with an understanding that warfare must now be politically acceptable. With the ghost of Vietnam still alive, this meant that America's supremacy in bombs, planes, satellites, and tanks had to be used to limit U.S. casualties and that military performance would be based on the use of technology, either to directly attack an enemy or to support a proxy, such as the Kurdish groups in northern Iraq, the KLA in Kosovo, and the Northern Alliance in Afghanistan, to absorb the brunt of the conflict. The rapid victories—in the Persian Gulf War in 1991, in Kosovo in 1999, and in Afghanistan in 2001–2002—were all accomplished at a minimal cost of American lives.

The life-and-death struggle to monopolize energy resources lies at the heart of this strategy because oil remains the lifeblood of the modern world economy. Superpower status naturally requires control of oil at every stage—from its discovery to its pumping, refining, transporting, and marketing. A brief look at a map of so-called terrorist sanctuaries and enemy rogue states reveals it to be "a map of the world's principal energy resources,"[32] and a few days before September 11, 2001, the U.S. Energy Information Administration documented Afghanistan's strategic "geographical position as a potential transit route for oil and natural gas exports from Central Asia to the Arabian Sea," including the construction of pipelines through Afghanistan.[33]

Central to this concern about control of oil is the Caspian Sea basin, which the Washington-based American Petroleum Institute, voice of the major U.S. oil companies, called "the area of greatest resource potential outside of the Middle East."[34] Vice President Dick Cheney, speaking of the Caspian Sea basin in 1998 as a representative of the oil industry, noted, "I cannot think of a time when we have had a region emerge as suddenly to become as strategically significant as the Caspian."[35] This leaves three basic questions looming over the future of this important region: Who owns these rich oil and natural gas resources? Who will control their transportation to world markets? Who will provide for the security of this sensitive transportation? The answers to these questions will substantially reconfigure the world's economy in this century and the international order that governs it.

But more is at stake in this competition than the fate of the resources of the Caspian Sea basin: The fate of OPEC and the U.S. dollar as the world's reserve currency hangs in the balance. Caspian oil thus far is "non-OPEC oil," meaning that oil supplies from this region are less likely to be affected by OPEC price and supply policies.[36] This would allow the flow of large volumes of Caspian oil through non-OPEC lands to erode the power of OPEC to maintain high oil prices and to use oil as a mode of political blackmail.[37] U.S. strategists do not want only to obtain oil, which could be accomplished simply by purchasing it. They want to eliminate all potential competitors, safeguard the area politically and militarily, and control the flow of oil to the big world markets in the West and in Southeast Asia.[38]

Caspian Sea oil has been a major concern in internal and unpublicized documents generated since before the beginning of the Bush administration. Because the United States is the world's largest consumer of petroleum, and because its appetite is growing, it needs control over the oil fields of the Caucasus to avoid price shocks. U.S. consumers spend over $558 billion per year on energy, with purchases of petroleum-derived products including gasoline, diesel, heating oil, and jet fuel accounting for almost half of this total. Total U.S. energy consumption in 2000 was 98.5 quadrillion British thermal units (Btu), representing one-fourth of the world's energy use. While industry is the largest user of energy, with 38 percent of the total, the transportation, residential, and commercial sectors are also major consumers, respectively accounting for 27 percent, 19 percent, and 16 percent of energy consumption.[39] However, U.S. interest in controlling oil is not limited to its own consumption, but extends to denying this control to other important industrial powers, particularly the European Union, China, and Japan.[40]

THE EURO AS A WEAPON OF MASS DESTRUCTION

Since the United States emerged as the dominant global superpower at the end of World War II, U.S. hegemony has rested on three unchallengeable pillars: overwhelming U.S. military superiority over all its rivals, the superiority of American production methods and the relative strength of the U.S. economy, and control over global economic markets, with the U.S. dollar acting as the global reserve currency.[41] Of these three, the role of the dollar may be the greatest among equals, but before the euro there was no potential challenge to this dollar hegemony in world trade.

With the creation of the euro in late 1999, an entirely new element was added to the global system of world economic trade relations that has the potential to rival the dollar as reserve currency. In just a few years the euro has emerged as a real alternative, establishing itself as the second most important currency in the world's financial markets. Just prior to the introduction of the euro, the amount of outstanding bonds and notes denominated in the legacy currencies of the euro accounted for barely 28 percent of world issues, compared to 45 percent for dollar-denominated bonds and notes. By mid-2003, the gap had become much smaller: The share of issues in dollars had fallen to 43 percent, while the euro's share had increased to 41 percent. On the money markets, the shift was even more spectacular: At the end of 1998, money market instruments denominated in the euro's predecessor currencies accounted for just over 17 percent of world issues, compared to 58 percent for dollar-denominated instruments, but by mid-2003 the share of issues in dollars had fallen to 30 percent while the share of euro issues had climbed to almost 46 percent.[42] Today, the euro accounts for one-quarter of the global market.[43]

The interplay between the reserve currency role of the dollar and its support through petrodollar relationships can be seen in the threat posed when an OPEC member breaks rank and attempts to revalue its oil in euros. In November 2000, Iraq announced that it would revalue its considerable petroleum reserves from dollars to euros. This was the first time an OPEC country dared violate the dollar price rule,[44] and since then the value of the euro has increased and the value of the dollar has steadily declined. Libya has been urging for some time that oil be priced in euros rather than dollars, and Iran, Venezuela, and other countries have indicated that they would like to denominate their petroleum trade in euros. Since the oil trade is a central factor underpinning the dollar's hegemony, all these are potentially very significant threats to the strength of the U.S. economy in particular, and U.S. global hegemony in general.[45]

Today, America borrows from practically the entire world without keeping reserves of any other currency. Because the dollar is the de facto global reserve currency, U.S. currency accounts for approximately two-thirds of all official exchange reserves. America does not have to compete with other currencies in interest rates, and even at low interest rates capital flies to the dollar. The more dollars are circulating outside the United States, the more the rest of the world has had to provide the United States with goods and services in exchange for these dollars. The United States even has the luxury of having its debts denominated in its own currency. The United States has enjoyed this position for more than thirty years, which means that the domestic U.S. economy has been receiving a huge subsidy from everyone else in the world since petrodollars were created in 1974. While this has produced undeniable benefits for U.S. political and economic elites, it has left the U.S. economy intimately tied to the dollar's role as reserve currency.[46]

World trade is now a game in which the US produces dollars and the rest of the world produces things that dollars can buy. The world's interlinked economies no longer trade to capture a comparative advantage; they compete in exports to capture needed dollars to service dollar-denominated foreign debts and to accumulate dollar reserves to sustain the exchange value of their domestic currencies. To prevent speculative and manipulative attacks on their currencies, the world's central banks must acquire and hold dollar reserves in corresponding amounts to their currencies in circulation. The higher the market pressure to devalue a particular currency, the more dollar reserves its central bank must hold. This creates a built-in support for a strong dollar that in turn forces the world's central banks to acquire and hold more dollar reserves, making it stronger. This phenomenon is known as dollar hegemony, which is created by the geopolitically constructed peculiarity that critical commodities, most notably oil, are denominated in dollars. Everyone accepts dollars because dollars can buy oil. The recycling of petro-dollars is the price the US has extracted from oil-producing countries for US tolerance of the oil-exporting cartel since 1973.[47]

Oil is not just the most important commodity traded internationally; it is the lifeblood of all modern economies. If you do not have oil, you have to buy it, and if you want to buy oil on the world markets, you commonly have to purchase it with dollars.[48] If a significant part of the petroleum trade were to use euros instead of dollars, many more countries would have to keep a greater part of their currency reserves in euros. The dollar would then have to directly compete with the euro for global capital. Not only would Europe not need dollars anymore, but Japan, which imports more than 80 percent of its oil from the Middle East, would have to convert most of its dollar assets to euros. The United States, too, being the world's largest oil importer, would have to hold a significant amount of euro reserves. This would be disastrous for American attempts at monetary management, because the United States would not only lose a large part of its annual subsidy of effectively free goods and services, but the switch to euro reserves from dollar reserves would bring down the value of U.S. currency. According to a June 2003 HSBC report, even a modest shift away from dollars, or a change in the flow, would create significant changes. "If the Euro becomes a bigger reserve currency [if the United States were to share its reserve currency status with the euro] it is also likely to mean either the U.S. buys more Euros or the Europeans reduce their dollar holdings and buy Euros."[49] This shows a clear and definite oil (and petrodollar) connection in the recent military conflict in Iraq and demonstrates that finance is a dimension of the power game with great geopolitical significance.

Yet it is surprising how little attention the issue of reserve currencies receives in international geopolitical analysis. As of December 30, 2003, the euro was worth 25 percent more than the dollar, and with an additional ten member states since May 2004, the EU represents an oil consumer bloc that is one-third larger than that of the United States. From a purely economic perspective, because following this enlargement 60 percent of OPEC oil is being imported by the EU, it would therefore make sense for Iraq and all other OPEC countries to require payment for oil in euros, not dollars.[50] If OPEC were to decide to accept euros for its oil, then American economic dominance would be practically over.[51]

The United States, in alliance with the British, intervened in Iraq militarily in March 2003 and installed its own authority to run the country. Soon after the invasion, it was announced that payment for Iraqi oil would be in dollars only.[52] But the story does not end there. Paradoxically, despite all these recent military and political advances and the rapidly increasing grip of U.S. military power in Eurasia, for a variety of economic and political reasons a growing number of oil producers in the Middle East, South America, and Russia are talking about openly trading oil for euros instead of dollars, or oil in a "basket of currencies."[53] To do so would accelerate the U.S. dollar's fall[54] and boost the euro's claim to become the world's second reserve currency.[55] If a nation's economy is only as good as its currency, and the dollar continues to lose value, the U.S. economy would be headed for a steep fall under these conditions.

U.S. MILITARY POWER BUTTRESSES A WEAKENING ECONOMIC HOLD

> The de facto role of the United States Armed Forces will be to keep the world safe for our economy and open to our cultural assault. To those ends, we will do a fair amount of killing.[56]

An important underlying thread runs from the collapse of the former Yugoslavia and various post-Yugoslav wars to American/NATO responses to numerous political and economic crises in the post-Soviet space, and more recently to America's "war on terrorism" in Afghanistan and Operation Iraqi Freedom. Although these various wars and conflicts had and have specific regional dimensions, they are primarily a U.S. response to new challenges and problems emerging from the demise of the Soviet Union, which can be seen as a synoptic plan of action: maneuvers by the United States and its allies in Europe to control the division of resources in Eurasia. All interventions thus far undertaken have advanced the ability of the United States to gain a strong military foothold in the lands between Europe to the west, the Russian Federation to the north, and China to the east, and turn this strategic region increasingly into an American sphere of influence.[57] The essential question that remains is whether the economic decline of the only superpower in the twenty-first century can be reversed by military means alone.[58]

U.S. global control cannot be understood in military terms alone. As William Wallace observes, real "hegemony rests upon a range of resources, of hard military power, economic weight, financial commitments, and the soft currency of hegemonic values, cultural influence and prestige."[59] It is not just the scale and power of its military might; it is more complicated than this. U.S. hegemony from 1945 onward has rested equally on its ability to homogenize the political cultures of its allies around sets of ideological values and on cultural perceptions constructed to reshape the world system along the lines designed by U.S. policymakers.[60] Most of these are symbolic structures loosely connected to the experience of World War II embodying such highly sensitive symbols as "Hitler," "genocide," "ethnic cleansing," "totalitarianism versus freedom and democracy," "individual rights," and so on.[61] With the demonization of political Islam during the Persian Gulf War and after, "Islamic fundamentalism" and more recently the "axis of evil" and "weapons of mass destruction" have been added to the list of dominant themes of this new era in world politics.

"As in the cold war, we can be assured that it is a blessed and righteous war. 'It is both our responsibility and our privilege to fight freedom's fight,' declared Bush, reminding us that 'God is near' as the U.S. government sets forth to root out evil the world round. A rapture of patriotism, triumphalism, and militarism has seized America."[62] This value structure has been repeatedly and effectively embedded within Western political cultures through repeated international polarizations and military interventions, as well as various racist campaigns against blacks, Asians, Muslims, and other non-European cultures. Since 1991, within this culture of "new American imperialism," a sharply increased level of xenophobia and racism aimed at those who are "uncivilized" has again become the order of the day, and the so-called intelligentsia in the Western world, conservatives and liberals alike, boldly echo the preferred euphemistic triumph of "Western civilization."[63]

> Since the end of the cold war, a new opportunity has arisen. The economic and political crises in the developing world, largely the result of imperialism, such as the blood-letting in the Middle East and the destruction of commodity markets in Africa, now serve as retrospective justification for imperialism. Although the word remains unspeakable, the western intelligentsia, conservatives and liberals alike, today boldly echo Bush and Blair's preferred euphemism, "civilisation." Italy's prime minister, Silvio Berlusconi, and the former liberal editor Harold Evans share a word whose true meaning relies on a comparison with those who are uncivilised, inferior and might challenge the "values" of the west, specifically its God-given right to control and plunder the uncivilised.[64]

As the only superpower remaining after the dismantling of the Soviet bloc, the United States is inserting itself into the strategic regions of Eurasia and anchoring U.S. geopolitical influence in these areas to prevent all real and potential competitors from challenging its global hegemony. The ultimate goal of U.S. strategy is to establish new spheres of influence and hence achieve a much firmer system of security and control that can eliminate any obstacles that stand in the way of protecting its imperial power. The intensified drive to use U.S. military dominance to fortify and expand Washington's political and economic power over much of the world has required the reintegration of the post-Soviet space into the U.S.-controlled world economy. The vast oil and natural gas resources of Eurasia are the fuel that is feeding this powerful drive, which may lead to new military operations by the United States and its allies against local opponents as well as major regional powers such as China and Russia.[65] Were any of its adversaries—or a combination of adversaries—to effectively challenge this emerging U.S.-led security system in the region, it would call into question the dominant role of the United States in the post–Cold War era. For the present U.S. administration, the most effective way to secure this system of stability and imperial control is through use of its mighty military machine.

America's war against the Taliban in Afghanistan and the violent military clashes still ongoing in Iraq are the latest in a series of interventions that have been played out in this strategically significant supercontinent. These recent wars have significantly increased U.S. military control over the lands of Eurasia, and the United States is using the attacks of 9/11 to carry out its foreign policy agenda on a truly aggressive level. Bush's "war on terrorism" has resulted in the projection of U.S. military power into a significant part of the post-Soviet lands, and within the context of this war on terrorism, central Asia is splattered with new American military bases, the Pacific and Indian Oceans are patrolled by aircraft carriers and accompanying fleets of awesome size, and hundreds of U.S. Special Forces have been shipped off to the Philippines to train government soldiers in active combat with the Islamic Abu Sayyaf guerrillas. U.S. Special Forces are also being sent to the former Soviet Republic of Georgia, where a small number of Arab and Chechen fighters are reported to be hiding out. U.S. military power "is now dominant and its limitations are minimal."[66] Never in history has the military supremacy of a single power been so great.[67]

All these are significant developments regarding the security architecture of the post–Cold War world. The expansion of U.S. military control, however, did not start with the attacks of 9/11, but has been in place since 1989.[68] The hijacked planes that crashed into the World Trade Center and the Pentagon simply provided an additional rationale for the unilateral increase in U.S. political and military control in the Eurasian region. As a result, neoconservative influence has also increased tremendously because a majority in the U.S. political and economic power structures now find these neoconservative views useful in pressing for an aggressive new U.S. role in the world. Within this new ideological climate, the Bush administration seized on the terror attacks of September 11, 2001, as a welcome pretext to replace anti-Communism with terrorism as the new millennium's all-purpose rationale for further U.S. military and political expansion around the globe.

While its huge military is an indispensable instrument in maintaining the American empire, it cannot supplant the essential role played by economic hegemony and the dollar's vital role as a reserve currency. Equipped with advanced precision-guided munitions, high-performance aircraft, and intercontinental-range missiles, the American armed forces can unquestionably deliver death and destruction to any target on earth and expect little in the way of retaliation. But as its own political theorists have acknowledged, "The dominant power concentrates (to its detriment) on the military; the candidate for successor concentrates on the economy. The latter has always paid off, handsomely. It did for the United States."[69]

OIL, MONEY, AND ILLUSIONS OF U.S. POWER

Illusions of power tend to arise during times of collective political crisis. As with the Ghost Dance, such illusions also commonly take a religious form where religion has historically served the politics of the nation. In this regard, the historical conditions of Native American nations in the late nineteenth century have some parallels with those of the present-day United States.[70] As defining as they were, the illusions of power represented in the Ghost Dance were fixed in time and place. They were illusions shared only among the Native Americans that embraced the Ghost Dance, and only at the moment when the final collapse of their traditional societies was at hand. As the wheel of history moved beyond them and their time, it encountered other illusions of power invoked for similar reasons and to similar effect. What has changed in the intervening century is the means through which illusions of power are created and the audience to which they are directed. Under these conditions, we can no longer assess the power of the United States according to its claims to be an unassailable political, economic, and military power, but by an enquiry into its actual power—its ability to shape and control perceptions, behaviors, and events that lie at the vital center of its existence.

Many illusions employed in the depiction of U.S. power in the twenty-first century need to be closely examined. Claims about racial, gender, and generational equality have faded in light of evidence that the worst effects of inequality have been only restrained. Claims about democracy appear in the shabby shadow of an electoral politics dominated by money, media, and a drive to deny rather than empower voting.[71] Claims of economic equality face defrocking in the face of thirty-five years of almost uninterrupted decline in the average standard of living and equitable distribution of national wealth. Even claims of free speech have suffered recently under the steady decline of independent and critical media.[72] Internationally, other claims are being made with regard to

U.S. economic, political, and military power. In each case, the claims are vigorously promoted through media that have little or no accountability for the truth of those claims. These too appear more illusion than fact, as the evidence demonstrates.

NOTES

1. With widespread starvation, conditions were so bad on the reservations at that time that the situation was ripe for a major uprising. Karen Strom, "Ghost Dance," http://www.hanksville.org/daniel/lakota/Ghost_Dance.html; "The Ghost Dance," *Last of the Independents*, http://www.lastoftheindependents.com/wounded.htm; "Ghost Dance," *Wikipedia*, http://en.wikipedia.org/wiki/Ghost_Dance.

2. They referred to Wovoka as the Christ as a reference to his vision of how the Christ had flown over them on their ride from the railroad station, teaching them Ghost Dance songs.

3. "Wounded Knee Massacre, *Wikipedia*, http://en.wikipedia.org/wiki/Wounded_Knee_Massacre; Library of Congress, "Wounded Knee Massacre," http://memory.loc.gov/ammem/today/dec29.html.

4. Ironically, the Ghost Dance itself was a mixture of European Christianity and traditional mysticism.

5. Frederick Jackson Turner, *The Frontier in American History* (Mineola, NY: Dover, 1996). Turner's thesis about the role of the frontier in shaping American history has since been challenged, but the reality of the closing of the frontier as the consummation of the Europeanization of North American remains.

6. Susan Strange, *Sterling and British Policy* (Oxford, UK: Oxford University Press, 1971), 5.

7. Tommaso Padoa-Schioppa, European Central Bank, November 22, 2002, http://www.ecb.int.

8. Armand Van Dormael, "The Bretton Woods Conference: Birth of a Monetary System," http://www.imfsite.org/origins/confer.html; de Rato and Wolfensohn, "What Is Bretton Woods?," http://jolis.worldbankimflib.org/Bwf/whatisbw.htm.

9. "It was not only the loss of an empire but also the loss of a self-sustaining international currency that left Britain in search of a role." Strange, *Sterling and British Policy*, 73.

10. "About Fort Knox Gold," http://www.apfn.net/Doc-100_bankruptcy10.htm.

11. The principal culprits in this decline were Germany and Japan, whose new and more efficient systems of production gave them a competitive advantage

over the U.S. aging infrastructure. http://economis.about.com/od/foreigntrade/a/foreign_trade.htm.

12. Gregory Bresiger, "Creating More Fiat Money and Winning an Election," http://www.fame.org/#Fiat%20money.

13. Committee to Restore the Constitution, "The Silent Revolution of Federal Regionalism—A Solution, Part 4: The Feudal State: National Crisis and Executive Orders," http://weba.viawest.net/users/comminc/Crisis.html.

14. Christopher Mayer, "Consequences of a Dollar Standard," December 3, 2003, http://www.gold-eagle.com/gold_digest_03/mayer120503pv.html.

15. Department of the Treasury, "Jeddah, Saudi Arabia, Joint Statement: U.S.-Saudi Arabian Economic Dialogue," press release, March 6, 2002, www.ustreas.gov/press/releases/po1074.htm.

16. Richard Heinberg, "The Endangered US Dollar," *Museletter*, August 2004, http://www.museletter.com/archive/149.html.

17. http://www.commericaldiplomacy.org/cd_dictionary/dictionary_legislation.htm.

18. Richard B. Du Boff, "US Hegemony: Continuing Decline, Enduring Danger," *Monthly Review* (December 2003), http://www.globalpolicy.org/empire/analysis/2003/12decline.htm.

19. The topic was raised at the May 1971 Bilderberger meeting in Saltsjoebaden, Sweden. C. Gordon Tether, "Introduction," *The Banned Articles of C. Gordon Tether*, http://bilderberg.org/bilder.htm#tether.

20. F. William Engdahl, "Iraq and the Hidden Euro-Dollar Wars," http://www.gasandoil.com/goc/news/ntm42655.htm.

21. The East European economies were among those countries unable to pay for their imports by exporting more. Even securing the most basic commodities and simple technologies involved adding to a mounting burden of foreign debt. By the end of the 1980s, the burden of debt remained heavy for the six Eastern European members of the COMECON (except Romania, which completely wiped out its debt by 1989). The strain of debt servicing had far-reaching economic and political consequences. The most important was that Western creditors, such as the IMF, could demand austerity measures as conditions for rescheduling, and the Communist rulers themselves were held responsible for such measures.

22. Eric J. Hobsbawm, *The Age of Extremes: A History of the World, 1914–1991* (New York: Vintage, 1994), 9–11.

23. Bülent Gökay, "The Most Dangerous Game in the World: Oil, War and U.S. Global Hegemony," *Alternatives* 1, no. 2 (2002), http://www.alternativesjournal.net/volume1/number2/gokay.htm.

24. C. Clover, "Dreams of the Eurasian Heartland," *Foreign Affairs* 78 (March/April 1999): 9.

25. On a lighter note, the Caspian Sea is now to be memorialized as the setting and plot device for the latest James Bond movie.

26. Since the collapse of the Communist regimes in Eastern Europe, the United States has been involved in virtually nonstop military operations: the invasion of Panama in 1989, the Persian Gulf War in 1990–91, Somalia in 1992–93, Bosnia in 1995, air attacks in the Gulf in 1998–99, the bombing campaigns in Kosovo and Yugoslavia in 1999, the attack on Afghanistan that began in 2001 and continues as a low-level war, and most recently the invasion and occupation of Iraq that began in 2003 and continues to the present.

27. Andre Gunder Frank, "NATO, Caucasus/Central Asia Oil," *World Socialist Web Site*, http://www.wsws.org/index.html (June 16, 1999): 1.

28. Z. Brzezinski, "A Geostrategy for Asia," *Foreign Affairs* (September/October 1997).

29. U.S. Energy Secretary Bill Richardson telling Stephen Kinzer, "On Piping Out Caspian Oil, U.S. Insists the Cheaper, Shorter Way Isn't Better," *New York Times*, November 8, 1998.

30. T. L. Thomas, "Al Qaeda and the Internet: The Danger of 'Cyberplanning,'" *Parameters* (Spring 2003): 112–23, http://www.au.af.mil/au/awc/awcgate/army-usawc/alqaida_net.htm.

31. Barry C. Collin, "The Future of CyberTerrorism: Where the Physical and Virtual Worlds Converge," 11th Annual International Symposium on Criminal Justice Issues, http://afgen.com/terrorism1.html; Yossi Melman, "Virtual Soldiers in a Holy War," *Ha'aretz*, September 17, 2002, http://www.haaretz.com; Barton Gellman, "FBI Fears Al-Qaeda Cyber Attacks," *San Francisco Chronicle*, June 28, 2002, pp. 1, 10.

32. F. Viviano, "Energy Future Rides on U.S. War, Conflict Centered in World's Oil Patch," *San Francisco Chronicle*, September 26, 2001.

33. M. Cohn, "The Deadly Pipeline War: US Afghan Policy Driven by Oil Interests," *Jurist* (December 7, 2001): 1.

34. M. Cohn, "Cheney's Black Gold," *Chicago Tribune*, August 10, 2000.

35. Quoted in the *Guardian*, October 23, 2001.

36. OPEC is the Saudi-dominated organization of oil-exporting countries. OPEC official Web site, http://www.opec.org/home/index.aspx?.

37. B. Shaffer, "A Caspian Alternative to OPEC," *Wall Street Journal*, July 11, 2001.

38. S. Parrott, "Pipeline Superhighway Replaces the Silk Road," *RFE/RL*, November 19, 1997.

39. Energy Policy Division, "Energy Highlights of the United States," http://www.iedc.in.gov/Energy/ERO_Highlights1.pdf, April 2002.

40. Since America perceives China as its potential rival and U.S. policymakers have already begun planning how to counter China's growing power in Eurasia, it is quite a significant reason for the Bush administration to persistently keep China out

of the oil regions of Eurasia. E. Marquardt, "China's Distant Threat to U.S. Dominance in Asia," September 8, 2003, http://pinr.com/report.php?ac=view_report&report_id=87&language_id=1.

41. The dollar has been the hub and all other currencies were dependent upon the dollar, analogous to spokes.

42. Romano Prodi, president of the European Commission, speech to Economic Club of New York, November 3, 2003, http://Europa-eu-un.org/article.asp?id=2985.

43. Tommaso Padoa-Schioppa, European Central Bank, November 22, 2002, http://www.ecb.int.

44. C. Recknagel, "Iraq: Baghdad Moves to Euro," Radio Liberty/RFE press release, November 1, 2000. The wire was picked up for about forty-eight hours by CNN and other media and quickly disappeared from the headlines.

45. Michael Wines, "For Flashier Russians, Euro Outshines the Dollar," *New York Times*, January 31, 2003.

46. Tommaso Padoa-Schioppa, member of the executive board of the European Central Bank, November 22, 2002, http://www.ecb.int.

47. Henry C. K. Liu, "US Dollar Hegemony Has Got to Go," *Asia Times*, April 11, 2002.

48. Ibid.

49. HSBC, "Currency Outlook," June 2003, http://www.hsbc.com.tw/tw/product/fund/images/gs_200307_e.pdf.

50. Richard Benson, "Oil, the Dollar, and US Prosperity," August 11, 2003, www.prudentbear.com.

51. Bülent Gökay, "The Most Dangerous Game in the World: Oil, War, and U.S. Global Hegemony," Summer 2002, http://www.alternativesjournal.net/volume1/number2/gokay.htm.

52. Carola Hoyos and Kevin Morrison, "Iraq Returns to International Oil Market," *Financial Times*, June 5, 2003.

53. Robert Hunter Wade, *International Herald Tribune*, February 12, 2004.

54. Since mid-2001, the euro has dropped only a couple of percent against gold, while the dollar has dropped 30 percent. The figures suggest a clear move away from the dollar toward gold and the euro. The dollar has lost a third against the euro since mid-2001. Richard C. B. Johnson, "The Fundamentals of a Falling Dollar," Ratio Institute in Stockholm, December 15, 2003, http://mises.org/fullarticle.asp?control=1394&id=63.

55. "In Round 2, It's the Dollar vs. Euro," *Newsweek*, April 23, 2003.

56. In Johan Galtung, "On the Coming Decline and Fall of the US Empire," January 28, 2004, http://www.transnational.org/forum/meet/2004/Galtung_USempireFall.html.

57. The "temporary" U.S. bases in Afghanistan, Pakistan, and the Caspian states appear to be putting down roots. U.S. military tent cities have now been established in thirteen places in the states bordering Afghanistan. More than 60,000 U.S. military personnel now live and work at these forward bases. New airports are being built and garrisons expanded. W. Arkin, *Los Angeles Times*, January 6, 2002; G. Monbiot, *The Guardian*, February 12, 2002.

58. The historian Paul Kennedy has dubbed this condition "imperial overstretch." Paul Kennedy, *Preparing for the Twenty-First Century* (Toronto: Harper-Collins, 1993), 290–328.

59. William Wallace, "Living with the Hegemon: European Dilemmas," Social Science Research Council, *After 11 September*, http://www.ssrc.org/sept11/essays/wallace, p. 9.

60. "Although the word [hegemony] comes from the ancient Greek and refers to the dominance of one state over others in the system, it is used in diverse and confused ways. Part of the problem is that unequal distribution of power is a matter of degree, and there is no general agreement on how much inequality and what types of power constitute hegemony. All too often, hegemony is used to refer to different behaviors and degrees of control, which obscures rather than clarifies that analysis." Joseph S. Nye Jr., "The Changing Nature of World Power," *Political Science Quarterly* 105, no. 2 (Summer 1990): 185.

61. Peter Gowan provides a comprehensive analysis of this process, around the events of NATO's attack on Yugoslavia in 1999. See Peter Gowan, "The Euro-Atlantic Origins of NATO's Attack on Yugoslavia," in T. Ali (ed.), *Masters of the Universe* (London: Verso, 2000), 30–45; and "Contemporary Intra-Core Relations and World Systems Theory," paper presented in June 2000, Ukraine Centre, University of North London.

62. T. Barry, "A Global Affairs Commentary: Onward Christian Soldiers," January 31, 2002, http://www.fpif.org/pdf/gac/0201onward.pdf.

63. William Bowles, " 'Why the Little Yellow Bastards!' Imperialism, Nationalism and Racism," March 19, 2004, http://www.williambowles.info/ini/ini-0210.html.

64. John Pilger, in Andre Gunder Frank, "Doublespeak," http://rrojasdatabank .info/agfrank/doublespeak.html.

65. *New York Times*, March 8, 1992.

66. P. Rogers, *OpenDemocracy*, January 22, 2002, http://www.opendemocracy.net/home/index.jsp.

67. P. Beaumont and E. Vulliamy, "Armed to the Teeth," *The Observer*, February 10, 2002; B. Jones, assistant secretary for European and Eurasian affairs, *AMBO-News*, February 11, 2002.

68. Frank, "NATO, Caucasus/Central Asia Oil."

69. I. Wallerstein, "The Eagle Has Crash Landed," *Foreign Policy* (July-August 2002), http://www.uni-muenster.de/PeaCon/global-texte/g-m/n/wallerstein-eagle.htm.

70. The concept of a divinely conferred national American mission to "civilize" non-Christian peoples can be read as a subtext in much of Samuel Huntington's widely influential polemic, *The Clash of Civilizations*.

71. Alexander Cockburn and James Ridgeway provide ample proof that by the 1980 election what mattered most in the presidential campaigns were political perceptions generated by media coverage of the candidates, with little effort to actually explore important national policies. Alexander Cockburn and James Ridgeway, "The World of Appearance: The Public Campaign" in *The Hidden Election: Politics and Economics in the 1980 Presidential Campaign*, ed. Thomas Ferguson and Joel Rogers (New York: Pantheon, 1981).

72. This commercialization of politics through media can be found where the neoliberal discourse of market-based policies is reinforced by the rapid expansion of commercial radio and television, which engages in a parallel discourse of corporate-dominated consumerism. It can also be seen in the attacks on independent media, like the attacks on the Pacifica radio network during the late 1990s, which sought to eliminate, limit, or take over independent media.

CHAPTER 2

Controlling Governments

As stated in the introduction and chapter 1, our general aim is to set out both the historical and structural framework within which America's new imperialism has developed. Andrew J. Bacevich's *American Empire* similarly reflects this, and its tone is set right in the introduction:

> Though garnished with neologistic flourishes intended to convey a sense of freshness or originality, the politico-economic concept to which the United States adheres today has not changed in a century: the familiar quest for an "open world," the overriding imperative of commercial integration, confidence that technology endows the United States with a privileged position in that order, and the expectation that American military might will preserve order and enforce the rules.[1]

Influenced by the work of revisionist American historians such as Charles A. Beard (1874–1948) and William Appleman Williams (1921–90), Bacevich places President Clinton's "liberal and democratic" strategy in the 1990s in perspective. He sees it in direct continuity with the overall strategic framework of the two preceding Republican administrations of Ronald Reagan and George H. W. Bush, and indeed in continuity with all administrations, whether Republican or Democratic, since World War II. Bacevich argues that Clinton's strategy of openness derived primarily from the country's domestic environment and needs, which was first and foremost the drive of its elite to increase their economic profits and consolidate their positions, whether political, economic, or military. He goes on to specify further his central thesis:

The events of 1989–1993 did not make an end to history.... Even to declare that a "new world order" was at hand was to sow confusion, making it difficult to recognize all that had *not* changed: first, that US foreign policy remained above all an expression of domestically generated imperatives; second, that economic expansionism abroad, best achieved by opening the world to trade and foreign investment, was a precondition of America's own well-being and therefore the centerpiece of US strategy; and third, that the cause of peace was best served by the United States' occupying a position of unquestioned global pre-eminence. The events of 1989 and thereafter had altered none of these firmly held convictions.[2]

Having examined the key features of U.S. monetary/economic strategy after World War II, we try here to reach a comprehensive understanding of the political nature of U.S. neo-imperialism. We do this by qualifying further the Bacevich thesis and by reviewing U.S. foreign policymaking and U.S. foreign policy initiatives since World War II. In this context, we compare, contrast, and assess some key policy documents produced by various U.S. government agencies during and after the end of the Cold War. We argue that the key political instruments and methods of America's neo-imperial system were established in the 1940s and early 1950s and that they were based on a very sophisticated and complex set of policies whose fundamental objective was to make all capitalist states dependent upon Washington's decision-making process. Thus, substantial U.S. efforts had to concentrate on controlling key governmental agencies of the "free world," chiefly in Western Europe, the Near and Middle East, and Southeast Asia, in order to succeed in the global fight against Communism. Although we are not the only ones—let alone the first ones—to do this, we call this system of U.S. global neo-imperial governance the "hub-and-spoke" system—Washington being the hub and all other states of the free world the spokes. We also argue that what has been happening after the end of the Cold War, particularly after 9/11, should be seen as a radical expansion of the same hub-and-spoke system of neo-imperial governance. This neo-imperial expansion has been taking place in zones and states that had been either under the control of the Soviet Union (e.g., east-central Europe, central Asia) or regulated by the Cold War balance of power (e.g., the Middle East). Thus, the United States today is lacking a substantially new strategy to deal with the original political, economic, and social challenges it faces both at home and abroad.

THE UNITED NATIONS: A THWARTED ALTERNATIVE

"I am a war president," George W. Bush boasted after the 9/11 terrorist attacks on America. Since then, senior neocon officials of his administration, from Donald Rumsfeld and Paul Wolfowitz to Dick Cheney and their intellectual acolytes, have liked to portray themselves as being on a mission similar to that of Franklin Delano Roosevelt (henceforth FDR) and Harry Truman. September 11, 2001, is paralleled with December 7, 1941, the date of the Japanese attack on the U.S. naval base at Pearl Harbor in Hawaii, and the "reconstruction" of Iraq and Afghanistan is paralleled with that of Germany and Japan after World War II on the grounds that it will take as much time to "rebuild and democratize" Afghanistan and Iraq as it more or less took to achieve this in Germany and Japan. The policy of regime change via preemptive action and projection of overwhelming force in order to refashion the greater Middle East would have to be accompanied with the rhetoric of spreading democracy and human rights. Because it takes time to do these things, Americans have to be patient. They also have to develop thick skins to remain unscathed by television images showing American and British soldiers torturing Muslim prisoners, making Samuel Huntington's theory of a clash of civilizations come true.[3] But at least until Bush's second-term inaugural address on January 19, 2005, a corporate event where more than $40 million was spent, Bush and his New American Century neocons and Christian Evangelicals held on to this historically misleading and preposterous argument.[4] Historical parallels can and must be drawn, but for the right reasons and the right purposes.

As early as May 1942, FDR began expounding his ideas about how America would like the world to be ruled after the end of the conflict. On the occasion of a visit to Washington by Soviet Foreign Minister Vyacheslav Molotov, Roosevelt made reference to his idea of "four policemen." He spoke to Molotov about a regulatory institutional framework, administered internationally by Great Britain, the USSR, the United States, and possibly China, provided it overcame its problems with advancing Communism and achieved a coherent central government.[5] FDR had found common ground with Stalin, which was their mutual disgust with old-fashioned British and French colonialism. "There will no longer be need for spheres of influence, for alliances, for balance of power, or any other of the special arrangements through which, in the unhappy past, the nations strove to safeguard their security," Secretary of State Cordell Hull, an extreme advocate of free-trade liberalism, opined in November 1943.[6] At the Dumbarton Oaks conference in Georgetown (August–September 1944) and at Yalta (February 1945), FDR and his policy team systematized a policy framework for a new international organization, the United Nations. It was meant to be the substitute for the defunct League of Nations, that is, "the system of unilateral action, the exclusive alliances, the spheres of influences, the balances of power, and other expedients that have been tried for centuries—and have always failed."[7]

FDR's vision, apart from being against classic British imperialism, was seriously aiming at doing business with Stalin by way of fragmenting Europe, Germany in particular. His administration was determined to create such conditions that no war could break out again because of French-German antagonism. Thus, FDR addressed the territorial concerns of Stalin in east-central Europe and the Balkans during the Tehran conference (November–December 1943), whereas a year later he adopted the so-called Morgenthau Plan—after the name of his treasury secretary—which proposed the breakup of Germany into three to five states (Morgenthau himself talked of "pastoralizing Germany").[8] Accordingly, FDR's team envisaged the four policemen performing such an important role that it would have made even the stationing of U.S. troops in Europe after the war unnecessary and redundant. The solution, therefore, to the European question was the transformation of the four policemen into an all-powerful directorate—what, in fact, became the UN Security Council—that would have the power to enforce policy decisions across the globe wherever the interests of its members were at stake. FDR did not live to see his UN dream come true. He died a fortnight before the UN was officially launched at the San Francisco conference (April–June 1945).

In his *Diplomacy* (1994), Henry Kissinger portrays FDR as a good-intentioned man, an idealist at heart and very soft in his diplomatic approaches and actions.[9] In other words, FDR was the dove of his era, an exponent of soft power—the UN. This characterization is rather miles away from the truth. John Lamberton Harper remarks, "FDR had commissioned elaborate studies for an expanded chain of post-war US bases in the Atlantic and the Pacific."[10] China, which at that time was the demoralized and dictatorial regime of Chiang Kai-shek, was included in the four policemen not out of sympathy or courtesy, but because America wanted an Asian anchor to buttress its expansionist designs in Eurasia and elsewhere. As Gabriel Kolko put it, "the policy of trusteeships the United States took to the founding conference of the United Nations at San Francisco stressed the *form of control* rather than the substantive allocation of territories" (emphasis ours). He continued:

> The categories of trusteeships the Big Three defined at Yalta, Washington accepted, but the delegation was practically concerned *only with United States base rights*. The United States intended its proposed trusteeship system to attain, by agreement, "the maintenance of United States military and strategic rights . . . [and] such control as will be necessary to assure general peace and security in the Pacific Ocean area as well as elsewhere in the world. . . ." *The assumptions of this statement hardly concealed the strategic objectives of the United States, for it was perfectly clear that the United States sought to advance its national interests in the guise of performing erstwhile international obligations, obligations which threatened to take it to every corner of the globe.*[11]

But there is more to the affair than meets the eye. FDR's administration was putting enormous pressure on the USSR to allow east-central European peoples to build their own democratic institutions, based on the U.S.-sponsored liberal values of political democracy and human and civil rights. This, among other things, would have allowed U.S. agencies to meddle more easily in the internal affairs of the Soviet satellites, thus exploiting and manipulating their domestic tensions, be they ethnic, politico-ideological, or economic. "The men who made US policy" historian Melvyn Leffler asserts, "were anything but idealists." These men, Leffler continues, "cared little about human rights and personal freedoms inside the Soviet Union and the Soviet orbit." But they did care about "configurations of power in the international system" and the way in which these configurations affected U.S. interests abroad and at home.[12]

This moves us forward in time to a remarkable comment made by another apparent democratic dove of the U.S. foreign policy establishment, Zbigniew Brzezinski. In Paris in 1998, promoting the French edition of his *The Grand Chessboard*, a journalist queried the apparent paradox of the book, namely that it was steeped in Realpolitik, whereas in his days as national security advisor to President Jimmy Carter, Brzezinski had been "a defender of human rights." But Brzezinski waved the paradox aside. "There is no paradox," he replied. "I elaborated that doctrine in agreement with President Carter, as it was the best way to destabilize the Soviet Union. And it worked."[13] But even Henry Kissinger, who was often at odds with Brzezinski over a number of issues and who found "human rights issues largely irrelevant to superpower politics," negotiated successfully the human rights provisions of the Helsinki Final Act of 1975, essentially for the same reason.[14] Ever since FDR, America's neo-imperial establishments have selectively and systematically used the issues of democracy and human rights as political instruments to accomplish power-politics ends.

In 1945, America supplied almost half of the world's gross economic output and 55 percent of the world's manufacturing, and it was self-sufficient in energy and other hydrocarbon resources. The dollar, as we saw earlier, was the strong monetary link binding together the entire capitalist world. American economic growth at home necessitated expansion on a global scale and projection of power in places where American economic and financial interests were involved. This meant, above all, that America's foreign policy establishment had to find ways to open up European colonial empires to American business interests and also had to cajole the Soviet Union to enter into the global economic system and arrangements of American-led capitalism. FDR's team thought that the best way to do this was by politically controlling the relevant regional groups and governments of the world via the UN system of international regulation. This was a domineering and not a philanthropic scheme for global control, and the reason why it foundered as a general concept of post–World War II collective security was because the four policemen disagreed with each other. Simply put, the UN could not unify the world under America's flag. As Gabriel Kolko argued,

> No possibility of global unity and common action for peace via the United
> Nations mechanism ever existed, since the controlling power in the
> United Nations never intended it. The United Nations gave the partial
> division of the world into spheres of influence and competing blocs a formal
> legal structure, and thus the Great Powers both created and acknowledged
> reality.[15]

Under the influence of George Kennan and, mostly, Dean Acheson, the UN had been abandoned in the late 1940s as a vehicle that could serve America's expansionist strategy. Then, with the rise of Arab nationalism and the nonaligned movement in the 1950s and 1960s, third world countries increasingly used the general assembly of the UN as a vehicle through which their anti-Israel and anti-imperialist cause could find expression. Thereafter, the UN proved to be a thwarted neo-imperial alternative to traditional British colonialism, and America began viewing it as an alien child who had betrayed his parents. From 1945 to 1990, some 192 vetoes were cast in the UN Security Council, with the USSR having used "the veto nearly twice as much as had the US."[16] But the end of the Cold War did not bring better news for the United States, as the UN only marginally helped the United States to win international legitimacy by approving its neo-imperial projection of power and NATO plans. Even at times when a formal NATO consensus appeared on the surface, such as with the Kosovo crisis of 1999, ferocious differences remained unresolved in the background between the United States and its European and Asian allies.[17]

CONTAINMENT AND PRIMACY

FDR's scheme came to an end at the Potsdam conference in July–August 1945. Under the influence of Kennan and Acheson, the Truman administration abandoned the idea of dismembering Germany altogether. Kennan became the first director of the Policy Planning Staff in May 1947, but his famous "Long Telegram" from Moscow outlining the theory of containment was sent from Moscow in February 1946.[18]

Kennan's knowledge of the Soviet political system and his type of geostrategic reading of Eurasia ("from the standpoint of Berlin") induced him to argue that the Soviet occupation of east-central Europe would not add political and administrative strength to the USSR because it lacked institutions of liberal-democratic representation and legitimization. Kennan thus believed that the Soviet system suffered from structural weakness and, as he put it, was made up of a "tired and dispirited population working largely under the shadow of fear and compulsion."[19] At the same time, Kennan understood that the Soviets would always view the West as a hostile bloc. This view was due to their anticapitalist ideology, but more important, "the Stalinist regime would always remain hostile because it depended upon the existence of foreign threats to maintain its domestic authority."[20] Thus, "the main element of any U.S. policy toward the Soviet Union must be that of a long-term, patient but firm and vigilant containment of Russian expansive tendencies."[21] But to be successful, containment had to develop two policy pillars. The first was the re-building of a strong, united Germany and a strong Japan, both of which would be harassing the USSR from each end of Eurasia until it bent (the idea of fortified rim lands). The second was the recommendation that the United States force "upon the Kremlin a far greater degree of moder-ation . . . and in this way . . . promote tendencies which must eventually find their outlet in either the break-up or the gradual mellowing of Soviet power."[22] This view reinforced and institutionalized further within the U.S. foreign policy establishment the idea of an interventionist policy whose strategic aim would be the accentuation of the internal tensions of the Soviet system in order to break it up. This idea, as we saw earlier, has remained alive and kicking to the present day.[23]

But Acheson and other key members of the establishment began to realize that containment of the Soviet threat could not be possible if, among other things, some other crucial Eurasian peripheries were not brought into the equation. This had to be done, not least because pen-etration of Eurasian peripheries by the Soviet Union would undercut the ability of the United States to have independent access either to key water passages (e.g., the Suez Canal, the Turkish Straits) or to energy-rich regions, or to run in support of the faltering British position. Thus, the Truman administration and the Joint Chiefs of Staff considered expan-sion in the Near East in Greece, Turkey, and Iran almost as important as that in Western Europe and Japan. London, after all, with an official note on February 21, 1947, made clear to Washington that it could no longer meet its economic and defense commitments to the Near East.[24] Greece, ravaged by the German occupation and a protracted civil war between a demoralized nationalist bloc and a democratic alliance dominated by the Greek Communist Party, was about to give in to Communism. Turkey was allegedly under pressure by the USSR to return the former Russian provinces of Kars and Ardahan and to allow the Soviets to have a base in the Dardanelles. It was also commented that the USSR had demanded a share of Italy's former colonies. Moreover, Stalin refused to withdraw his troops from Iran on March 2, 1946, according to a treaty signed in 1942. But the Soviets backed down in all cases. As a matter of fact, Truman's address to the U.S. Congress (March 1947) included an explicit request

to prioritize military and economic aid to Greece and Turkey.[25] In front
of a group of prominent senators and General George Marshall, Undersecretary of State Dean Acheson gave a passionate speech explaining why
America must intervene in Greece:

> [If Greece fell] like apples in a barrel infected by one rotten one, the
> corruption of Greece would infect Iran and all to the East. It would also carry
> infection to Africa through Asia Minor and Egypt, and to Europe through
> Italy and France, already threatened by the strongest domestic Communist
> parties.[26]

U.S. intervention in Greece provided Acheson's best case study of
how the international struggle of the West against the "evil forces" of
Communism must be transplanted and guide the domestic environments
of states that were important to America's security. Installing puppet
regimes, then conducting "democratic" elections, supporting an authoritarian state of emergency, cracking down on the "enemy," and opening
up the domestic economy to world markets—this is the pattern Acheson
supported in Greece in 1948–49, and this is the pattern America followed
throughout the Cold War. Apparently, America is copying the same
pattern today in Afghanistan, Iraq, and elsewhere.

Kennan disagreed with this interpretation of "containment." He thought
that world politics could not be presented in Manichean terms, as "evil
Communism" against the "free world." But Acheson prevailed. The first
containment test for the Americans had been positive, but it had not been
the sort of containment Kennan had in mind.

Germany was another important testing ground for the new policies of
Acheson, Truman, and Marshall. At Potsdam, Stalin had accepted U.S.
Secretary of State James Byrnes's proposal that Germany's economy and
foreign trade would be managed on an East-West bizonal basis. But by the
spring of 1946, the United States had reneged on this agreement, insisting
that Germany's import and export activities had to be carried out as
if Germany were a unified economic zone. At this stage, the objective of
Britain and the United States was to present themselves as supporters of
German national unity and the Soviet Union as the great enemy of a
unified German state. "The ostensible aim of [British] policy," Anne
Deighton noted, quoting a British official, "is to make the Russians appear
to the German public as the saboteurs of German unity."[27]

In essence, however, this policy was implying that the Soviets could not have a free hand in East Germany and, by extension, all of east-central Europe. Churchill delivered his "iron curtain" speech on March 5, 1946, at Foulton, Missouri. A year later, General George Marshall, secretary of state since January 1947, explained to Stalin at a conference in Moscow that America's European Recovery Program would include all of Europe plus the USSR and the countries under its military control. But Marshall's offer was conditional, and the condition was that the Soviet Union and its satellites would have to open up to American, European, and Japanese capital and trade. The Soviets, therefore, "would either exclude themselves by unwillingness to accept the proposed conditions or agree to abandon the exclusive orientation of their economies."[28]

Clearly, as Alan Milward argued, "the Marshall Plan was predominately designed for political objectives,"[29] and its objectives were to regain the preeminence of the U.S. Department of State, to open European markets to American capital, and to sweep away the European system of nation-states. But the Soviets were not prepared to pulverize the bureaucratized system of their state-run economy, nor were the Europeans eager to give up the sovereignty of their states.[30] Stalin went ahead with his five-year economic plans, and the first Berlin crisis did not take long to come.[31] As far as the Europeans were concerned, they rescued their states through their European Payments Union and the European Coal and Steel Community, the precursor to the European Economic Community (EEC) and the European Union (EU).[32] But Acheson had something else in store: the Atlantic Pact and the State Department's agreement that a special relationship be developed between the United States and Britain.

Acheson privileged a special relationship with Britain, and not with West Germany, based on a preferred type of bilateral security and defense arrangement in which the leading role of the United States was guaranteed in advance. This framework would enable the United States in the future to play the divide-and-rule game between European states in case they got too close to forming a political union independent of the United States.[33] At the time, U.S.-UK relations were indeed privileged, and Paris and Bonn could get together only if they could count on Washington for protection. But the U.S.-UK special relationship has not always been smooth and perfect. For instance, during the Eisenhower presidency from 1953 to 1961, during which John Foster Dulles was secretary of state, U.S.-UK and U.S.-European relations reached the breaking point. The

Suez Canal crisis not only marked a major crisis in U.S.-UK relations but as Brzezinski did not fail to note in his last monograph—it created the conditions in which "European foreign policy could define itself *against* America."[34]

In the Pacific theater, the key bilateral arrangement was with Japan. Article 1 of the U.S. treaty with Japan (signed in 1951 and partly revised in 1960) stated that "Japan grants, and the United States of America accepts, the right, upon the coming into force of the Treaty of Peace and of this Treaty, to dispose United States land, air and sea forces in and about Japan." Article 6 of the same treaty stipulated that "for the purpose of contributing to the security of Japan and the maintenance of international peace and security in the Far East, the United States of America is granted the use by its land, air and naval forces of facilities and areas of Japan."[35]

America's instrument of domination over Europe was NATO. NATO, as a mechanism for collective security with a rigid command structure and a web of apparatuses and regional branches in Europe led by the Pentagon, would, first and foremost, institutionalize the dependence of Western European states upon the United States. The European Coal and Steel Community would have to operate under U.S. tutelage. This meant that the process of European integration would have to proceed "hand in hand with the extension of the American umbrella, not with its removal."[36] Germany must be checked at all times, the United States must stay in Europe, and the Soviets must stay out of Europe's affairs. Back in 1949, Lord Ismay, NATO's first secretary general, was speaking Acheson's and Nitze's language when, without any savoir faire, he said publicly, "NATO's aim is to keep the Americans in, the Russians out and the Germans down."[37] If Europe expanded eastward under Germany's drive, then NATO too should expand there to create new spokes. If Europe expanded southward under France's drive, then NATO too should expand there. Countries could work hand in hand to expand, but would it not be better if the U.S.-led NATO put its hand in first? This is exactly what happened after the end of the Cold War: two rounds of NATO enlargement in post-Communist east-central Europe went hand in glove with, or even preceded, two rounds of EU eastward enlargement.

In 1949, as in post–Cold War settings, the key decision makers of the American establishment had brushed off worries about the reaction of the USSR, or Russia after 1991. It was no great concern if the USSR cemented its domestic authoritarianism by way of NATO and intensified its rearmament program, because what mattered for Acheson was the superiority of U.S. power vis-à-vis the USSR and the materialization of U.S. leadership over the unified and free capitalist world. Similarly, it was no great concern for Clinton, Madeleine Albright, Brzezinski, and Wolfowitz if the Russians or the Chinese objected to NATO enlargement and U.S. projection of power in the Balkans, the Middle East, and central Asia. In fact, what mattered, and what matters now, is sheer superiority of U.S. power vis-à-vis their Eurasian competitors—the EU, China, and Russia—and the expansion of the hub-and-spoke system of dependency upon and control by the United States. As the dollar became the hub of the global monetary system, requiring that all other currencies move around it as spokes, so Washington aimed at becoming the political hub of the capitalist system, with all other states acting as Washington's dependable spokes. Thus, if Washington ordered an end to state sovereignty because the dollar-led world economic system of unregulated markets, private industries, and public utilities so dictated, then all others must obey. In a nutshell, this is the political essence of new American imperialism that continues unabated to the present day. But what about its political ideology and security dimension?

We deal with these questions in more detail in the next two chapters, but for the time being, suffice it to say that Acheson had taken seriously one part of Kennan's message—that the Soviet regime, for ideological reasons, was deeply hostile to the West. He completely ignored or deliberately discounted the other part of the message, namely that the Soviets were weak, overextended, and had neither the intention nor the means to attack.[38]

During the Berlin crisis, though not excluding the possibility of war, Kennan did not believe the Russians had either any interest in conquering Western Europe or the means to do so. Kennan was right in stressing the issue of structural weakness of the Soviet Union, exacerbated by its newly conquered zones and the devastating effects of the war upon it. The Soviets registered over 20 million deaths and their economy was shattered. In the words of Kissinger, "Stalin could not have simultaneously reconstructed the Soviet Union and risked a confrontation with the United States. The much advertised Soviet invasion of Western Europe was a fantasy."[39] If the Soviet Union was implacably hostile to the West, that was because of its domestic weakness and not its military strength. In fact, Kennan argued, the Soviet Union was more liable to collapse. In this context, thwarting Acheson's NATO project, was for Kennan essential because it provided "the very external threat that the Kremlin required to shore up its position in Eastern Europe and at home."[40] But what for Kennan was repulsive for Acheson was propulsive.

Acheson thought that by exaggerating the Soviet threat, the "free world" would have had no other option but to jump on the American bandwagon more easily. As far as the restructuring of the intelligence apparatus was concerned, the Truman administration had gone ahead with significant reforms. It restructured completely FDR's Office of Strategic Services (OSS) by setting up a professional intelligence agency, the Central Intelligence Agency (CIA). In June 1948, after the Communist coup in Czechoslovakia and the Berlin blockade, Truman "authorised the CIA to engage in a broad range of covert operations against the Soviet Union and communists elsewhere, including political and economic warfare and paramilitary activities."[41]

One project that held several lessons for future, not only during the Cold War but for the post–Cold War era as well, was the covert intelligence operations in Albania between 1949 and 1954. The Albanian operation is interesting because it was a joint U.S.-British effort that highlighted some of the contemporary problems in the relationship between these two states. The plan to subvert the small Albanian Communist regime was first originated by the British Secret Intelligence Service (SIS), which had greater prestige and longer experience in the area. The young CIA, on the other hand, had greater resources. That the idea of targeting Albania was first formulated by the British soon caused tensions. For example, the British preferred small amphibious landings to the American method of dangerous low-level parachute drops. Overall, the U.S. and British intelligence chiefs had greatly overestimated the strength of resistance to the Communists and the requirement for plausible deniability backfired. Since the British and Americans stressed deniability, some Albanian exiles were recruited and sent back to the country for the operation. The American CIA and the British SIS had fundamentally different views on the collection of intelligence and covert operations, which resulted in bitter disputes that damaged the operation's effectiveness, and in the end the failure of the Albanian operation was blamed on the Soviet penetration of the operation by the SIS liaison officer in Washington, Kim Philby. Yet overall the

Albanian experience showed that even apparently weak regimes could defend themselves against foreign-supported insurgents.[42] From that point forward, a pattern emerged based on the Albanian experience: The CIA's subversive role and covert operations abroad included Italy (1947–48), assisting the Christian Democrats to outflank the Left; Iran in 1952–53, overthrowing Mohammed Mossedegh after he nationalized the country's oil fields; Chile (1964–73); Greece and Cyprus, by installing a junta regime in the former (1967–74) and facilitating the partition of Cyprus (1974 to the present day); the list is endless.[43] The case of Cyprus is particularly striking:

> The morning of 20 July 1974, when the Turkish invasion of Cyprus was announced, Henry Kissinger was in San Clement, California, where President Nixon had his vacation residence. In California, it was late afternoon. Kissinger had continued telephone conversations with President Nixon, CIA Director William Colby, his British counterpart James Callahan and other State Department officials in Washington. Kissinger was trying to enact a strategy that was aimed at avoiding a war between Greece and Turkey and negotiating the Cyprus conflict after the successful landing of Turkish forces on the island. For this to succeed, Greece could not get involved in resisting the Turkish invasion and must treat the problem as one that merely concerned Cyprus. According to the testimony of Greek commander Nikolopoulos, at 6:00 a.m. on July 20, when it became evident that there were Turkish landing operations, he acted in his capacity as the information officer to appeal to the Greek Commander of the Armed Forces Gregorios Bonanos, asking him to give the order to mobilise his fleet. Bonanos answered, "Turks are attacking Cyprus, but we are Greece." The stance of the Junta leadership that events in Cyprus did not concern Greece, was also known to the Director of the CIA, William Colby, who explained it to Henry Kissinger in a telephone conversation at 7:35 a.m. on July 20. In that same conversation, Colby also told Kissinger that the Turks would not occupy the entire island and would only advance as far as Amohostos. The capture of Amohostos occurred twenty-four days later, on August 14.[44]

Some of the most acrimonious security debates between the Americans and the Europeans concern issues of burden-sharing and the notorious Article 5 of the North Atlantic Treaty. The burden-sharing idea, Paul Nitze explained in his 1989 autobiography, was an effort to "achieve an equitable distribution of NATO's economic burdens," thus committing Europeans to contribute equitably to the cost of running the alliance.[45] In a way, this was self-contradictory because, on the one hand, Acheson and

Nitze were propounding the weakness of European economies that could not fund a credible deterrence against the Soviet threat, while on the other they were asking these economies to contribute to the NATO project. But the intent of burden-sharing was and remains political: It creates for the Europeans an additional permanent commitment to follow NATO's U.S.-led initiatives across the globe, minimizing prospects to build their own separate defense and security structures.[46]

The debate on Article 5 should be read along the same lines. Article 5 of the NATO treaty stipulates that "an armed attack against one or more of [the parties of the treaty] shall be considered an attack against them all." This would have meant that if the Soviets had attacked the United States, then West Germany, France, and Britain would have to engage in hostilities against the USSR. This in turn would have turned the German-Austrian and Greek-Turkish zones into the main war theaters between the two superpowers. Precisely because of these strategic differences between the United States and Western Europe, Britain and France went ahead with building their own nuclear deterrents, a choice unavailable to West Germany. Greece and Turkey, geographically far from the European core, consumed their security and energy primarily over Cyprus after 1954, and the Aegean after 1973. As America's neo-imperial drive under the guidance of the neocons today challenges Europe to strengthen its political and strategic unity against America, so this type of American unilateralism at that time pushed Europeans toward greater nuclear cooperation.[47]

Let us now turn to NSC-68, a document drafted under the supervision of Paul Nitze, the successor to George Kennan in the influential Policy Planning Staff. Herein lies at its best the Achesonian idea of how America can achieve primacy in global affairs.

"BUILDING SITUATIONS OF STRENGTH"

Where Acheson and Kennan agreed was on the question of Palestine. Although always flanked by arch-Zionists such as Louis Brandeis and Felix Frankfurter, Acheson was never sympathetic to the establishment of a Jewish state, fearing that the mass emigration of Jews from postwar Europe into Palestine would lead to protracted war with the Arabs.[48]

Similarly, Kennan argued that the 1947 UN partition plan for Palestine should be ditched because of the damage it was doing to the oil-producing states of the Arab world, and because the United States might find itself in the awkward position of having to defend Israel in perpetuity. But Truman overruled their concerns, as well as the fierce diplomatic opposition of Saudi Arabia: "I'm sorry, gentlemen, but I have to answer to hundreds of thousands who are anxious for the success of Zionism. I do not have hundreds of thousands of Arabs among my constituents."[49] This set a precedent for America's pro-Zionist Middle Eastern policy that, with some important variations and turns, has lasted to the present day.

How can Acheson's anti-Zionism in particular be explained? Most probably, Acheson thought that a protracted Arab-Israeli conflict would undermine the cohesion of the anti-USSR shield in the Near East, composed of Greece, Turkey, Iran, and Afghanistan—what U.S. strategists at the time used to call the Northern Tier. This would have allowed the Soviets to break through into oil- and gas-producing regions, disrupting NATO and U.S. communication and defense lines. Our interpretation is that Acheson thought that the Zionist affair included the potential to break up the smooth expansion of the hub-and-spoke system in the Middle East, while at the same time creating huge problems within the Western alliance. This is a problem the United States is still experiencing today.

In 1949, the Chinese Communist Party, headed by Mao Tse-tung and assisted by the Soviet Union, achieved victory over the Nationalist forces. This further convinced Acheson that the UN was not at all an adequate instrument for America's neo-imperial strategy of expansion and domination. Moreover, the Soviet atomic test in September–October 1949 had pushed Washington to see the Soviets as attempting nuclear parity with the United States, whereas U.S. standing conventional forces were far inferior to those of the Soviets.[50] Immediately, Nitze, who took over from Kennan on January 1, 1950, and his staff began consulting senior military personnel about the possibility of testing a new thermonuclear weapon, the hydrogen bomb.[51] At the same time they began working on NSC-68.[52]

According to the authors of NSC-68, "the fundamental design of the Kremlin" was the consolidation of the Soviet system inside the USSR and the Soviet-controlled states of east-central Europe, as well as the system's expansion in the non-Soviet world. The frustration of the Kremlin's designs should, therefore, become one of America's major objectives.[53] This could be achieved only by what Acheson called "building situations of strength" all over the non-Soviet zones. In addition, he argued that the United States must foster a fundamental change in the nature of the Soviet system, although it would be "less costly and more effective if this change occurs as a result of internal forces in Soviet society."[54] "The Kremlin," the NSC-68 argument goes, "is inescapably militant" because it is the "inheritor of Russian imperialism" and its only apparent restraints on resort to war are "calculations of practicality."[55]

Admittedly, some of Kennan's thinking is present in the document— "a very weak Soviet economy," "lack of harmony between the Soviet elite and the Soviet people as the latter is coerced by the former," "external conflicts used to cover up the regime's deficiencies."[56] But crucial issues, such as the domination of Eurasia by the USSR or China, are placed in a different context altogether.[57] As far as the idea of containment was concerned, Nitze argued against Kennan, claiming that "without superior aggregate military strength, in being and readily mobilizable, a policy of 'containment'—which is in effect a policy of calculated and gradual coercion—is no more than a policy of bluff."[58] NSC-68 was about making the case for a substantial increase in defense spending to convince domestic skeptics and Congress about the Soviet threat while ideologizing it by presenting it in a confrontational framework of free world against evil dictatorships.[59] At the same time, the United States must exhaust all its efforts on the altar of keeping the free world together and under its tutelage:

> Strength at the center, in the United States, is only the first of two essential elements. The second is that our allies and potential allies do not as a result of a sense of frustration or of Soviet intimidation drift into a course of neutrality eventually leading to Soviet domination. If this were to happen in Germany the effect upon Western Europe and eventually upon us might be catastrophic.[60]

Nitze's recommended course of action was a "rapid build-up of political, economic and military strength of the free world." In fact, as Acheson explained in his memoirs, NSC-68 was "to bludgeon the mass mind of 'top government'" into recognizing the need to move away from primary reliance upon nuclear weapons and start strengthening the conventional forces.[61] In addition, NSC-68 concerned whether to go forward with testing the feasibility of a hydrogen bomb.[62] In a concluding passage that describes at its best the Achesonian-Nitzean neo-imperial idea of the hub-and-spoke system, NSC-68 argued:

> Our position as the center of power in the free world places a heavy responsibility upon the United States for leadership. We must organize and enlist the energies and resources of the free world in a positive program for peace, which will frustrate the Kremlin design for world domination by creating a situation in the free world to which the Kremlin will be compelled to adjust. Without such a co-operative effort, led by the United States, we will have to make gradual withdrawals under pressure until we discover one day that we have sacrificed positions of vital interest.[63]

NSC-68 was as much about building situations of strength around the world and encircling the Soviet Union as it was about making key capitalist states politically and militarily dependent upon the United States; as much about undermining the cohesion of the Soviet bloc from within through using issues such as human rights and ethnic pluralism, as it was about controlling and manipulating governments through the subversive action of globalizing intelligence apparatuses through the CIA. The priority was to preserve America's superpower status through a web of bilateral and security arrangements, and this became the most essential element of Acheson's powerful idea of primacy. If we brush aside neocon bias, a dose of historical exaggeration, and the underlying messianic belief of the author that "this neo-imperial system is the best and could last forever," then the following message by Josef Joffe, written in 1997 for *Foreign Affairs*, reads with pleasure:

> Imperial's Britain strategy was to capitalize on its great advantage of insularity—to stay aloof from the quarrels of Europe, if possible, and to intervene against the hegemonist of the day when necessary. . . . Bismarck's grand strategy was the opposite extreme: not intermittent intervention but permanent entanglement. To banish his "nightmare of coalitions" the Iron Chancellor sought to cement better relations with all contenders than they might establish among them. As long as these relationships converged like spokes in a hub, Germany would be the manager, not the victim of European diplomacy. . . . The US's global game is essentially a Bismarckian one, and that explains why the rest of the world is not moving in on the US. . . . The appropriate metaphor is that of hub and spoke. The hub is Washington, and

the spokes are Western Europe, Japan, China, Russia and the Middle East. For all their antagonism toward the US, their association with the hub is more important to them than are their ties to one another.[64]

Intellectuals such as Joffe are much better at performance than are politicians, such as Britain's callous and histrionic Prime Minister Tony Blair: When they both embrace neo-imperialism's key tenets, neocon intellectuals are frank, but neocon politicians are ostentatious liars.

William Kristol and Robert Kagan, two other neocon ideologues and key members of the Project for the New American Century (henceforth PNAC), are sincere when they argue that "containment alone did not characterize US strategy during the Cold War." Kagan also concedes that "from the end of WWII . . . Europe fell into a state of strategic dependence on the United States."[65] The neocons concede that "containment of the Soviet threat" did make sense only if it was seen as a form of double containment—containing both the Soviets and the allies—or, as Ronald Steel put it in 1995, as a "two-anchor strategy of containing and expanding: containment of Soviet territorial temptations through military and economic power; expansion through alliances, bases, investments and bribes."[66] Also, Kagan is frank when he says that "the September 11 attacks shifted and accelerated but did not fundamentally alter a course the US was already on."[67] Neocons are frank and outspoken when they insist that "the master of Eurasia is the master of the world" and that the United States must secure its mastery there forever. Last but not least, they are sincere when they set out the key aims of the United States as being sheer predominance in cyberspace, intelligence systems, applied research, and military technology. Since the end of the Cold War, these themes have reappeared more than explicitly in, among others, Zbigniew Brzezinski's *The Grand Chessboard* (1997) and the widely discussed neocon paper, "Rebuilding America's Defenses" (1997–98).[68]

FULL-SPECTRUM DOMINANCE

The key elements in the present phase of American neo-imperialism as experienced through the foreign and military policies of George W. Bush are radicalizations of earlier forms of U.S. neo-imperialism, namely of the

Achesonian/Nitzean hub-and-spoke model of attaining global primacy. U.S. expansion and projection of power today in Eastern Europe, the Balkans, and the greater Middle East, with NATO or not, with British assistance or not, is but a radicalized expansion of this model based on this sixty-year-old idea. The United States is trying to bring under its tutelage more strategic zones and states in Eurasia and the globe, while keeping under control its old Cold War allies, mainly the expanding EU and Japan.

Yet the world has changed dramatically since 1945. And what has changed even more dramatically is American society, which is full of tensions and ethnic/religious contradictions, along with America's worsening economic position in the world. In other words, neocon America lacks a new political strategy capable of articulating a dynamic response to the demanding requirements of the present, both at home and abroad. Some three thousand years ago, Thucydides saw Athens applying preemptive action on Melians and he explained that by virtue of its domestic economic and social decline. So is the case with America today. As with NSC-68 and the policies of U.S. expansionism during the Cold War, the hawks of the New American Century argue that the declining power presence of the USSR in the second half of the 1980s induced substantial sections of America's ruling elite, particularly in Congress, to demand from the Pentagon significant cuts in defense spending. The pressure mounted especially during Clinton's first term after the spectacular, high-tech ousting of Saddam's forces from Kuwait in January–February 1991.[69]

The answer to this demand, the neocon argument went, was a new initiative, which in fact began with the "Defense Planning Guidance" document, drafted by Paul Wolfowitz and I. Lewis Libby, which was leaked to the *New York Times* in March 1992. "This document was prophetic," the neocon editor of the *Weekly Standard*, William Kristol, boasted ten years later.[70] Prophetic in what sense? In the sense that it foresaw all the changes that the administration of George W. Bush adopted after 9/11 in order to face successfully the new global challenge of the "war of the civilized world against terror." We argue that the situation was and is far more complex. In fact, the analyses of the PNAC regarding U.S. defense spending before and after the Cold War are deeply flawed (table 2.1).

A superficial reading of table 2.1 might wrongly lead to the conclusion that President Clinton did indeed cut defense spending, which in turn alarmed the neocons. "Over the first seven years of the Clinton

Table 2.1. Annual Military Spending from 1945 to 1996 (in Billions of 1996 Dollars)

Year	Amount	Year	Amount
1945	962.7	1971	311.7
1946	500.6	1972	289.1
1947	133.7	1973	259.5
1948	94.7	1974	243.8
1949	127.8	1975	242.0
1950	133.0	1976	234.0
1951	225.7	1977	232.7
1952	408.5	1978	233.2
1953	437.0	1979	237.4
1954	402.1	1980	246.2
1955	344.5	1981	260.8
1956	320.7	1982	282.0
1957	322.4	1983	303.2
1958	317.9	1984	318.1
1959	306.9	1985	343.7
1960	289.6	1986	363.7
1961	291.1	1987	371.1
1962	300.0	1988	372.8
1963	293.3	1989	376.2
1964	294.8	1990	358.7
1965	268.3	1991	316.5
1966	297.3	1992	328.6
1967	354.1	1993	312.1
1968	388.9	1994	290.3
1969	371.8	1995	272.1
1970	346.0	1996	265.6

Source: Center for Defense Information, www.cdi.org/issues/milspend.html.

Note: Total cost of the Cold War (1948–91) in 1996 dollars = $13.1 trillion. Average annual military spending during Cold War = $298.5 billion. Average annual military spending during peacetime Cold War (excluding Korean and Vietnam War years) = $285.4 billion.

administration," a neocon document argued, "approximately $426 billion in defense investments were deferred" and "Clinton cut more than $160 billion from the Bush program from 1992 to 1996 alone."[71] This is entirely misleading and an aggregate comparison belies this conclusion.

Despite the post–Cold War decline in defense spending, America's military share as a percentage of the world total in 1996 had increased by 20 percent compared to a peak Reaganite year, 1985. Whereas in 1985 the United States was spending only 65 percent as much on defense as did the Soviet bloc, China, and Cuba, just few months before 9/11 it was spending more than twice as much as did all these former Communist threats.[72] Aggregate Pentagon spending during the whole of the 1990s "was 86.5 percent as high as the total for the 1980s, adjusted for inflation, or $3.11 trillion compared to $3.61 trillion." This gave a "financial peace dividend of approximately £500 billion—a sum equivalent to 15 months spending during the Reagan-Bush Sr. peak."[73] If calculated on a per capita basis, the Pentagon actually spent 11 percent more in real terms during the 1990s than during the 1980s. In fact, as already noticed by many commentators, it was during the Clinton years that the shift of power from the declining State Department to the rising Pentagon was completed. In 2001, the federal budget reaching the State Department was $6.6 billion, a reduction of 10 percent over 1993.[74] The "rise of proconsuls," that is, the tendency of serving officers to displace civilians in implementing foreign policy, a theme so eloquently analyzed by Bacevich, must be seen in the context of this shift of power from one bureaucratic branch to another. Herein lie the material roots of the so-called militarization of U.S. foreign policy after 9/11. Today, after the second Gulf War and the increasing military engagement of U.S. forces around the globe, the United States spends more than $400 billion per year on defense, which is more than one-half of the global total.

These are some quantitative aggregate data that say nothing about the sheer and increasingly qualitative superiority of the United States over all its other suspected rivals—the EU states, Russia, China, and Japan—for world dominance. But they help explain why the Clinton administration did not undermine this process, which has been further radicalized following 9/11 and the hijacking of the White House by the policy ideas of the PNAC.

However, Clinton's neo-imperial administration should not be considered identical to the neocon program: there are subtle differences between the two. For instance, neocons demanded, first from the first President Bush and then from Clinton, that U.S. forces should overthrow Saddam unilaterally, thus overruling the UN mandate that the war must end once Iraqi forces were driven out of Kuwait. Clinton followed a halfway approach: He periodically authorized bombing raids against Iraqi targets throughout the 1990s—the most serious being that of December 1998 on the pretext that Saddam was blocking the work of UN inspectors in their search for weapons of mass destruction—and we do not know how he would have reacted had 9/11 taken place during his years in office. At best, therefore, this is a difference between reformist neo-imperialism and radical neo-imperialism. At worst, there is no difference.

The Wolfowitz-Libby program of 1992 and the writings of the PNAC were put forward as an answer to post–Cold War conditions. Interestingly, these documents were also presented in almost identical fashion as an answer to post-9/11 conditions, which were considered to mark the beginning of a new era—the war on terror. Thus, for the purposes of our main argument, it is appropriate to deal with these documents as an integrated whole, avoiding a strictly chronological presentation. So what are the strategic policy essentials of this radical neo-imperial program and how has the United States attempted to infuse them into its allies?

From the first year of the George H. W. Bush administration in 1989, then Secretary of Defense Dick Cheney, Colin Powell, who was the head of the Joint Chiefs of Staff, and Paul Wolfowitz, then undersecretary of defense for policy, worked hard to find military responses to the USSR's declining global presence.[75] Powell argued that there should be a move from "global containment" to "forward deterrence" in Eurasia to prevent anarchy caused by the contraction of Soviet power. The use of overwhelming force and high-tech force should not be excluded, because it could produce favorable results quickly. This approach would reduce defense spending—which was good news for Congress—but not so much, as the structural transformation of U.S. forces based on high-tech weaponry could not be done on the cheap.

When confronted with events in Eastern Europe and the Balkans, U.S. policy planners refined this design. As well as moving the United States forward to become a truly global superpower, policy planners became more flexible in an effort to quickly deploy and successfully confront emergency situations and small-scale warfare, such as ethnic and religious conflicts. This approach was quickly transplanted into NATO and became known as NATO's new strategic concept in the wake of a NATO summit in Rome in November 1991. This followed precisely Powell's and Cheney's designs for America's global dominance. Adapted to the alliance's jargon, the new strategic concept emphasized out-of-area missions—that is, missions outside the security zone of western and southern Europe. This entailed a revisionist reading of Article 5 of the NATO treaty, because the new NATO could take political (e.g., expansion) or military action even if unprovoked and even outside western or southern Europe.[76]

The Wolfowitz-Libby "Defense Planning Guidance" document similarly appeared at a critical juncture—following the first Gulf crisis and at the beginning of the first Yugoslav crisis. It also appeared when the Europeans, in the run up to the Maastricht Treaty negotiations of December 1991–January 1992, were making their own arrangements for a military force separate from NATO, an independent foreign and security policy, and an independent reserve currency, the euro. Clinton did put the record straight, stating that "the Europeans can have a separable but not separate security and defence identity from NATO,"[77] as a separate identity would have dismantled the Achesonian-Nitzean hub-and-spoke system. But this left the hawks dissatisfied. They wanted to see Clinton implement a radical program of global dominance, now that no super rival existed, and well before a new one even thought to emerge. The image came straight from the Bible: America was presented as a heavily armed City on a Hill, ready to spread the light of its civilization, by all means available, across the globe.[78]

The neocon political program rested on three paramount policy objectives: first, the United States must employ a military strategy conducive to preventing the emergence of a rival superpower in Europe and Asia; second, the United States must grasp the opportunity and promote American values and culture, democracy and human rights, and a free-market economy and competitiveness in every country; and third, America must let it be known that it could and would sometimes act unilaterally, and take preemptive action to achieve "regime change." For March 1992, this was a tall order. But after 9/11 it was accepted as inevitable.

If the first Gulf War was a successful test for the "deter forward" idea using the projection of overwhelming force, the Bosnian crisis proved to be another successful testing ground for projecting power in Europe. The ousting of Saddam from Kuwait deepened and expanded the presence of U.S. power in the Middle East by establishing permanent bases in Kuwait and Saudi Arabia while slicing Iraq into northern and southern no-fly zones. The intervention in Bosnia preempted NATO's eastward expansion, warning both the Europeans and the Russians—and particularly the Germans—to abandon any separate design for politically securing east-central Europe according to their national interests. The radicalization of the hub-and-spoke scheme was in full reforming deployment: It was in action. But the neocons of the New American Century wanted more action. They wanted full-spectrum dominance: in Eurasia, cyberspace, intelligence, military activities and planning, high-tech military systems, and precision weapons. Clinton could not ignore their call, not least because a big section of his administration, particularly in the military, was dominated by similar ideas. Moreover, the NATO war on Yugoslavia (March–June 1999) over Kosovo, the first and perhaps last war the alliance will fight in its history, made clear the disagreements among the allies and the difficulties they had in reaching an understanding while in action. Thus, in a document titled *Joint Vision 2020*, produced by the Strategy Division of the Pentagon a year after Kosovo, we read:

> For the joint force of the future [the objectives of the national command authorities] will be achieved through *full spectrum dominance*—the ability of US forces, *operating unilaterally or in combination with multinational and interagency partners*, to defeat any adversary and control any situation across the full range of military operations. . . . The label full spectrum dominance implies that US forces are able to conduct prompt, sustained, and sychronized operations with combinations of forces tailored to specific situations and with access to and freedom to operate in all domains—space, sea, land, air and information.[79]

The radicalization of the hub-and-spoke system that began under Clinton was accelerated after 9/11, when the ruling elites were being presented with tangible evidence that a new enemy—global terrorism—had emerged. We do not imply here that international terrorism was not on America's black list before 9/11—it was. But after 9/11 it rose to the top of the U.S. enemies list. This new war on terror provided the neocons, now in power, with the excuse that was missing in the 1990s: an outstanding enemy, capable of inflicting as much damage on America as the Japanese did at Pearl Harbor or as the Soviets could do during the Cold War. The Clintonian human rights approach of the 1990s now had to be subordinated to the scheme of the war on terror, in order to give a humane and democratic appearance to America's preemptive wars and in case an international coalition was not willing to follow America. Others who were willing would now form "coalitions of the willing" under U.S. leadership. On June 1, 2002, at West Point in New York, George W. Bush presented the National Security Strategy of the United States. These words mark the last phase of post–World War II U.S. neo-imperialism:

> The United States has long maintained the option of preemptive actions to counter a sufficient threat to our national security.... the case for taking anticipatory action to defend ourselves, even if uncertainty remains as to the time and place of the enemy's attack. To forestall or prevent such hostile acts by our adversaries, the United States will, if necessary, act preemptively.[80]

The road to a preemptive strike on Afghanistan and Iraq was paved. It was, after all, the logical conclusion to Clinton's policy of embargo, periodic bombing, and other restrictions. NATO expanded again in 2004, becoming more and more a political instrument in the hands of Washington to control governments, arms sales, and decision-making processes in the crucial zones of east-central Europe, central Asia, and the Middle East. State sovereignty is now a thing of the past and Acheson's plan regarding the pulverization of the state system in Europe is back on the U.S. agenda on a global scale. States all over the world have to accommodate their domestic environments to this new war on terror and report back to America. Those who resist are against "us," America and its close allies. America is the strongest military force in the world. In that sense at least, it is an empire that can impose its will whenever it wants to use its force. On the other hand, the problem of foreign policy is not just to impose your will once, but to make it last.[81]

NOTES

1. Andrew J. Bacevich, *American Empire: The Realities and Consequences of US Diplomacy* (Cambridge, MA: Harvard University Press, 2002), 6.

2. Ibid., 77.

3. Samuel Huntington, *The Clash of Civilizations and the Remaking of World Order* (London: Simon and Schuster, 1997). Huntington's thesis of a clash between the West and the rest on religious grounds has been drawn from the work of Bernard Lewis, a Princeton University Orientalist who in 1990 had published in *Atlantic Monthly*, no. 26, an essay titled "The Roots of Muslim Rage." Huntington recast it in

a more elaborate and systematic form; on this issue, see also the incisive comments by Derek Gregory, *The Colonial Present* (Oxford, UK: Blackwell, 2004), 56–58 passim.

4. See James Harding, "A Polarizing President Gets His Chance to Become a Republican Roosevelt," *Financial Times* (January 19, 2005): 17.

5. See John Lamberton Harper, *American Visions of Europe* (Cambridge, UK: Cambridge University Press, 1996), 82.

6. Cordell Hull in *U.S. Department of State Bulletin* ix, no. 230 (November 20, 1943): 343.

7. FDR, quoted in Robert Dallek, *Franklin D. Roosevelt and American Foreign Policy, 1932–1945* (New York: Oxford University Press, 1979), 520.

8. Among others, Marc Trachtenberg, *A Constructed Peace: The Making of the European Settlement* (Princeton, NJ: Princeton University Press, 1999), 16.

9. Henry Kissinger, *Diplomacy* (New York: Simon and Schuster, 1994), 394ff.

10. Harper, *American Visions*, 96.

11. Emphasis ours. Gabriel Kolko, *The Politics of War: The World and United States Foreign Policy, 1943–1945* (New York: Random House, 1968), 467.

12. Melvyn P. Leffler, *The Spectre of Communism: The United States and the Origins of the Cold War, 1917–1953* (New York: Hill and Wang, 1944), 49.

13. For Brzezinski as defender of human rights, see the acute remarks by Diana Johnstone, "Humanitarian War: Making the Crime Fit the Punishment," in *Masters of the Universe? NATO's Balkan Crusade*, ed. Tariq Ali, 153 (London: Verso, 2000). For Brzezinski denying a paradox, see Vassilis K. Fouskas, *Zones of Conflict: US Foreign Policy in the Balkans and the Greater Middle East* (London: Pluto Press, 2003), 5ff.

14. See John J. Maresca, *To Helsinki: The Conference on Security and Co-operation in Europe, 1973–1975* (Durham, NC: Duke University Press, 1985), 158.

15. Kolko, *The Politics of War*, 474.

16. David M. Malone, "US-UN Relations in the UN Security Council in the Post–Cold War Era," in *US Hegemony and International Organizations*, ed. Rosemary Foot et al., (Oxford, UK: Oxford University Press, 2003), 74, n.2.

17. For a detailed discussion of the issue, see K. Drezov, B. Gökay, and D. Kostivicova (eds.), *Kosovo, Myths, Conflict and War* (Keele, UK: Keele European Research Centre, 1999).

18. An edited version of it titled "The Sources of Soviet Conduct" appeared in *Foreign Affairs* in July 1947, signed by "Mr. X." Our quotations from Kennan's classic text are drawn from George F. Kennan, *American Diplomacy, 1900–1950* (Chicago: University of Chicago Press, 1951), 107–29.

19. George F. Kennan, "The Sources of Soviet Conduct," in *American Diplomacy, 1900–1950* (Chicago: University of Chicago Press, 1951), 122–23.

20. John Lewis Gaddis, *The United States and the Origins of the Cold War* (New York: Columbia University Press, 2000), 316 (first published in 1972).

21. Kennan, "The Sources of Soviet Conduct," 119.

22. Ibid., 127.

23. See U.S. documents on dealings with Afghanistan, National Security Archive Electronic Briefing Book No. 59, ed. William Burr, October 26, 2001, http://www2.gwu.edu/~nsarchiv/NSAEBB/NSAEBB59/.

24. See James Chase, *Acheson: The Secretary of State Who Created the American World* (Cambridge, MA: Harvard University Press, 1998), 162.

25. See Harry Truman, "The Truman Doctrine," in *Public Papers of the Presidents of the United States: Harry S. Truman, 1947* (Washington, DC: Government Printing Office, 1963), 179–80.

26. Dean Acheson, *Present at the Creation: My Years in the State Department* (New York: W.W. Norton, 1969), 219.

27. Anne Deighton, *The Impossible Peace: Britain, the Division of Germany and the Origins of the Cold War* (Oxford, UK: Clarendon, 1990), 108.

28. Kennan, quoted in Richard Crockatt, *The Fifty Years War: The United States and the Soviet Union in World Politics, 1941–1991* (London: Routledge, 1995), 78.

29. Alan S. Milward, *The Reconstruction of Western Europe, 1945–51* (London: Routledge, 1984), 5.

30. "Invaded by Germany in June 1941, the Soviet Union fought a lone, heroic struggle on the European mainland against Nazi Germany and her allies from that date until the opening of the Second Front in the D-Day invasion in June 1944. She suffered by far the greatest casualties of any country on either side." Joseph V. O'Brien, "World War II: Combatants and Casualties (1937–45)," http://web.jjay .cuny.edu/~jobrien/reference/ob62.html.

31. The first Berlin blockade of June 1948–May 1949, however, was the direct result of the London conference, which Kennan opposed, where the Western powers alone, without consulting the Soviets, decided to support the creation of an independent German state. Stalin refused to abide by that decision. Thus, on April 1, 1948, the Soviets began imposing certain restrictions on the movement of military supplies into Berlin. In June, France, the UK, and the United States announced a currency reform for their respective zones of occupation, excluding Berlin. The Soviet response was to further restrict movements into Berlin. But when the Western powers introduced their monetary policy in West Berlin, the Soviet authorities responded with an all-out blockade of all land routes to Berlin. The three western powers began airlifting supplies into Berlin, something that the Soviets did not challenge, and the blockade was eventually called off in May 1949.

32. On this issue, see the perceptive work by Alan Milward, *The European Rescue of the Nation State* (London: Routledge, 1992). Europe would have recovered even without the Marshall Plan. Prompted by the Czechoslovak crisis, the plan was

endorsed by the U.S. Senate in March 1948, and between 1948 and 1952 America delivered $13 billion to Western Europe and Yugoslavia, a sum that would have been proportionately much thinner had the USSR and its satellites been among the participants.

33. In fact, the prospect of the "Europe of Six" getting too close was contemplated in 1952 by senior members of Acheson's staff and by William Draper, U.S. permanent representative to NATO. The conclusion was that a "third pillar independent from NATO" was an undesirable development; ibid., 323–24.

34. Author's emphasis. Zbigniew Brzezinski, *The Choice: Global Domination or Global Leadership?* (New York: Basic Books, 2004), 70. For an appraisal of U.S.-UK relations, see Andrew Gamble, *Between Europe and America: The Future of British Politics* (London: Palgrave, 2003); John Dumbrell, *A Special Relationship: Anglo-American Relations in the Cold War and After* (London: Macmillan, 2001).

35. See "Security Treaty between the United States and Japan," in Armin Rappaport, *Sources in American Diplomacy* (New York: Macmillan, 1966) 349, 351.

36. Harper, *American Visions*, 309.

37. One of us has dwelled extensively on this point. See Fouskas, *Zones of Conflict*, chapter 3 passim.

38. Harper, *American Visions*, 224.

39. Kissinger, *Diplomacy*, 433.

40. Harper, *American Visions*, 206.

41. These words come from two authors who can hardly be suspected of an anti-American bias: Stephen Ambrose and Douglas Brinkley, *Rise to Globalism: American Foreign Policy Since 1938* (Harmondsworth: Penguin, 1997 [1971]), 93.

42. Christopher Andrew, *Secret Service* (Kent: Sceptre, 1987), 686–87.

43. See in particular William Blum, *Killing Hope: US Military and CIA Interventions since WWII* (London: Zed Books, 2003).

44. Makarios Drousiotis, "Kissinger's Secret Phone Calls Concerning Cyprus," *Eleftherotypia*, July 20, 2004. See also Vassilis K. Fouskas, "Uncomfortable Questions: Cyprus, October 1973–August 1974," *Contemporary European History* 14, no. 1 (2005): 45–63.

45. Paul H. Nitze, *From Hiroshima to Glasnost: At the Centre of Decision* (New York: Grove Weidenfeld, 1989), 125.

46. For a good summary on the issue of burden-sharing, see Alan Tonelson, "NATO Burden-Sharing: Promises, Promises," in *NATO Enters the 21st Century*, ed. Ted Galen Carpenter, 29–58 (London: Frank Cass, 2001).

47. On this question, see Beatrice Heuser, *NATO, Britain, France and the FRG: Nuclear Strategies and Forces for Europe, 1949–2000* (London: Macmillan, 1998).

48. Chase, *Acheson*, 131.

49. Quoted in William Eddie, *FDR Meets Ibn Saud* (New York: American Friends of the Middle East, 1954), 37; see also ibid., 132.

50. It was perceived that the Soviets had 175 divisions while the United States had 7. Later, Nitze himself confirmed, American intelligence had estimated that of the 175 Soviet divisions, "one third were at full strength, one third were at partial strength and the final third were cadres," Paul Nitze, "The Development of the NSC-68," *International Security* 4, no. 4 (Spring 1980): 173.

51. Paul H. Nitze, *From Hiroshima to Glasnost*, 87–93. Nitze's rationale was that since the Americans were able to go ahead with the H-bomb, then the possibility that the Soviets might also be able to do so could not be excluded.

52. John Lewis Caddis reminded us, during his debate with Nitze on this document, "Until 1975 no one without top secret clearance could read it;" John Lewis Caddis, "NSC-68 and the Problem of Ends and Means," *International Security* 4, no. 4 (Spring 1980): 165.

53. Nitze informs us about the key authors that worked under his supervision: John Paton Davies coined the phrase "to frustrate the Kremlin design," a phrase that later was picked up by Foster Dulles and inserted in the 1952 Republican platform; Robert Hooker wrote the sections on the ideological struggles between East and West. Bob Tufts was another key contributor; Nitze, *From Hiroshima to Glasnost*, 94.

54. NSC-68, 5; all quotations from NSC-68, "NSC-68: United States Objectives and Programs for National Security (April 14, 1950): A Report to the President Pursuant to the President's Directive of January 31, 1950," National Security Council, http://www.fas.org/irp/offdocs/nsc-hst/nsc-68.htm.

55. Ibid., 8.

56. Nitze, "The Development of NSC-68," 172.

57. See in particular, Nitze, *From Hiroshima to Glasnost*, 31–33, 39 passim.

58. NSC-68, 14.

59. Ibid., 22 passim. As John Lamberton Harper remarks sharply, "NSC-68 exaggerated the *direct* threat to US soil" in order to convince skeptics in the Congress and the administration—including Truman himself and Defense Secretary Louis Johnson—to approve budgets with exceedingly high spending ceilings in defense; *American Visions*, 293.

60. NSC-68, 23.

61. Acheson, *Present at the Creation*, 374.

62. Nitze, "The Development of NSC-68," 172, 176. As in his autobiography, Nitze argues that the principal consultant to the Policy Planning Staff, Robert Oppenheimer, felt that any H-bomb testing would be costly and that its conversion to a proper weapon was rather impractical. All of those propositions, Nitze argued, were wrong; thus, the Soviets "developed a hydrogen bomb before we did," 176.

63. NSC-68, 41.

64. Josef Joffe, "How America Does It," *Foreign Affairs* 76, no. 5 (September–October 1997): 16–17, 21.

65. Robert Kagan, *Paradise and Power* (London: Atlantic Books, 2003), 18.

66. Ronald Steel, *Temptations of a Superpower* (Cambridge, MA: Harvard University Press, 1995), 22.

67. Kagan, *Paradise and Power*, 91.

68. The paper can be downloaded from www.newamericancentury.org. For a perceptive discussion on how this project finally hijacked the Pentagon and the White House establishments, beginning with Wolfowitz's "Defense Planning Guidance" document of 1992, see David Amstrong, "Dick Cheney's Song of America: Drafting a Plan for Global Dominance," *Harper's Magazine* (October 2002), 76–83.

69. This is the argument, for example, followed by Steven W. Hook, *US Foreign Policy* (New York: CQ Press, 2004), 146–48 passim; and, to a lesser extent, by Fraser Cameron, *US Foreign Policy after the Cold War* (London: Routledge, 2002), 53–60.

70. See the discussion between Barton Gellman (*The Washington Post*), John Lewis Gaddis, William Kristol, and Dennis Ross (former State Department official and Mideast envoy), Public Broacasting Service Web site, www.pbs.org/wgbh/pages/frontline/shows/iraq/themes/1992.html.

71. *Rebuilding America's Defenses: Strategy, Forces and Resources for a New Century*, September 2000, www.newamericancentury.org.

72. See Project on Defense Alternatives, www.comw.org/pda.

73. Ibid.

74. Cameron, *US Foreign Policy*, 47.

75. Here we follow Amstrong, "Dick Cheney's Song of America," 77–78.

76. Among others, Ted Galen Carpenter, "NATO's New Strategic Concept: Coherent Blueprint or Conceptual Muddle?," in *NATO Enters the 21st Century*, ed. Ted Galen Carpenter, 7–28 (London: Frank Cass, 2001).

77. See Fouskas, *Zones of Conflict*, chapter 3.

78. "Defense Planning Guidance," 1992, www.pbs.org/wgbh/pages/frontline/shows/iraq/etc/wol.html (accessed March 16, 2004).

79. Emphasis ours. *Joint Vision 2020* (Washington, DC: Government Printing Office, June 2000), 8. The approval authority was General Henry H. Shelton, chair of the Joint Chiefs of Staff.

80. Office of the President of the United States of America, *The National Security Strategy of the United States of America* (Washington, DC: Government Printing Office, September 2002), 15.

81. Henry Kissinger, "Henry Kissinger at Large, Part Two," *Think Tank with Ben Wattenberg*, February 5, 2004, http://www.pbs.org/thinktank/transcript1139.html.

CHAPTER 3

The New American Way of War

> The hidden hand of the market will never work without a hidden fist—McDonald's cannot flourish without McDonnell Douglas, the builder of the F-15. And the hidden fist that keeps the world safe for Silicon Valley's technologies is called the United States Army, Air Force, Navy and Marine Corps.[1]

The decline of U.S. economic power and the relative retreat of its dominant position in the world economic system has promoted a militarist drift in U.S. foreign policy. The belief that the United States can still reshape the world solely through military means has led to an increasing need for American troops to get involved in remote corners of the globe, something that Andre Gunder Frank called "US imperial political military blowback."[2]

In the decade since the end of the Cold War and the disintegration of the Soviet bloc, the United States has spent over $2 trillion on national security, more than all of its adversaries combined. This is not an anomaly, and today "the Pentagon's budget is equal to the combined military budgets of the next 12 or 15 nations" and "the US accounts for 40–45% of all the defence spending of the world's 189 states."[3] Even with this enormous spending, the Joint Chiefs of Staff argue that current military readiness is frayed and that the long-term health of the U.S. military is in jeopardy.[4] In a world constantly at war, only the military can command such a disproportionate share of a nation's wealth.

The so-called war on terror has allowed for U.S. military penetration into areas of the world where it previously was absent. During the war in Afghanistan, the U.S. military was able to establish thirteen new military bases in bordering ex-Soviet states, with Uzbekistan as the first central Asian state to host a permanent U.S. military base in early 2002. Shortly thereafter, other bases appeared in Kyrgyzstan and Tajikistan, and the attendant policy and praxis of common military exercises has reached to include distant Kazakhstan.[5] The establishment of these military bases in central Asia represents a major advance for the United States and ready access to the rich oil and gas resources of the Caspian Sea basin. At the same time, these military advances dampen and limit Russian influence in the area. U.S. leaders regard this trans-Caspian area as a backup for Middle East oil supplies, and some insist that the United States must "take the lead in pacifying the entire area," including the possible overthrow of uncooperative governments. All this also has strengthened the position of the United States in relation to Russia and Europe, but also against China, a power identified since the end of the Cold War as a likely challenger to U.S. hegemony in Eurasia.[6]

Today, the United States deploys more than half a million soldiers, spies, technicians, and other related staff in these Eurasian countries. In addition, some thirteen naval task forces dominate the oceans and seas of the world, and U.S. intelligence and security services operate in a dense network of bases beyond U.S. territory in an effort to monitor what the people of the world are saying, faxing, or e-mailing to one another.[7] It is not easy to assess the exact size of this U.S. "empire of bases," but partial records from the U.S. State Department show that the number of countries where the United States has a presence is at least 192.[8] All of these countries except one, Vatican City, are members of the UN, but according to a U.S. Department of Defense publication, *Active Duty Military Personnel Strengths by Regional Area and by Country*, the United States has managed to deploy troops in at least 135, or 70 percent, of all the UN member countries listed below[9]:

Afghanistan	Australia	Bangladesh
Albania	Austria	Barbados
Algeria	Azerbaijan	Belgium
Antigua	Bahamas	Belize
Argentina	Bahrain	Bolivia

Bosnia and
  Herzegovina
Botswana
Brazil
Bulgaria
Burma
Burundi
Cambodia
Cameroon
Canada
Chad
Chile
China
Colombia
Congo
Costa Rica
Côte d'Ivoire
Cuba
Cyprus
Czech Republic
Denmark
Djibouti
Dominican Republic
East Timor
Ecuador
Egypt
El Salvador
Eritrea
Estonia
Ethiopia
Fiji
Finland
France
Georgia
Germany
Ghana
Greece
Guatemala

Guinea
Haiti
Honduras
Hungary
Iceland
India
Indonesia
Iraq
Ireland
Israel
Italy
Jamaica
Japan
Jordan
Kazakhstan
Kenya
Kuwait
Kyrgyzstan
Laos
Latvia
Lebanon
Liberia
Lithuania
Luxembourg
Macedonia
Madagascar
Malawi
Malaysia
Mali
Malta
Mexico
Mongolia
Morocco
Mozambique
Nepal
Netherlands
New Zealand
Nicaragua

Niger
Nigeria
North Korea
Norway
Oman
Pakistan
Paraguay
Peru
Philippines
Poland
Portugal
Qatar
Romania
Russia
Saudi Arabia
Senegal
Serbia and
  Montenegro
Sierra Leone
Singapore
Slovenia
Spain
South Africa
South Korea
Sri Lanka
Suriname
Sweden
Switzerland
Syria
Tanzania
Thailand
Togo
Trinidad and Tobago
Tunisia
Turkey
Turkmenistan
Uganda
Ukraine

United Arab Emirates   Venezuela   Zambia
United Kingdom   Vietnam   Zimbabwe
Uruguay   Yemen

Others could be added to this list, including the Indian Ocean territory of
Diego Garcia, Gibraltar, and the Atlantic Ocean island of St. Helena,
all which are controlled by Great Britain but not considered as inde-
pendently sovereign. Greenland also is home to U.S. troops, but is tech-
nically part of Denmark. Troops in two other regions, Kosovo and Hong
Kong, could be included here, but the Department of Defense's *Personnel
Strengths* document includes U.S. troops in Kosovo under Serbia and U.S.
troops in Hong Kong under China.[10]

Once upon a time, one could trace the spread of imperialism by
counting colonies. In the neo-imperial version, colonies are military
bases. Some of these bases are so large that they require as many as nine
internal bus routes to transport soldiers and civilian contractors. Camp
Bondsteel, a massive U.S. base located in the hills just east of the
southern Kosovo town of Urosevac, is the biggest "from scratch" foreign
U.S. military base since the Vietnam War. It is known as the grand dame
in a network of U.S. bases running on both sides of the border between
Kosovo and Macedonia, and is so large that the U.S. General Accounting
Office likens it to "a small town" of some 360,000 square meters.[11] After
NATO's bombing campaign in March 1999, the United States spent
$36.6 million to build Camp Bondsteel, the work being completed by the
Brown and Root Division of Halliburton, the world's biggest oil services
corporation, which was run by Dick Cheney before he became the U.S.
vice president.[12]

Following the U.S.-led invasion of Iraq in 2003, plans were drawn up to
establish even bigger and more long-lasting military bases. By late 2003,
recreational areas throughout Baghdad had been taken over by American
forces. Baghdad's former weekend attractions—the Martyr's Monument,
the Games City theme park, the Wedding Island marriage venue, and the
Saddamiyat al-Tharthar—were declared military zones. Only the zoo
remained open to the public. By late January 2004, engineers from the
First Armored Division were midway through an $800 million project to
build half a dozen camps for the incoming First Cavalry Division—the
new outposts, dubbed Enduring Camps, will improve living quarters for

soldiers and allow the military to return key infrastructure sites within the Iraqi capital to the emerging government, military leaders say. "The plan is for the camps to last five to 10 years," said Colonel Lou Marich, commander of the First Armored Division engineers. "They will last longer if we take care of them."[13] The largest of the new camps, Camp Victory North, will be twice the size of Camp Bondsteel. Camp Victory North lies northeast of Baghdad International Airport, known to troops as BIAP.[14]

While Camp Victory North is the division's largest encampment, work continues on several other camps. North of the city, about 5,000 troops will live in Taji, a former Iraqi base. To the east, camps Dragoon and War Eagle combined will have room for about 2,200. What troops now call Camp Muleskinner sits on Al-Rastimiya, the former Iraqi officer's war college. About 2,100 U.S. troops will share the base with the new Iraqi army. At Camp Falcon, on the southern outskirts of Bagdad, room for 5,000 is planned. Soldiers from the Fort Hood, Texas-based First Cavalry Division began arriving in late January 2004 and continued to flow in through March. The transfer of authority between the First Armored Division and First Cavalry Division took place in mid-April 2004. The incoming soldiers are occupying the new camps.[15]

Further, the establishment of new military bases

> may in the long run be more critical to U.S. war planners and the enemies of the U.S. than the wars themselves. The attack on September 11 was not directly tied to the Gulf War—Osama bin Laden had backed the Saudi fundamentalist dictatorship against the Iraqi secular dictatorship. Rather, the attacks had their roots in the U.S. decision to leave behind bases in Saudi Arabia and other Gulf states.[16]

In fact, the widespread presence of the U.S. military was a major cause of terrorism against the United States in the first place.[17] In 1997, the Defense Science Board—a panel of experts that advises the Secretary of Defense—noted the link between an activist American foreign policy and terrorism against the United States:

> As part of its global position, the United States is called upon frequently to respond to international causes and deploy forces around the world. America's position in the world invites attack simply because of its presence. Further, an examination of historical data show a strong correlation between U.S. involvements in international situations and an increase in terrorist attacks against the United States.[18]

It is not easy being a global military power. It takes a lot of effort—both money and troops—spread all over the globe. But it became possible for the United States as a consequence of the reorganization of the American military and security apparatuses during the 1990s under the so-called revolution in military affairs (RMA).[19] The concept of an RMA itself, its constituent elements, and the timing of its occurrence, however, remain subjects of continuing debate.[20] But it is clear that a sea change was occurring in military planning, as planners attempted to learn from their collective experiences in unconventional and modern warfare.

There are several interpretations of the exact number and constituent elements of earlier RMAs. One analyst counts as many as ten RMAs since the fourteenth century.[21] The infantry revolution and the artillery revolution took place during the Hundred Years' War. In the first of these, infantry displaced the dominant role of heavy cavalry on the battlefield; in the second, advances in technology led to the development of effective cannons and siege warfare, which could quickly degrade the formerly strong defenses of cities. The outcome of the Battle of Crécy, a battle of the Hundred Years' War—which marked the end of cavalry supremacy—provides an example of the overwhelming dominance that followed an RMA.[22] In that battle the French lost 1,542 knights and lords and suffered over 10,000 casualties among crossbowmen and other support troops. The victorious English, relying on disciplined formations of infantry with unprecedented use of longbowmen, lost two knights, one squire, forty other men-at-arms and archers, and "a few dozen Welsh."[23]

In 1991, in the wake of the Persian Gulf War, a debate broke out asking whether the world had witnessed an RMA.[24] Although some commentators had identified as many as ten previous RMAs, the term used in this debate evolved from a form, "military technical revolution," that was used by Soviet military theorists. In the early 1970s, Soviet defense experts had begun exploring this idea, and had identified two periods of fundamental military change in the twentieth century: one driven by the emergence of aircraft, motor vehicles, and chemical warfare in World War I, and the second driven by the development of nuclear weapons, missiles, and computers after World War II. The next military technical revolution, the Soviets thought, would involve advances in microelectronics, sensors, precision-guided automated control systems, and directed energy.

Other RMAs took place at sea, where the advent of sail-powered warships and cannon transformed the nature of naval warfare. A fortress revolution in the sixteenth century resulted from the development of fortifications better able to withstand the siege artillery of the day. The development of muskets and tactics to overcome their weaknesses and exploit their power led to another revolution. The large squares of pikemen and archers that had earlier overcome mounted cavalry now became targets for artillery and musket fire. The Napoleonic revolution took place when the French were able to standardize and improve their artillery, greatly increased the size of their armies, and greatly advanced the organization and command of their military formations; as a result of the Napoleonic revolution, total war became possible on a scale such as even Clausewitz had never envisaged.[25]

The expansion of railroads and fast telegraph communication, and the introduction of rifling for muskets and artillery created another land warfare revolution in the nineteenth century. The American Civil War was fought by taking advantage of these developments. A second naval revolution occurred at the end of the century as rifled cannons, steel ships, and steam power changed the face of warfare at sea. The end of this period witnessed the introduction of the submarine and torpedo. The culmination of the tactics, organizations, and technology of the two nineteenth-century revolutions was achieved in the early stages of World War I with static trench warfare on land and submarine warfare at sea.

The new technology and improved organization that existed by the end of World War I set the stage for the revolutions in mechanization, aviation, and information that took place in the interwar period. Some commentators claimed that the tank revolutionized warfare.[26] These revolutions led to the great military innovations of World War I: blitzkrieg by the German army,[27] carrier aviation by Japan and the United States, amphibious warfare by the United States, and strategic bombing by Great Britain and the United States. In the context of the recent debate on the RMA, it should be noted that all of the elements of the later revolution—motor vehicles and tanks, airplanes and radios—were already present in World War I. It was, rather, the combination of their technical development in the 1920s and 1930s, along with new doctrine and improved organization, that created later revolutions. Finally, the nuclear revolution took place as a result of the coupling of nuclear weapons with intercontinental bombers and ballistic missiles.

A defining characteristic of the last half of the twentieth century was very swift, accelerating, inescapable technological change; one of the major elements needed for an RMA is therefore technological change. At the same time, rapid societal change and organizational adaptations by military forces were also taking place. Some commentators use the term *RMA* to refer to the revolutionary technology itself that is driving change, while others use the term to mean revolutionary adaptations by military organizations that may be necessary to deal with the changes in technology or the geopolitical environment, and still others use the term to mean the revolutionary impact of geopolitical or technological change on the outcome of military conflicts—regardless of the nature of the particular technology or the reaction of the participants to the technological change. Members of each group use the term *revolution*, but in reference to different phenomena. The difference in terms of reference leads to different suggested alternatives.

Marshal Nikolai Ogarkov, then chief of the Soviet general staff, argued in the early 1980s that a military technical revolution was underway.[28] He expressed a concern that the emergence of "automated reconnaissance and strike complexes," including new control systems and very accurate long-range precision weapons, would bring the destructive potential of conventional weapons closer to that of weapons of mass destruction. The swift success of U.S.-led forces in Operation Desert Storm convinced the Soviets that the integration of control, communications, electronic combat, and delivery of conventional fires had been realized for the first time.[29] One of the leading military theorists of the Soviet Union and Russian Federation, Makhmut Akhmetovich Gareev, analyzed the trends affecting changes in military art by considering certain political-military assumptions about the course of world affairs during the post–Cold War era. He stressed the low probability of a conventional world war, but thought that states would instead rely on two means to achieve their objectives: subversive actions against other states, and gradually accomplishing limited goals through local wars, both of which offered the potential to evolve into large-scale armed confrontations.[30] This Soviet analysis of a military technical revolution quickly gained the attention of the U.S. Department of Defense, and "the often dazzling successes of integrated battlefield technologies (i.e., electronic combat, communications, imaging, precision strike weapons, and stealth technology) employed during the First Gulf War led many to conclude that an RMA was indeed taking place."[31]

During these 1990 debates, three basic concepts of the current RMA were identified. The first focused primarily on changes in the organization of the nation-state and its need for completely different types of military force and organizations to apply force in the future. The second highlighted the evolution of weapons, military organizations, and operational concepts that made these changes possible through advancing technology. The third held that a true revolution in military affairs was unlikely, but in its place a continuing evolution was occurring in equipment, organizations, and tactics in an effort to adjust to changes in technology and the international political and economic environment.[32]

These debates illuminated definitions of an RMA that emphasized the way that improvements in computer technology, precision targeting, and smart weapons created a realistic possibility for a new form of network-centric warfare. As a result, technological developments will increasingly promote a higher number of specialists, scientists, computer experts, and so on in the U.S. military.[33] The three major components of an RMA that were considered—intelligence, surveillance, and reconnaissance; command, control, communications, and intelligence processing; and precision force—would imply that in the future there would be not a single RMA, but a series of almost continuous revolutions based on the rapid pace of technological change.

Information warfare emerged as one of an RMA's central features following the debate, and has now achieved a prominent place in the works of military systemologists. This involves first either attacking, influencing, or protecting military reconnaissance, surveillance, dedicated communications, command and control, fire control, and intelligence assets; second, protecting, influencing, or attacking the basic communications links of a society (voice, video or data transfer, electric power or telephone system control commands, etc.); and finally, what formerly were called psychological operations. All these involve using television, radio, or print media to attack, influence, or protect the attitudes of soldiers, civilian populations, or leaders. Some commentators have suggested that the information warfare of the RMA is changing the very nature of the threat, as well as threat deterrence. Even though nuclear weapons still remain a reliable deterrent, nuclear confrontation is losing its momentum and information superiority is becoming the goal. "Smart weapons, with their precision strikes on strategic targets, now make non-nuclear deterrence realistic. It is no longer necessary to cross the enemy's borders, because it is possible to destroy the enemy without occupying his territory—the enemy can be destroyed without using nuclear weapons, and his communication and transportation structures can be incapacitated so he cannot retaliate."[34]

The continuing rapid advances in computer technologies are driving all of the above elements in the RMA. The improvements in computer speed and reliability, combined with new or more sensitive types of sensors, has made possible dramatic increases in weapons accuracy and lethality, intelligence gathering and dissemination, and communications. The ability to model or simulate processes, activities, or objects has grown exponentially in recent years. The desire to take advantage of the increasing sophistication of modeling and simulation activities has been one of the major aspects in the plans of the U.S. military services to adapt to the future.[35]

A war involving a participant possessing the elements of this vision of an RMA would take place at a very rapid pace, involving synoptic battlefield awareness, the use of extremely lethal precision-guided weapons, and control of the entire electromagnetic spectrum, and would be highly integrated among all the components and services. This type of warfare would be most effective against conventional but less technologically advanced powers, and obviously less effective against unsophisticated opponents or guerrillas.

Some of the consequences of accepting this technology-based view of the RMA would be a new focus on relatively small, highly sophisticated, technologically advanced weapons and organizations. The word *relatively* is emphasized because the size of the force would be generally considered to be a consequence of the size of the threat. Information and various strike technologies will provide much greater combat effectiveness to smaller systems and units. This capability, and the need to reduce unit sizes, will result in smaller, lighter, and more mobile forces—with more flexible organizational requirements.

> In the foothills of the Colorado Rockies earlier this year [2001], a group of Air Force officers gathered at a highly secure military base for five days of unprecedented war games. The scenario was familiar enough—the growing tension between the United States and a fictitious country that resembled China. But the battlefield was out of this world: a simulated war raging for the first time in space.... The year was 2017, and space was bristling with

futuristic weapons. During the exercise at Schriever Air Force Base, the United States and its adversary deployed microsatellites—small, highly maneuverable spacecraft that shadowed the other side's satellites, then neutralized them by either blocking their view, jamming their signals or melting their circuitry with lasers. Also prowling the extraterrestrial battlefield were infrared early-warning satellites and space-based radar, offering tempting targets to ground stations and aircraft that harassed them with lasers and jamming signals.[36]

The full consequences of many of the changes highlighted by the debate over the RMA may take place in the relatively distant future. However, the U.S. military has been making the most of this technology explosion, energetically exploiting it, and experimenting with it in its extensive global campaigns since the end of the Cold War. The real results of this effort will change the way the United States conducts military operations forever and will set the tone for many of the world's armies. It already has in many instances.[37] Some major organizational steps taken by the U.S. Department of Defense to institutionalize the examination of long-term change include the following.

- *Joint Requirements Oversight Council* (JROC). To the U.S. military, the establishment of requirements is the first step in the acquisition process. Formerly, each service essentially defined its own requirements. Created in the mid-1980s and consisting of the Vice Chiefs of Staff of the military services and the vice chair of the Joint Chiefs of Staff, the JROC has become a focal point both for furthering jointness in the acquisition process and, more important, for assessing future requirements. It is from the work of this forum that many of the new concepts currently in use by U.S. military chiefs have been developed.
- *National Defense University and colleges.* An Information Resources Management College has been created at the National Defense University, which together with various war colleges offers courses on the RMA and on aspects of information warfare. The Information Resources Management College hosted a conference at National Defense University in May 1995 on the global information explosion and potential consequences for U.S. national security. All these units are actively organizing seminars, short courses, and workshops on various components of the RMA.
- *Louisiana Maneuvers Task Force.* Named after a set of corps-sized army exercises conducted in 1941 to determine how U.S. troops might fight opponents with armor and attack aircraft, the modern incarnation of the Louisiana Maneuvers Task Force was created by General Sullivan in 1992 to examine the steps needed to be taken by the army to make the transition to the post–Cold War era. Initially concentrating on working through army exercises and advanced

simulation technology, in April 1994 the task force was also made responsible for integrating and synchronizing the creation of the design of Force XXI. One result of their efforts is the Force XXI Campaign Synchronization Matrix, which resulted in an extensive analysis of the new aspects of warfare. The matrix is significant because, first, it indicates the complexity of the steps that the army is taking to put into practice the general ideas behind the RMA, and second, it indicates the difficulty of integrating various new concepts and required changes throughout the army in a systematic fashion.

- *Army Digitization Office.* This is one of the three axes of Force XXI implementation. The mission of the Army Digitization Office is to act as the coordinator for army efforts to apply digital technology to all aspects of army activities: combat, combat support, logistics, intelligence, and training. The training element is quite important, as army leadership—and the Louisiana Maneuvers Task Force—have fostered the development of disaggregated, digitized simulation and training programs to examine the consequences of implementing Force XXI. In the context of applying information technology, one of the most interesting factors has been the development of a very sophisticated Internet World Wide Web site for Force XXI. The site makes available to all army personnel the goals of Force XXI, Force XXI history, texts of doctrinal statements, Force XXI development scheduling, and a range of background and supporting material. For fiscal year 1995, Congress authorized $95 million for the army's Digital Battlefield Program.[38]

- *Battle Labs.* Established in 1992, the nine army Battle Labs were designed to form hypotheses about new technology and changing methods of operations, and then to conduct experiments using soldiers and leaders in realistic, live environments. Battle Labs are used to identify, develop, and experiment with new war fighting concepts and capabilities offered by emerging technologies. The Battle Lab concept is intended to provide hands-on user involvement during the early part of the requirements and acquisition process. This is expected to produce better requirements definitions during the research and advanced technology stages of programs, when decisions that determine most of the system's life cycle costs are made.[39]

- *Future Technologies Institute.* A small, independent organization set up early in 1995 under the auspices of the Army Research Laboratory in Adelphi, Maryland, to concentrate upon the technology and doctrine the army will need twenty to twenty-five years in the future.[40]

Among the most recent key air force doctrinal white papers are *Global Reach, Global Power,* and *Global Presence,* each dealing with aspects of the RMA in the present and the near future.[41] Another project, Spacecast 2020, was conducted at the Air University at Maxwell Air Force Base to study and report on emerging technologies for space in the year 2020 and beyond. It was a space study directed by the chief of staff of the air force, challenged to identify and conceptually develop high-leverage space technologies and systems that will best support the war fighter in the twenty-first century. The study made significant progress regarding future space capabilities and the possible benefits for the U.S. military. Begun at the behest of Air Force Chief of Staff General Merrill McPeak in September 1993, the final report for Spacecast 2020 was completed in June 1994. The 350 participants in the study included faculty and class members at the Air Command and Staff College and the Air War College, scientists at the Air Force Institute of Technology at Wright Patterson Air Force Base in Ohio, members of the other services, government agencies and laboratories, universities, think tanks, and independent scholars. A majority of the military participants came from the operational line forces of all of the services. The final report consisted of two parts, one classified.[42]

> The date is 3 December 2020. It had been five minutes since the tingling sensation in her arm had summoned her from her office. Now she was standing alone in the darkened battle-assessment room wondering how she would do in her first actual conflict as commander in chief (CINC). "Computer on, terrestrial view," she snapped. Silently, a huge, three-dimensional globe floated in front of her. "Target: Western Pacific. Display friendly and enemy orders of battle, unit status, and activity level," was the next command. The globe turned into a flat battle map showing corps, division, and battalion dispositions. Lifelike images appeared before her, marking the aircraft bases with smaller figures showing airborne formations. Beside each symbol were the unit's designator, its manning level, and the plain-text interpretation of its current activity. The friendly forces were shown in blue, and the enemy in red. All the friendlies were in the midst of a recall. The map showed two squadrons of air-domination drones, a wing of troop-support drones, and an airborne command module (ACM) heading toward the formations of enemy forces. Shaded kill zones encircled each formation. Enemy forces floated before her, also displaying textual information. The image displayed enemy units on the move from their garrisons. Speed, strength, and combat radii were marked for each unit. Some enemy units showed—still in garrison—but with engines running, discovered by sensitive seismic, tactile, and fume-smelling sensors. "Manchuria," came the next command. The map changed. The CINC was now in the middle of a holographic display. Ground superiority vehicles (GSV), identified by the reliable structural sensory signature system (S4), moved below her, and drones flew around her. She could see her forces responding to the enemy sneak attack and monitored their progress. The engagement clock showed 10 minutes to go before the first blue and red squadrons joined in battle.

Aboard the ACM, the aerospace operations director observed the same battle map the CINC had just switched off. By touching the flat screen in front of him, he sent target formations to his dozen controllers. Each controller wore a helmet and face screen that "virtually" put him or her just above the drone flight being maneuvered. The sight, feel, and touch of the terrain profile—including trees, buildings, clouds, and rain—were all there as each controller pressed to attack the approaching foe.

On the ground, a platoon sergeant nervously watched his face-shield visual display. From his position, he could see in three-dimensional color the hill in front of him and the enemy infantry approaching from the opposite side. If the agency had had enough time before the conflict, it could have loaded DNA data on the opposing commander into the data fusion control bank (DFCB) so he could positively identify him, but such was the fog of war. The driving rain kept him from seeing 10 feet in front of him, but his monitor clearly showed the enemy force splitting and coming around both sides of the hill.[43]

Similar to the fictionalized version above, the authors of Spacecast 2020 stated that although they could not know in detail what the future would hold, they could speculate in an informed fashion on the technologies that would be of the most value for space and which were not beyond plausibility. In the introduction and overview, the authors stated that the most fundamental characteristic of space from a military perspective is that it possesses unprecedented vantage or view. The global view given by space is the enabler for the basic air force concepts of global reach and global power. According to the study, implementing the concept of global view as a reality would depend on three things: creation of an integrated on-demand information system for command users, development of increased and improved sensing capabilities, and availability of relatively inexpensive space lift. Before presenting the papers in the report, the authors of Spacecast 2020 set out four alternative future international environments and the consequences for military and commercial space arising from the characteristics of each. The four possible futures were (1) A Spacefaring World, (2) A Rogue's World, (3) Mad Max Incorporated, and (4) a Space Baron's World.[44]

Over 500,000 photographs were processed during Operation Desert Storm. Over its 14-year lifetime, the Pioneer Venus orbiter sent back 10 terabits (10 trillion bits) of data. Had it performed as designed, the Hubble Space Telescope was expected to produce a continuous data flow of 86 billion bits a day or more than 30 terabits a year. By the year 2000, satellites will be sending 8 terabits of raw data to earth each day.[45]

To the chiefs of the U.S. Army, the experiences of the 1990s—from the Gulf War to Somalia to Kosovo—provided ample evidence of the need for lighter, faster forces. Somalia and Kosovo demonstrated the price of building army doctrine around the seventy-ton M1A1 Abrams tank, which cannot be airlifted into battle in large numbers using the rough, smaller airfields of the developing world. No ground war ever developed in Kosovo, but had the United States decided to invade, the army's tanks would have taken months to show up.[46]

Although the debate as to whether there truly exists—or will exist in the near future—an RMA continues, U.S. military services are actively discussing the question and implementing various components of it.

> Today, no other nation even approximates America's singular combination of technological prowess, economic vitality, military strength, internal stability. . . . America's substantial security margin is reinforced by the strength of its allies. The NATO and OECD countries now constitute three-quarters of the world economy, these states plus other long-time American allies . . . account for more than 70 percent of world military spending . . . thus, not only has the general diffusion of military power slowed dramatically, it has come substantially under the control of the United States and its allies.[47]

Almost all of the participants in the process agree on the elements that created earlier RMAs. These are new technologies, new organizations and operational concepts to incorporate the technologies, and new doctrine to encompass the technology and organization. There are many analogies with the period following World War I, but the vigor of the current formal efforts in the United States to examine the state of technology and necessary adaptations to military purposes distinguishes the efforts today. To the greatest extent, the U.S. Army has formally structured itself to examine future conflict and has taken steps to adapt itself to function—and win—in that environment. The air force and more recently the navy have undertaken more active formal efforts to examine future warfare possibilities. In addition, the very sophisticated war games initiated under the Department of Defense-RMA initiative and by each of the services have also served to highlight likely future environments and available technology. The overall trend in combat was toward fewer soldiers in a given battle space; at the same time, the greatly increased situational awareness and more capable joint weapons able to reach farther accurately would contribute to the expansion of the battle space.

As in the time of the telegraph, railroad, and rifled guns, the world faces a situation in which most of the technologies that matter are available in the civil sector. It is for this and related reasons that the really interesting issues over the next few decades will be not so much about technology as about operational and organizational lag. We are probably in the early stages of a true RMA. Even though there is a dramatic increase in the use of precision munitions, exponential increases in information volume and variety, and a corresponding decrease in sensor-to-shooter decision cycles, which are among the technical symptoms of the state of the RMA, there have not been enough fundamental changes in organization and operational concepts.[48] However, there have been some signs of possibly significant organizational change, such as the recent stand-up by the U.S. Air Force of Unmanned Aerial Vehicle and Information Warfare squadrons. It is also interesting to see an apparent trend toward small special operations units now fielded in the United States and the units in the U.S. Marine Corps.

All of this is designed to reduce domestic pressures on U.S. political leaders conducting global military operations by reducing U.S. casualties. Yet the significant changes associated with the RMA do not automatically provide a safer world for the United States.

> The tactical transformations accompanying the RMA create such a severe
> conventional military disadvantage for US adversaries that the response
> to the asymmetric military situation in which they find themselves will almost
> certainly involve the increased use of terrorism and other direct threats to
> US political and civilian targets. The less vulnerable US military forces
> are the more US adversaries are likely to increase attacks against US political
> targets, and even US civilians.[49]

AMERICA'S SECRET INTERNATIONAL SPY NETWORK

Airplanes taking a north-by-northwest approach into Denver International Airport often fly over a cluster of eerie white objects in the Aurora suburbs that rival the eclectic architecture of Denver International Airport, which the public and press ridiculed as a giant circus tent or a cluster of teepees. From some angles, the one hundred-foot spires that erupt in this urban landscape mimic the rough outline of Colorado's Rocky

Mountains that lie in the distance. But on these plains east of Denver, the white-domed landscape is never at rest as new towers rise silently, increasing their numbers year by year.

During the more than thirty years since Buckley Air Force Base became a primary U.S. intelligence base,[50] radomes have been added to the site on Sixth Avenue in Aurora with hardly an outcry from the local population. Resembling giant white golf balls, radomes—which weather-protect the huge satellite-commanding/data-receiving antennas—seem to sprout from every direction. Similar domes are now a regular part of the Federal Aviation Administration's air traffic control network, and many citizens thus have little reason to suspect that the Buckley "golf balls" serve anything other than a benign purpose. The base includes three separate land areas totalling 3,250 acres, and the airfield complex consists of one runway 11,000 feet long by 150 feet wide. Flying operations are active and all facilities are fully occupied and in use. Buckley's location provides a necessary and ideal refueling stop, particularly for military aircraft traveling the country in all directions. In addition to supporting all base-assigned aircraft, Buckley services up to 6,000 transient military aircraft per year, representing every aircraft type in the Department of Defense inventory and from every service and command, of which approximately 2,000 remain at least one night on base.[51] Each year, billions of dollars are thought to enter the Colorado economy through funding for top-secret facilities, such as Buckley Air National Guard Base and Lockheed Martin Corp.'s rocket and satellite factory, which sits only a few miles away at the mouth of Waterton Canyon in southern Jefferson County.[52]

The U.S. intelligence establishment, once dominated by covert CIA operations, is now largely conducted through the high-tech monitoring networks created by the National Security Agency (NSA) and National Reconnaissance Office (NRO).[53] However, most U.S. citizens either remain unaware of these agencies or, if they know of them, assume that their activities are far more benign than those of the CIA. Both approaches miss the significance of how these agencies currently operate. For example, since the Persian Gulf War in 1991, space power has become increasingly vital to the United States's high-tech style of war. Experts say the technical edge the United States gets from satellites has been critical to the U.S. role in Afghanistan: Where ex-superpower Soviet Russia crumbled against the harsh, mountainous terrain, the

United States operates from high above. "We'll be getting space support that the Russians back in the '80s could never have dreamed of," said John Pike, director of Globalsecurity.org, a national security analysis firm. Operations at Buckley Air Force Base Aurora give meaning to his words, as government spies listen in on terrorist networks using the radar stations inside the white domes. "It's generally assumed that at least some of the golf balls out there are NSA," Pike said. "There's spooky stuff at Buckley. So," he continued, "if there are radio and cell phone conversations in Afghanistan that U.S. intelligence satellites can pick up, Buckley is one of the places they would be downloaded and processed."[54]

The NSA is one of the most secret and secretive branches of the U.S. intelligence community.[55] Its predecessor, the Armed Forces Security Agency (AFSA), was established on May 20, 1949, within the Department of Defense under the command of the Joint Chiefs of Staff. In theory, the AFSA was to direct the communications intelligence and electronic intelligence activities of the military service signals intelligence units—consisting of the Army Security Agency, Naval Security Group, and Air Force Security Service. But in practice, the AFSA had little power, with its functions being defined in terms of activities not performed by the service units.[56] The December 10, 1951, memo sent by Walter Bedell Smith to James B. Lay, executive secretary of the National Security Council, which laid the basis for the modern NSA, observed that "control over, and coordination of, the collection and processing of Communications Intelligence had proved ineffective," and it recommended a survey of communications intelligence activities. The proposal was approved on December 13, 1951, and the study authorized on December 28, 1951. The report, known as the Brownell Committee Report, was completed on June 13, 1952. It surveyed the history of U.S. communications intelligence activities and suggested the need for a much greater degree of coordination and direction at the national level, and thus the NSA was born. As the new security agency's name indicated, the role of the NSA was to extend beyond merely assembling reports from the armed forces, but the agency itself remained virtually unknown until 1956, when a spy scandal at NSA headquarters was reported in the press.[57]

NSA influence was as broad and deep as was its early anonymity. In the 1950s, it was responsible for setting most of the directions for the U.S. computer industry, and from its inception it was instrumental in setting up the system of U.S. spy bases all over the non-Communist world in the early years of the Cold War. Many countries on the periphery of the Soviet bloc, such as Turkey, Greece, Norway, and Pakistan, were made hosts to several classified NSA-run antenna and radar sites, and in most cases local parliaments were either unaware of or had no input into the treaties that established these installations. Even today, members of parliaments in western allies of the United States, like Great Britain, are usually barred from entering or asking questions about how these installations operate and for what purpose. The NSA's goal in developing this extensive network was nothing less than the maintenance of a twenty-four-hour worldwide intelligence system capable of intercepting any communication of interest to the U.S. government, including the regular interception of domestic communications within the United States. The NSA has long been one of the most highly technological agencies in the federal government, and a building at NSA headquarters contains the world's largest collection of supercomputers in one place: a Cray Triton supercomputer used by the agency can handle 64 billion instructions per second and is commonly used for making as well as breaking codes.[58]

In the 1998 movie *Enemy of the State*, starring Will Smith and Gene Hackman, the NSA was portrayed as an evil Big Brother that spied on Americans. The plot centers on an NSA deputy director who oversaw the murder of a congressman because of his opposition to a bill that the NSA official wanted passed. As the plot continues, an attorney gets entangled in a web of national politics when a reporter friend accidentally records the murder. Unaware that he is in possession of the reporter's video, the attorney becomes the target of an NSA investigation, which nearly succeeds in destroying his personal and professional life. Only when he meets the mysterious Brill, a surveillance and information professional, does he begin to understand the stakes in this game. While he was waiting for his confirmation as the new NSA director, Lieutenant General Michael Hayden saw the movie in a South Korean theater filled with other military personnel. Sensing an image problem, General Hayden launched an NSA public relations campaign, remarking, "I made the judgment that we couldn't survive with the popular impression of this agency being formed by the last Will Smith movie." Whether General Hayden did more is open to question, but when questioned about NSA activities, he simply said, "Could there be abuses? Of course, there could, but I am looking you and the American people in the eye and saying there are not."[59]

The establishment of the NRO in 1960 set the stage for a new space intelligence agency that would become among the largest.[60] The NRO began as a virtual paper agency charged with coordinating the space missions of the CIA, NSA, and the air force's Space and Missile Systems Organization. It continues that mission in the present, although it acts more like a budget manager than a true agency with thousands of people in the field. Even though the NRO centrally established and managed photographic and radar imaging satellites, which played a major role in Vietnam and the Middle East during the 1960s, its name was never mentioned in public. Although it had been in existence for more than twenty years, public knowledge of it was so limited that it emerged only as a rumor in the mid-1980s and was publicly acknowledged only in September 1992 when its existence was declassified.[61] Beginning in the early 1970s, the core missions of the NRO began turning away from imaging to directly providing the NSA with space-based communications intelligence. This shift was openly promoted by high-tech advocates in the Ford and Carter administrations, and today the NRO acts "as part of the 14-member *Intelligence Community* whose mission is to achieve information superiority for the U.S. Government and Armed Forces."[62]

During the last two decades of the twentieth century, U.S. intelligence services made a show of consolidating or phasing out certain listening stations in Turkey, Crete (Greece), and Germany. However, most of these changes were public relations gambits, as the bases were simply shifted from one country to another. For example, when the United States was kicked out of Iran, China allowed two new U.S. signal bases to be constructed at Qitai and Korla in Xinjiang province. As reported by the London, New York, and Los Angeles *Times*, the United States and the People's Republic of China reached a basic agreement in January 1980, and actual intelligence operations began in the fall of 1980. The CIA's Office of SIGINT Operations constructed these stations, and in return the CIA provided technical training for the Chinese technicians that operated them and periodically visited the stations to advise them and to service the equipment as required.[63]

With the inauguration of the Clinton administration, a new era in intelligence gathering began in which multibillion-dollar satellites lofted into orbit by the Titan IV missile provided unprecedented opportunities to intercept communications in a wide range of frequencies from space. These more sophisticated satellites, bearing names such as Advanced

Jump-seat, Advanced Vortex, and Advanced Orion, have been launched with virtually no coverage from the U.S. media. However, Colorado residents often get an indirect confirmation that a launch has occurred because Lockheed Martin likes to take out full-page ads in the daily paper to congratulate its employees on a successful launch, such as a "next-generation military communications satellite, Titan IV, for the U.S. Air Force."[64]

The relentless development of ever more sophisticated spy technologies has a policy goal to ensure that every U.S. military engagement can be turned into a "turkey shoot," similar to the slaughter of Iraqis on the road to Basra during the Persian Gulf War in 1991.[65] Following the trauma of the war in Vietnam, the political perception has been that the American public will accept military interventions only where U.S. casualties are limited. In practice, military planning now includes choices that allow for potentially no casualties for "our side." Spy satellites, drones, motion sensors, and smart bombs have all become familiar high-tech weapons of choice to be used against real and potential enemies. The NSA supports these policies by directing spy satellites to photograph and listen to suspects' activities, while the agency's supercomputers search recordings for clues to the identities and whereabouts of the "enemy personnel." The Air Force then uses unmanned drone aircraft to record images and sounds using sophisticated radar and imaging tools. Only then do U.S. ground troops get involved by scouting for hostile forces using hidden sensors buried in the ground or dropped from the air by reconnaissance aircraft the size of large birds.[66] Over 500 satellites are now operating in space, of which more than 220 belong to the United States. This represents over a $100 billion investment and, *U.S. News and World Report* speculates, in the near future another 1,800 satellites will be added.[67] As a consequence, the Space Command has grown steadily bolder in using intelligence as a "force multiplier," and proactively using intelligence in preparation for preemptive missions has become a key part of the "New American Way of War."[68]

ECHELON: EYE IN THE SKY

The new technology available in the post–Cold War world has transformed the U.S.-led West's leading spymasters into sinister shadows manipulating a massive surveillance system that can capture and study every telephone call, fax, and e-mail message sent anywhere in the world. These high-tech espionage agents, backed up by a web of ships, planes, and radar and communication interception sites that ring the earth, have established the greatest spy network in history. Its name is Echelon. Echelon is the popular name for the automated, global, quasi-total surveillance system operated by the combined intelligence agencies of the United States (NSA), the United Kingdom (GCHQ), Canada (CSE), Australia (DSD), and New Zealand (GCSB). The network is very much an Anglo-American show, with the Americans as senior partners running it from Fort Meade in Maryland, Menwith Hill in Yorkshire, and GCHQ at Cheltenham, UK. In Germany, 750 Americans run the operation in an intercept station near Bad Aibling that was inherited by the U.S. Army in 1952.[69]

Echelon intercepts huge amounts of ordinary phone calls, e-mails, Internet downloads, satellite transmissions, and so on, gathering all of these transmissions indiscriminately and distilling the most desirable information through artificial intelligence programs. Some sources claim that Echelon sifts through an estimated 90 percent of all traffic that flows through the Internet. The United States has gone to great lengths to keep Echelon a secret, even though Australia and New Zealand have acknowledged its existence. As a highly classified system, Echelon operates with little or no oversight by national parliaments or courts, so there is no way to know how the information is used or whether that use is lawful. The U.S. Congress and other governments have raised serious privacy concerns about Echelon with interesting results.[70] Recently, the Scientific and Technical Options Assessment program office of the European Parliament commissioned two reports, both of which confirmed the existence of Echelon and described its activities.[71] These reports unearthed a startling amount of evidence that suggested how Echelon's powers may have been underestimated and how it has been used for other than purely military purposes. As the reports note, "Echelon is designed for primarily non-military targets: governments, organizations and businesses in virtually every country."

Echelon is now perhaps the most powerful intelligence-gathering organization in the world. Data is collected in multiple ways: massive ground-based radio antennae intercept satellite transmissions and tap surface traffic, and satellites are used to catch spillover data from transmissions between cities and beam this information down to pro-cessing centers on the ground. Echelon also intercepts Internet trans-missions through numerous "sniffer" devices that collect information from data packets as they traverse the Internet via several key junctions. It also uses search software to scan for Web sites that may be of interest.[72] Echelon has even used special underwater devices that tap into cables carrying phone calls across the seas. States that are involved with Echelon also train special agents to install a variety of special data collection devices, such as information-processing kits the size of a suitcase and sophisticated radio receivers that are as small as a credit card. All of the information collected is sifted through a system of computers known as Dictionaries that pick out relevant information. This vast quantity of voice and data communications is then processed through sophisticated filtering technologies.[73]

SPYING ON "FRIENDS"

In March 2003, just before the U.S. invasion of Iraq, the United Nations began a top-level investigation into the bugging of its delegations by the United States. The smoking gun was "a memorandum written by a top official at the National Security Agency, and circulated to both senior agents in his organization and to a friendly foreign intelligence agency," recommending that office telephones and the e-mails of U.N. delegates be monitored. Details of the memo, sent by Frank Koza, defense chief of staff for regional targets, which monitors international communications at the NSA, were published in the London *Observer*, showing that this memo was specifically directed against UN delegations from Angola, Cameroon, Chile, Bulgaria, and Guinea, with "extra focus on Pakistan."[74]

The memo was dated five days before Secretary of State Colin L. Powell's dramatic presentation to the UN General Assembly during which he played NSA intercepts of Iraqi officers and showed satellite photos of efforts to hide banned weapons. The memo advised NSA of-ficials that the agency was "mounting a surge" aimed at gleaning infor-mation on how delegations on the Security Council would vote on any second resolution on Iraq and on policies, negotiating positions, alliances, and dependencies. The agency wanted any information "that could give

US policy makers an edge in obtaining results favourable to US goals or to head off surprises," the memo reportedly said. The memo went on to say that the eavesdropping push would probably peak after Powell's speech.[75]

The leaked memorandum made clear that the targets of this heightened surveillance effort were the delegations from Angola, Cameroon, Chile, Mexico, Guinea, and Pakistan at the UN headquarters in New York—the so-called Middle Six delegations whose votes were "being fought over by the prowar party, led by the United States and Britain, and the party arguing for more time for UN inspections, led by France, China and Russia."[76] All the named countries, except Bulgaria, were among the Middle Six on the UN Security Council whose votes were being sought by pro- and antiwar factions. Though Pakistan had indicated it was likely to back the United States, and Bulgaria had been a strong supporter of the U.S. and British position, it appeared that the United States wanted to leave nothing to chance: nine votes were needed in the fifteen-member Security Council to approve any resolution and with the opposition of several permanent members the United States needed every vote.[77] As the *Observer* concluded in its story, this spying activity represented an "aggressive surveillance operation [by the United States]. . . . Sources in the office of UN Secretary General Kofi Annan confirmed that the spying operation had already been discussed at the UN's counter-terrorism committee and would be further investigated."[78] The United States was looking for any information that could help the NSA put pressure on these countries to vote for a U.S.- and UK-sponsored resolution that would authorize a war against Iraq.

What Koza never suspected was that someone outside the NSA would be so shocked by his request that they would leak his memo, or that it would end up in the hands of the *Observer*. By end of that week, the leaked memo and the story in the *Observer* combined to create the biggest spy hunt of the post–Cold War era.[79] As news of the spying operation spread, the British police moved in and arrested Katherine Gun, a twenty-eight-year-old whistleblower who worked as mathematician alongside code breakers and linguists at GCHQ in Cheltenham. She was charged under the Official Secrets Act with passing information to unauthorized persons.[80] But the charges against Gun eventually were dropped after prosecutors said they would offer no evidence against her.[81] In the NSA's Maryland headquarters, incredulity at the leak turned to fury with the knowledge that someone in a partner intelligence organization had de-liberately disclosed information that would cause severe damage to America's attempts to secure a second Security Council resolution au-thorizing war against Iraq.[82]

U.S. and British intelligence agencies extend their reach not only to those still working for the United Nations, like Secretary General Kofi Annan, but even to those who have retired. Hans von Sponek, a former UN diplomat, speaking from his home in Geneva, said he had strong reasons for believing his phone had been bugged by the United States. "I am a small fish in all this," he said. "But I feel uncomfortable at times, without being paranoid." Von Sponek, a strait-laced Prussian who was based in Baghdad for the UN, is not the kind given to paranoia. But as a leading campaigner against Iraq sanctions, he had been troublesome to the United States and Britain and was a natural target for the wide net thrown by the NSA's operation.[83] Former UN Secretary General Boutros Boutros-Ghali similarly has said he always assumed he was an espionage target, and Richard Butler, the former chief weapons inspector, has also admitted that at least four permanent members of the UN Security Council—the United States, Britain, France, and Russia—monitored his calls.[84]

The uncovering of this spy operation caused deep embarrassment to the Bush administration at a key point in its sensitive diplomatic nego-tiations to gain support for a second UN resolution. White House spokesman Ari Fleischer and Defense Secretary Donald Rumsfeld were both challenged about it as an illegal spying operation but said they could not comment on security matters. The operation was thought to have been authorized by U.S. National Security Adviser Condoleezza Rice, but American intelligence experts told the *Observer* that a decision of this kind would also have involved Donald Rumsfeld, CIA Director George Tenet, and NSA chief General Michael Hayden. President Bush himself must have been informed at one of the daily intelligence briefings held every morning at the White House, whether or not he accepted respon-sibility for it.

The *Observer* story caused a political furor in Chile, where President Ricardo Lagos demanded an immediate explanation of the spying oper-ation. The Chilean public is extremely sensitive to reports of U.S. dirty tricks after decades of American Secret Service involvement in the country's internal affairs, and has its own memories of September 11 as the day in 1973 when the CIA supported a coup that toppled the democratically elected socialist government of Salvador Allende, resulting in Allende's suicide. That coup brought to power the hated dictator General Augusto Pinochet, whose military and civilian supporters tortured, killed, or abducted some four thousand people in their seventeen years in power.[85] President Lagos spoke on the telephone with Prime Minister Tony Blair about the memo immediately after the publication of the story, and twice again the following week. Chile's foreign minister, Soledad Alvear, also raised the matter with Foreign Secretary Jack Straw. Chile's ambassador to Britain, Mariano Fernández, told the *Observer*: "We cannot understand why the United States was spying on Chile. We were very surprised. Relations have been good with America since the time of George Bush Senior." He went on to remind Straw that the position of the Chilean mission to the UN was published in regular diplomatic bulletins, which were public documents openly available. Mexico also sent a letter to Britain and the United States asking them to explain accusations that they spied on countries before the Iraq war, and Mexico's former UN ambassador—who said he had been spied on—called on Mexico to file a formal complaint with the UN Secretary General. U.S. State Department spokeswoman Brenda Greenberg declined to comment on Mexico's request, offering, "We don't comment on allegations concerning intelligence matters."[86]

While bugging foreign diplomats at the UN is permissible under the U.S. Foreign Intelligence Services Act, it still represents a breach of the Vienna Convention on Diplomatic Relations, according to one of America's leading experts on international law, Professor John Quigley of Ohio University. His analysis of the convention finds that "The receiving state shall permit and protect free communication on the part of the mission for all official purposes. . . . The official correspondence of the mission shall be inviolable."[87]

In a *London Times* article that appeared a few days after the bombshell in the *Observer*, it noted that the leaked memo was at least an "embarrassing disclosure." And the embarrassment was nearly worldwide—from Russia to Japan to Chile to Mexico to Australia, the story was big mainstream news, but not in the United States. Several days after the "embarrassing disclosure," not a word about it had appeared in America's supposed paper of record. The *New York Times*—the single most influential media outlet in the United States—still had not printed anything about the story. Why? "Well, it's not that we haven't been interested," *New York Times* deputy foreign editor Alison Smale said, nearly ninety-six hours after the *Observer* broke the story. "We could get no confirmation or comment" on the memo from U.S. officials. However, the *New York Times* opted not to relay the *Observer's* account, because, according to Smale, "We would normally expect to do our own intelligence reporting." She added, "We are still definitely looking into it. It's not that we're not."[88]

Eventually, the matter of Washington's spying at the UN remained off the American media map for several months. Delayed coverage would be better than none at all, but readers have a right to be suspicious when the *New York Times* fails to cover a story of this importance during its crucial first days. "At some moments in history, when war and peace hang in the balance, journalism delayed is journalism denied."[89] Overall, the thin U.S. coverage that did emerge seemed eager to downplay the importance of the *Observer's* revelations. On March 4, 2003, the *Washington Post* ran a back-page 514-word article headlined "Spying Report No Shock to U.N.," while the *Los Angeles Times* published a longer piece that began by emphasizing that U.S. spy activities at the United Nations were "long-standing."[90] The U.S. media's sharply different coverage did not go unnoticed in other countries. "While some have taken a ho-hum attitude in the U.S., many around the world are furious," says Ed Vulliamy, one of the *Observer* reporters who wrote the March 2 article. "Still, almost all governments are extremely reluctant to speak up against the espionage. This further illustrates their vulnerability to the U.S. government."[91]

THE PERVERSIONS OF PSYCHE-WAR

American citizens may be unaware of how Washington exercises its global hegemony, since so much of this activity takes place either in relative secrecy or under comforting rubrics. U.S. intelligence services conduct numerous covert operations in the name of keeping the United States safe and protecting its interests. They topple governments, train military and paramilitary forces, and conduct propaganda campaigns, all while denying their activities to the press and the public.[92] From 1950 to 1962, the CIA conducted massive, secret research into coercion and the malleability of human consciousness, which by the late 1950s was costing a billion dollars a year, including the testing of LSD on unsuspecting subjects.[93] Like the Nazi doctors who experimented upon concentration camp inmates during World War II, the CIA victimized people who were unable to resist: prisoners, mental patients, the terminally ill, sexual deviants, ethnic minorities. Evidence of this can be found in the extensive CIA drug studies conducted at the Addiction Research Center of the U.S. Public Health Service Hospital in Lexington, Kentucky.

Lexington was ostensibly a place where heroin addicts could go to shake a habit. Although it was officially a penitentiary, all the prisoners were identified as "patients," and the patients referred to the doctors as "hacks" or "croakers" who patrolled the premises in military uniforms. The patients at Lexington had no way of knowing that it was one of fifteen penal and mental institutions operated by the CIA in its super-secret drug development program during the 1950s. To conceal its role, the agency enlisted the aid of the navy and the National Institute of Mental Health (NIMH), which served as conduits for channelling money to Dr. Harris Isbell, a gung-ho research scientist who remained on the CIA payroll for over a decade. According to CIA documents, the directors of NIMH and the National Institutes of Health were fully cognizant of the agency's interest in Isbell's work and offered "full support and protection."[94] The CIA's LSD experiments were conducted on many unsuspecting subjects in studies referred to as Operation Midnight Climax. In almost all cases, the victims were marginalized persons: prisoners, patrons of brothels set up and run by the agency, war resisters, mentally retarded people, the elderly, terminally ill patients, schizophrenics, drug addicts, foreigners, and, of course, any other man, woman, or child who would fit the bill of need. The agency installed two-way mirrors to allow observation of the drug's effects.[95] In 1975, a U.S. Senate committee criticized the program in the following words:

> From its beginning in the early 1950s until its termination in 1963, the program of surreptitious administration of LSD to unwitting non-volunteer human subjects demonstrates a failure of the CIA's leadership to pay adequate attention to the rights of individuals and to provide effective guidance to CIA employees. Though it was known that the testing was dangerous, the lives of subjects were placed in jeopardy and were ignored. . . . Although it was clear that the laws of the United States were being violated, the testing continued.[96]

While these CIA drug experiments eventually produced little of value, and in some cases were most effective in producing lawsuits, research into mind control has continued. In particular, this research is now focusing on sensory deprivation as an alternative and more effective psychological rather than physical torture—sometimes described as "no-touch" torture. Interest in using mind control as part of the national security apparatus started during World War II with research on hypnosis for interrogation, secure courier duties, and reducing fatigue. The Korean War gave mind control research a name, brainwashing, which has remained as part of our popular lexicon.[97]

CIA tortures carried out in recent history have often involved these new forms of psychological terror—sensory deprivation, bodily function deprivation, and sleep deprivation in rooms with no windows and continuous light. Other forms of mind control involved a wide variety of drugs that induce comas, brain surgeries including prefrontal lobotomies, massive Page-Russell electric shocks, and electroconvulsive treatments that were combined with endless tape-recorded interrogations. These interrogations were calculated to induce required answers from the "patient," and the tape-recorded sessions were played back to the patient by means of a helmet fitted with headphones. The helmet might be worn for days with the tape playing endlessly. In some cases, a combination of these techniques was used until the broken patient died. Many that entered these psyche-war laboratories never saw family, friends, or the light of day again. To say it was a living hellish nightmare for most would be to put it mildly.[98] These "special operations" are run by the CIA through various intermediaries, some of whom have large financial interests in the experiments. One such company, Eli Lilly, told the CIA at its height of LSD manufacture that it could supply tons of the drug.[99] George Herbert Walker Bush, who became a CIA director and later president, was also a member of the Eli Lilly board of directors from 1977 to 1979.[100]

The CIA's psychological torture paradigm is based on two methods, sensory disorientation and self-inflicted pain, both of which are aimed at causing victims to feel responsible for their own suffering and so to capitulate more readily to their torturers. A week after the Abu Ghraib scandal broke, General Geoffrey Miller, U.S. prison commander in Iraq (and formerly in Guantanamo Bay, Cuba), offered an unwitting summary of this two-phase torture. "We will no longer, in any circumstances, hood any of the detainees," the general said. "We will no longer use stress positions in any of our interrogations. And we will no longer use sleep deprivation in any of our interrogations." Although seemingly less brutal than physical methods, the CIA's no-touch torture actually leaves deep, searing psychological scars on both victims and their interrogators. Victims often need a long period of treatment to recover from a trauma many experts consider more crippling than physical pain. Perpetrators can suffer a dangerous expansion of ego, leading to escalating acts of cruelty and lasting emotional disorders.[101] When applied in actual operations, the CIA's psychological procedures have frequently led to unimaginable cruelties, physical and sexual, by individual perpetrators whose improvisations are often horrific and only occasionally effective.[102]

Once the war on terror started, the U.S. military and security agencies started again widely using no-touch torture, first surfacing at Bagram Air Base near Kabul in early 2002, where Pentagon investigators found two Afghans who had died during interrogation. In reports from Iraq, the methods are strikingly similar to those detailed over forty years ago in the CIA's notorious no-touch interrogation manual that was later used by U.S.-trained security forces worldwide. Upon careful examination, those photographs of nude bodies at Abu Ghraib expose the CIA's most basic torture techniques—stress positions, sensory deprivation, and sexual humiliation.[103] Thanks to recent revelations from Abu Ghraib prison[104] and the Guantanamo detention camps,[105] these new techniques of psychological torture are becoming all too familiar, even if Americans do not recognize their history in earlier wars.[106]

NO BAD NEWS

U.S. intelligence agencies have not limited themselves to torturing individual suspects. During the 1950s, the CIA undertook several missions into Communist China, where it trained assassins to kill a CIA-drafted list of political officials in advance of a coup in Guatemala. The successful coup overthrew the democratically elected president, Arbenz, and put in his place a procession of dictators who ruthlessly ruled the country through military force and brutal suppression for the next four decades. Despite a series of gaffes, in 1953 the CIA successfully overthrew the popular government of Mossedegh and installed the Shah in Iran, whose oppressive looting of the nation benefited the United States for several decades, but ultimately led to the Islamic revolution in 1979 that brought the Ayatollah Khomeini and his Islamic government to power. In February 1963, working with British intelligence, the CIA backed a bloody coup d'état in which the Baath Party seized power in Iraq for the first time, but which also secured British interests in the area. The coup of 1963 was the worst bloodbath in the history of Iraq and can be compared only to the bloodbath that followed the September 11, 1973, CIA-backed coup d'état in Chile.

The new Iraqi government, in which the young Saddam Hussein was a notable figure, suited Western interests "pretty well," wrote Sir Roger Allen, the British ambassador in Baghdad. He told the Foreign Office a week later that "the present government is doing what it can, and therefore it is my belief that we should support it and help it in the long term to establish itself so that this communist threat may gradually diminish."[107] Immediately after the coup, Britain and the United States recognized the new regime in Baghdad. Things were "almost back to normal" from the ambassador's point of view. Following a succession of governments and infighting, the Baath Party consolidated its grip on power in 1968. A subsequent 1968 CIA-inspired coup d'état brought Saddam Hussein to power as the Iraqi vice president to Ahmed Hassan al-Bakr, where he remained until he assumed the presidency in 1979, with a U.S. blessing.[108] Similarly, the CIA created and supported Osama bin Laden and his organization in Afghanistan in the early 1980s as "freedom fighters" against the Soviet "evil empire,"[109] and only later "discovered" them to be Islamic fundamentalists. In each case, the American mass media at the time treated these events as if they had not happened, only reporting them and U.S. involvement as a passing reference in an event characterized as liberating a country from Communist influence. This treatment rings familiar, as the German people were told that reports on Nazi crimes were no more than Jewish or Communist propaganda.

During the Three Mile Island nuclear power plant accident in Pennsylvania in 1979, a Japanese journalist, Atsuo Kaneko of the Japanese Kyoto News Service, interviewed many people who were temporarily housed at a hockey rink. He discovered that none of them had ever heard of Hiroshima.[110] *National Geographic* reported in 2003 that

85% of young Americans (18–24) couldn't identify Iraq, Afghanistan or Israel on an unmarked map, 56% couldn't find the Indian subcontinent dangling there so conspicuously into none other than the Indian Ocean, and only 19% could name four countries that acknowledge having nuclear weapons. Fortunately, a whopping 70% could identify the Pacific Ocean, but that's probably because it's the biggest thing on the planet and lies just to the west of the U.S. Such levels of ignorance can't be found in most other industrialized countries.[111]

Even those Americans who say they are paying attention, at least to television, are highly misinformed. A massive University of Maryland study found that most who got their news from commercial television held at least one of three fundamental misperceptions regarding the recent war in Iraq: (1) that Iraq had been directly linked to 9/11, (2) that weapons of mass destruction had been found in Iraq, or (3) that world opinion supported the U.S. invasion of Iraq.[112] The great mass media channels

are always changing the reason for the invasion, and if one of them is proven false they invent another. In a national survey about which television channels were most watched by the population, it was discovered that the majority watch news on the Fox chain. Of these, 80% said that weapons of mass destruction were found in Iraq: in other words the great mass media seems to confuse rather than inform their viewers—a conclusion sadly made that in the U.S. with its ubiquitous television coverage and mass circulation newspapers the people are the least-informed in the world.[113]

The CIA was shaped out of the Office of Strategic Services in 1947 as an intelligence-gathering agency directed against "plots" by "Communist spies" who were undermining U.S. freedom. It was reported that these "Commie spies" were using propaganda and brainwashing techniques to dupe Americans into accepting "Communist socialism." They were assured that this was required to counteract these insidious plots, and that this was part of a Cold War between U.S. freedom and Russian "brainwashing."[114] This value structure has been repeatedly and effectively embedded within the Western political culture even as international relations have evolved, shifted, and dramatically changed since the end of the Cold War.[115] Yet the Cold War discourse never dies or fades away: It is merely reborn with a new enemy. "The only way America is able to attack and invade nations is to first portray their regimes as threats to our security. Serbia's Milosevic is thus a Balkan 'Hitler' who must be stopped. And Iraq must be invaded because Saddam is building weapons of mass destruction, to give them to Osama bin Laden."[116]

Many Americans continue to deeply believe that their role in the world is virtuous and that their government invariably acts for the good of others as well as themselves.[117] Even when their country's actions lead to disaster, they assume that the motives behind them were honorable, in spite of a mountain of evidence that virtue and honor are political slogans rather than political principles. It would appear that the mind control that U.S. intelligence and security agencies have so freely exercised in other places in the world has had its greatest success in those agencies' home country and in their own artificially constructed world. Have they been brainwashed into believing their own propaganda? Or is this too another form of propaganda?

NOTES

1. Thomas L. Friedman, "A Manifesto for the Fast World," *New York Times*, March 28, 1999.

2. Andre Gunder Frank, "US Economic Overstretch and Military/Political Imperial Blowback," in *September 11 and World Politics*, ed. G. Bacik and B. Aras, 125 (Istanbul: Fatih University Press, 2004). The term *blowback*, which CIA officials first invented for their own internal use, refers to the unintended consequences of policies that were kept secret from the American people.

3. Niall Ferguson, "American Colossus," http://www.channel4.com/history/microsites/H/history/a-b/american.html.

4. PBS, "A Chronology of U.S. Military Interventions: From Vietnam to the Balkans," http://www.pbs.org/wgbh/pages/frontline/shows/military/etc/cron.html; Tim Kane, "Global U.S. Troop Deployment, 1950–2003," Center for Data Analysis Report 04-11, October 27, 2004, http://www.heritage.org/Research/NationalSecurity/cda04-11.cfm.

5. Martin McCauley, *Afghanistan and Central Asia* (London: Longman, 2002), 153; Andre Gunder Frank, "Doublespeak," December 2000, http://rrojasdatabank.info/agfrank/doublespeak.html.

6. Patrick Martin, "US Bases Pave the Way for Long-Term Intervention in Central Asia," January 11, 2002, http://www.wsws.org/articles/2002/jan2002/base-j11.shtml; Ivan Eland, "The U.S. Military: Overextended Overseas," July 24,

1998, http://www.cato.org/dailys/7-24-98.html. "The big concern here obviously would be China. China is going to dominate Asia because it's going to have the biggest domestic market there, just like we dominate the Western hemisphere." Thomas Barnett, professor and senior strategic researcher, United States Naval War College, February 11, 2003, http://www.cfr.org/publication.php?id=5569.

7. Michael Eisenstadt, "U.S. Military Capabilities in the Post Cold-War Era: Implications for Middle East Allies," *Middle East Review of International Affairs* 2, no. 4 (November 1998), http://meria.idc.ac.il/journal/1998/issue4/jv2n4a5.html.

8. Bureau of Intelligence and Research, "Fact Sheet: States in the World," January 28, 2005, http://www.state.gov/s/inr/rls/4250.htm.

9. http://www.dior.whs.mil/mmid/M05/hst0309.pdf.

10. Michael Mainville, "U.S. Bases Overseas Show New Strategy," *Pittsburgh Post-Gazette*, July 26, 2004, http://www.post-gazette.com/pg/04208/351890.stm.

11. U.S. Office Pristina, "Bush Says Vision of Peaceful Balkans 'Within Reach,'" http://pristina.usmission.gov/bondst.htm; Jolyon Naegele, "Yugoslavia: U.S. Troops in Kosovo to Be Well Housed by Winter," *Radio Free Europe*, http://www.b-info.com/tools/miva/newsview.mv?url=news/1999-08/text/aug25c.rfe.

12. M. Cohn, "Pacification for a Pipeline," *Jurist* (April 27, 2001) in http://jurist.law.pitt.edu/forum/forumnew22.HTM.

13. "Baghdad Coalition Facilities," June 2005, http://www.globalsecurity.org/military/world/iraq/baghdad-usa.htm.

14. "U.S. Military Occupation Facilities," June 2005, http://www.globalsecurity.org/military/facility/iraq.htm.

15. "Baghdad Coalition Facilities."

16. U.S. Department of State, *Patterns of Global Terrorism 2001* (Washington, DC: Author, 2002), 171, 176.

17. Zoltan Grossman, "New U.S. Military Bases: Side Effects or Causes of War?" *Bu-lat-lat* 2, no. 5 (March 10–16, 2002), http://www.bulatlat.com/news/2-5/2-4-reader-grossman.html.

18. Defense Science Board, *The Defense Science Board 1997 Summer Study Task Force on DoD Response to Transnational Threats* (Washington, DC: U.S. Department of Defense, October 1997), vol. 1, Final Report, p. 15.

19. "A military revolution occurs when the application of new technologies into a significant number of military systems combines with innovative operational concepts and organizational adaptation in a way that fundamentally alters the character and conduct of conflict. It does so by producing a dramatic increase 'often an order of magnitude or greater' in the combat potential and military effectiveness of armed forces." Steven Metz and James Kievit, *Strategy and the Revolution in Military Affairs: From Theory to Policy* (Carlisle, PA: Strategic Studies Institute of the US Army War College, June 27, 1995), 3.

20. Ahmed S. Hasim, "The Revolution in Military Affairs Outside the West," *Journal of International Affairs* 51, no. 2 (Winter 1998), http://www.comw.org/rma/fulltext/hasim.html.

21. PLA Senior Colonels on Strategy and Geopolitics, "Unrestricted Warfare: Part IV," *A February 2000 Report from U.S. Embassy Beijing,* http://www.fas.org/nuke/guide/china/doctrine/WEBRES4.htm; "Buck Rogers or Rock Throwers? Conference Report," October 14, 1999, http://www.fas.org/irp/nic/buck_rogers.htm; Report of the *Commission to Assess the Ballistic Missile Threat to the United States,* Pursuant to Public Law 201 104th Congress July 15, 1998, http://www.fas.org/irp/threat/missile/rumsfeld/execsum.htm.

22. "An Account of the Battle of Crecy 1346: A Battle of the Hundred Years War," from the *Chronicles* of Jean Froissart, http://www.chronique.com/Library/Knights/crecy.htm.

23. "The Hundred Years War—Battle of Crécy," http://www.archeryweb.com/archery/crecy.htm.

24. Metz and Kievit, *Strategy and the Revolution in Military Affairs,* 3.

25. Peter Paret, "Napoleon and the Revolution in War," in *Makers of Modern Strategy,* ed. Peter Paret, 124 (Princeton, NJ: Princeton University Press, 1986).

26. Karl Lautenschläger, Senior Staff, Los Alamos National Laboratory, "The Tank as RMA: A Case Study in Real World Technical Revolution," September 2001, http://web.mit.edu/ssp/fall01/lautenschlager.htm.

27. Blitzkrieg means "lightning war." Blitzkrieg was a German tactic used in World War II based on speed and surprise. It needed a military force based on light tank units supported by planes and infantry (foot soldiers). The tactic was developed in Germany by an army officer called Hans Guderian. He had written a military pamphlet called "Achtung Panzer," which got into the hands of Hitler. The tactic was used to devastating effect in the first years of World War II and resulted in the British and French armies being pushed back in just a few weeks to the beaches of Dunkirk and the Russian army being devastated in the attack on Russia in June 1941. http://www.historylearningsite.co.uk/blitzkrieg.htm.

28. *Canadian Centre for Management,* "Thoughts on the Emerging RMA," September 30, 2003, http://www.vcds.forces.gc.ca/dgsp/pubs/rep-pub/dda/rma/Primer2_e.asp.

29. FAS (Federation of American Scientists), "The National Defense Panel Assessment of the May 1997 Quadrennial Defense Review," http://www.fas.org/man/docs/ndp/ndp_assess.html.

30. General Makhmut Akhmetovich Gareev, *Esli zavtra voyna* (Moscow: Valdar, 1994), 112, 113. It is interesting to note that in June 1997, the Russian army proclaimed its own "RMA-based military reform," which failed due to lack of funding.

31. Canada Defence Planning and Management, "Thoughts on the Emerging RMA," http://www.vcds.forces.gc.ca/dgsp/pubs/rep-pub/dda/rma/Primer2_e.asp, September 30, 2003.

32. Congressional Research Service Reports Military and National Security, http://www.fas.org/man/crs/N_2_.

33. Edward N. Luttwak, *Strategy: The Logic of War and Peace* (London: Belknap, 1987), 77–80.

34. S. A. Modestov and N. Turko, "Geopoliticheskie I geostrategicheskie aspekty obespecheniya natsional'noy bezopasnosti," in *Protecting National Security*, Bezopasnost', no. 9 (1995): 23.

35. Army Research Laboratory, http://www.arl.army.mil/main/Main/default.cfm; http://www.usmilitary.com/army.html.

36. Jonathan Broder, "Forward, March . . . into Space," MSNBC News, Washington, April 27, 2001, http://www.msnbc.com/news/546843.asp?cp1=1.

37. J. D. Kenneth Boutin, "Prospects for a Revolution in Military Affairs in Southeast Asia," Institute of Defence and Strategic Studies, Nanyang Technological University, Singapore, November 2001, http://www.ntu.edu.sg/idss/Perspective/research_050108.htm.

38. Office of the Army Chief Information Officer (CIO/G-6), U.S. Army, http://www.army.mil/ciog6/digitization.html.

39. U.S. Army Battle Labs, February 20, 2003, http://www.army.mil/spectrum/library/battle_labs.htm.

40. Congressional Research Service Reports: Military and National Security, http://www.fas.org/man/crs/N_26.

41. Spacecast 2020 Air University, September 10, 1993, http://www.au.af.mil/Spacecast/Spacecast.html.

42. Ibid.

43. "Leveraging the Infosphere, Surveillance and Reconnaissance in 2020," *Airpower Journal* (Summer 1995), http://www.airpower.maxwell.af.mil/airchronicles/apj/spacast1.html.

44. Jay W. Kelley, Air Univ Maxwell AFB AL, Spacecast 2020, Vol. 1, June 1992, http://www.stormingmedia.us/24/2415/A241592.html.

45. Don Herskovitz, "On the Road from Data to Intelligence," *Journal of Electronic Defense* (October 1993): 95–96.

46. Michael Moran, "In the Navy, Size Does Matter," MSNBC, April 12, 2001, http://www.msnbc.com/news/550115.asp.

47. Carl Conetta and Charles Knight, "U.S. Defense Posture in a Global Context: A Framework for Evaluating the Quadrennial Defense Review," *Background on the QDR*, (May 1997), 2.

48. Max Boot, "The New American Way of War," *Foreign Affairs* 82, no. 4, (July/August 2003), http://www.foreignaffairs.org/20030701faessay15404/max-boot/the-new-american-way-of-war.html.

49. L. George, "On Pharmacotic War," in *11 September 2001: War, Terror and Judgement*, ed. B. Gökay and R. B. J. Walker, 164 (London: Frank Cass, 2003).

50. Buckley became an active-duty Air Force Base on October 2, 2000. On that date, the base was handed over from the Colorado Air National Guard to Air Force Space Command.

51. Air National Guard, "Prosecuting the Global War on Terrorism," http://www.ngb.army.mil/ll/04posture/content/air_ng_terrorism.html.

52. Ian Olgeirson, "Spy Chief to Head Colo. Firm," *Denver Business Journal*, July 26, 1996, http://www.bizjournals.com/denver/stories/1996/07/29/story5.html.

53. National Security Agency home page, http://www.nsa.gov/home_html.cfm.

54. Mike Soraghan, "US Has Mof Spy Techniques," *Denver Post*, September 27, 2001.

55. http://www.nsa.gov/.

56. National Security Archive Electronic Briefing Book No. 24, http://www.gwu.edu/~nsarchiv/NSAEBB/NSAEBB23/.

57. Loring Wirbel, "Confronting the New Intelligence Establishment: Lessons from the Colorado Experience," http://www.fas.org/irp/eprint/wirbel.htm.

58. In 1972, the FBI's Administrative Index (ADEX) included 15,000 Americans considered to be subversives, subject to mass arrest in the event of a national security emergency. *Paul Wolf*, "Echelon," http://www.icdc.com/~paulwolf/echelon/echelon.htm.

59. Echelon On Line Connaître le réseau Echelon, http://progsystem.free.fr/echelononline.htm.

60. The National Security Archive Electronic Briefing Book No.35, http://www2.gwu.edu/~nsarchiv/NSAEBB/NSAEBB35/01-01.htm.

61. Ibid.

62. The National Reconnaissance Office, http://www.nro.gov/.

63. Robert C. Toth, "U.S., China Jointly Track Firings of Soviet Missiles," *Los Angeles Times*, June 18, 1981, 1, 9; David Bonavia, "Radar Post Leak May Be Warning to Soviet Union," *London Times*, June 19, 1981, 5; Philip Taubman, "U.S. and Peking Jointly Monitor Russian Missiles," *New York Times*, June 18, 1981, A1, A14.

64. Newswire, "Titan IV Rocket Successfully Launches from California," May 24, 1999, http://newswire.spaceimaging.com/archives/5-24-99.htm; Rednova.com, "Successful Launch of Titan IV-B Rocket," http://www.rednova.com/news/display/?id=5167.

65. Human Rights Watch, *Report on the Gulf War 1991*, http://www.hrw.org/reports/1991/gulfwar/.

66. "U.S. May Use High-Tech Tools vs. Low-Tech Terrorists," *USA Today*, September 24, 2001, http://www.usatoday.com/tech/news/2001/09/24/tech-anti-terrorism-tools.htm.

67. Commander in Chief, U.S. Space Command, "'The Promise of Space' for the United States Space Foundation's 1997 National Space Symposium," United States Space Foundation's 1997 National Space Symposium, http://www.fas.org/spp/military/docops/usspac/speech3.htm; Howell M. Estes III, "Protecting America's Investment in Space," Aerospace Corporation, http://www.aero.org/news/newsitems/protecting-may98.html.

68. FAS Space Policy Project, "US Space Command Doctrine," http://www.fas.org/spp/military/docops/usspac/.

69. David Ensor, "The NSA: Spying on You?," http://www.cnn.com/SPECIALS/2001/nsa/stories/privacy/index.html.

70. Peter Goodspeed, "The New Space Invaders," *National Post*, February 19, 2000.

71. *Elizabeth de Bony*, "Satellite Spying?," July 6, 2000, http://www.infoworld.com/articles/hn/xml/00/07/06/000706hnechelon.html?0706thpm.

72. Vernon Loeb, "Making Sense of the Deluge of Data," *Washington Post*, March 26, 2001.

73. Peter Goodspeed, "The New Space Invaders: Spies in the Sky," *National Post Online*, February 19, 2000, http://www.fas.org/irp/program/process/docs/000219-echelon.htm.

74. Ibid.; Philippe Rivière, "How the United States Spies on Us All," *Le Monde Diplomatique*, January 1999, http://mondediplo.com/1999/01/04echelon.

75. Scott Shane and Ariel Sabar, "Alleged NSA Memo Details U.S. Eavesdropping at U.N.," *Baltimore Sun*, March 4, 2003, http://www.baltimoresun.com/news/nationworld/iraq/bal-te.md.nsa04mar04,0,7914034.story.

76. Ibid.

77. Daily press briefing by the Office of the Spokesman for the UN Secretary-General, February 26, 2004, http://www.un.org/News/briefings/docs/2004/db022604.doc.htm.

78. "UN Launches Investigation into US Spying on Envoys," March 10, 2003, http://www.taipeitimes.com/News/front/archives/2003/03/10/197437/.

79. The Age, March 2, 2003, http://www.theage.com.au/articles/2003/03/02/1046540068572.html?oneclick=true.

80. Martin Bright, Ed Vulliamy, and Peter Beaumont, "Revealed: US Dirty Tricks to Win Vote on Iraq War," *The Observer*, March 9, 2003.

81. "U.N.: UK Spying 'Illegal' if True," February 26, 2004, http://www.cnn.com/2004/US/02/26/un.britain/.

82. "Pre-War Spy Scandal Hits Blair," March 1, 2004, CBS News, http://www
.cbsnews.com/stories/2003/03/03/iraq/main542516.shtml.

83. *The Guardian*, February 27, 2004.

84. "Pre-War Spy Scandal Hits Blair."

85. *Intelligence Activities, Senate Resolution 21*, Vol. 7 (Washington, DC: Government Printing Office, 1976).

86. Mark Stevenson, "Mexico Asks Britain, United States for Answer to Spying
Accusations," Associated Press, February 12, 2004, http://www.sfgate.com/cgi-bin/
article.cgi?f=/news/archive/2004/02/12/international0853EST6239.DTL.

87. Stephen Pritchard, "Our Spy Story Spelt Conspiracy to Some," *The Observer*,
March 9, 2003.

88. Norman Solomon, "American Media Dodging U.N. Surveillance Story,"
March 6, 2003, http://www.epic.org/alert/EPIC_Alert_10.05.html.

89. Norman Solomon, "American Media Dodging U.N. Surveillance Story: U.S.
'Paper of Record' Still Hasn't Mentioned Spying Scandal," October 3, 2003, http://
www.workingforchange.com/article.cfm?ItemID=14622.

90. Norman Solomon, "Bugging Kofi Annan: UN Spying and the Evasions of US
Journalism," February 26, 2004, *CounterPunch*, http://www.counterpunch.org/
solomon02262004.html.

91. Pritchard, "Our Spy Story Spelt Conspiracy to Some."

92. *Supplementary Detailed Staff Reports on Foreign and Military Intelligence*, Book
IV, Final Report (Washington, DC: Government Printing Office, 1976).

93. "Acid Dreams: The CIA, LSD, and the Sixties Rebellion," http://www
.historyhouse.com/book/0802130623/.

94. "Weird CIA Drug Experiments in Lexington, Kentucky," http://www.levity
.com/aciddreams/samples/lexington.html.

95. *History House*, "LSD and the CIA: Government Operated LSD Whore-
houses? Believe It!," http://www.historyhouse.com/in_history/lsd/.

96. Given in Jon Elliston, "MKULTRA: CIA Mind Control," http://www
.meta-religion.com/Secret_societies/Conspiracies/Mind_Control/mkultra.htm.

97. Tom Porter, "Government Research into ESP & Mind Control," March
1996, http://www.totse.com/en/conspiracy/mind_control/162399.html.

98. "CIA: Bastion of Integrity," June 25, 1997, http://www.thewinds.org/1997/06/
cia.html. Stephen R. Weissman, in his book *American Foreign Policy in the Congo:
1960–1964* (Ithaca, NY: Cornell University Press, 1974), describes how the CIA got
deeply involved and used the most extreme "techniques" there at a time when
certain U.S. business and financial interests were at risk.

99. Eli Lilly and Company, "History," http://www.lilly.com/about/history.html.

100. "CIA: Bastion of Integrity"; Bruce Levine, "Eli Lilly, Zyprexa & the Bush Family (& the CIA MK-ULTRA LSD Experiments)," http://www.antidepressantsfacts.com/Bush-Lilly-CIA-serotonin.htm; Bruce E. Levine, *Z Magazine Online*, May 8, 2004, www.zmag.org.

101. Cheryl Welsh, "U.S. Human Rights Abuse Report," January 1998, http://www.mindjustice.org/7.htm; Alan Scheflin, "Freedom of the Mind as an International Human Rights Issue," *Human Rights Law Journal* 3 (1982):1–64.

102. Allen L. Barker, "50-Year History of CIA Torture," September 15, 2004, http://www.talkaboutgovernment.com/group/alt.politics.org.covert/messages/4424.html.

103. Ibid.

104. In the era of Saddam Hussein, Abu Ghraib, twenty miles west of Baghdad, was one of the world's most notorious prisons, with torture, weekly executions, and vile living conditions. Following the U.S.-led operations in Iraq in 2003, Abu Ghraib became a U.S. military prison. Most of the prisoners, however—several thousand, including women and teenagers—were civilians, many of whom had been picked up in random military sweeps and at highway checkpoints. A fifty-three-page report, obtained by the *New Yorker* (February 24, 2005), written by Major General Antonio M. Taguba and not meant for public release, made it clear that there were serious institutional failures of the army prison system. Specifically, Taguba found that between October and December of 2003 numerous instances of "sadistic, blatant, and wanton criminal abuses" occurred at Abu Ghraib. This systematic and illegal abuse of detainees, Taguba reported, was perpetrated by soldiers of the 372nd Military Police Company, and also by members of the American intelligence community. Seymour M. Hersh, "American Soldiers Brutalized Iraqis. How Far Up Does the Responsibility Go?" *New Yorker*, May 5, 2004, http://www.theiraqmonitor.org/article/view/25553.html.

105. Since the U.S. operations in Afghanistan in 2002, hundreds of people of around thirty-five different nationalities remain held in a legal black hole at the U.S. Naval Base in Guantanamo Bay in Cuba, many without access to any court, legal counsel, or family visits. Denied their rights under international law and held in conditions which may amount to cruel, inhuman, or degrading treatment, the detainees face severe psychological distress. There have been numerous suicide attempts. Recently new evidence surfaced that the abuse of Guantanamo detainees has been widespread (http://www.globalsecurity.org/military/facility/guantanamo-bay_x-ray.htm). The U.S. administration defines torture so narrowly that only activities resulting in "death, organ failure or the permanent impairment of a significant body function" qualify. It also claims, absurdly, that Americans can defend themselves if criminally prosecuted for torture by relying on the criminal law defenses of necessity and/or self-defense, based on the horror of the 9/11 terrorist attacks J. W. Dean, "The Torture Memo by Judge Jay S. Bybee That Haunted Alberto Gonzales's Confirmation Hearings," January 14, 2005, http://writ.news.findlaw.com/dean/20050114.html.

106. S. M. Hersh, "Torture at Abu Ghraib," *New Yorker Fact*, May 10, 2004, http://www.newyorker.com/fact/content/?040510fa_fact.

107. Ghali Hassan, "Iraq: History of Imperialism and Eurosupremacy," February 13, 2005, http://houston.indymedia.org/news/2005/02/37440.php.

108. "Central Intelligence Agency," http://www.rotten.com/library/conspiracy/cia/.

109. A. Brigot and O. Roy, *The War in Afghanistan* (New York: Harvester, 1988); "Who Is Osama Bin Laden?," BBC News, September 18, 2001, http://news.bbc.co.uk/1/hi/world/south_asia/155236.stm.

110. The accident at the Three Mile Island Unit 2 nuclear power plant near Middletown, Pennsylvania, on March 28, 1979, was the most serious in U.S. commercial nuclear power plant operating history, even though it led to no deaths or injuries to plant workers or members of the nearby community. But it brought about sweeping changes involving emergency response planning, reactor operator training, human factors engineering, radiation protection, and many other areas of nuclear power plant operations. It also caused the U.S. Nuclear Regulatory Commission to tighten and heighten its regulatory oversight. Resultant changes in the nuclear power industry and at the NRC had the effect of enhancing safety. Saul Landau, "More Nuclear Disasters: The Lesson Unlearned," Znet, November 8, 1999, http://www.zmag.org/ZSustainers/ZDaily/1999-11/08landau.htm.

111. Gary Leup, "The Matrix of Ignorance—Unplugging the Sixty-Nine Percent," *CounterPunch*, September 13, 2003, http://www.counterpunch.org/leupp09132003.html.

112. Jeff Cohen, "Bush and Iraq: Mass Media, Mass Ignorance," *CommonDreams.org*, http://www.commondreams.org/views03/1201-13.htm.

113. Interview with Howard Zinn, http://www.walterlippmann.com/zinn-cuba-5-2004.html.

114. "CIA: Bastion of Integrity."

115. Bülent Gökay, "Oil, War and US Global Hegemony," in *September 11 and World Politics*, ed. G. Bacik and B. Aras, 190–191 (Istanbul: Fatih University Press, 2004).

116. Patrick J. Buchanan, "Why America's Empire Will Vanish," *The American Cause*, May 5, 2003, http://www.theamericancause.org/patwhyamericasempirewillvanish.htm.

117. Biography of Patrick Buchanan, http://www.townhall.com/spotlights/archive/8-28-95/buchbio.html.

CHAPTER 4

Neo-Imperialist Ideology

The wind whistles through Midland, a remote town in Texas surrounded by open fields where nodding donkeys silently extract oil from the ground. It was here in the 1950s that the future President George W. Bush spent years as a boy and later returned to find his faith in God.

While many Europeans remain cynical over Bush's impassioned rhetoric about spreading liberty around the globe, the president's old friends from Midland are in no doubt that it springs from his religious convictions. . . .

Bush became a born-again Christian in the 1980s after attending a men's Bible study group in the town, 300 miles from Dallas, the nearest city. "If you want to understand me, [you] need to understand Midland," he has said.[1]

In *Leo Strauss and the Politics of American Empire*, Anne Norton attempts to trace the intellectual origins of neoconservative ideology.[2] Hers is a narrative full of useful information, which is based partly on her personal experience and contacts with neocons during her/their studies at various Ivy League American universities and partly on her knowledge as a political theorist. She argues that the cultural and ideological formation of neocons comes straight from the work of conservative Jewish philosophers and strategists, such as Leo Strauss and Albert Wohlstetter, both at the University of Chicago. They and their pupils, Paul Wolfowitz, Zalmay Khalilzad, Abram Shulsky, and others, blossomed and created a wide network of professional contacts in various policymaking bodies, think tanks, universities, the business world, and the media. As Alex Callinicos put it, all neocons seem to have endorsed Strauss's view, which Strauss himself attributed to Xenophon: "The best regime is then an aristocracy guised as democracy."[3] The end result of their political activism and pro-Israeli militancy was the hijacking of the Pentagon and the White House after 9/11. In *America Alone*, Stefan Halper and Jonathan Clarke reach a similar conclusion, although their focus is not so much on Strauss and Wohlstetter as on political processes.[4] They declare themselves conservatives, but castigate the neocons on a number of substantial issues. Other authors, such as Ivo H. Daalder and James M. Lindsay, see no connection between Strauss and the neocons.[5]

We come back to these themes in the last section of this chapter. But the main reason why we have made reference to these works is because some of them, particularly Norton's, rest on the work of German theoretician Carl Schmidt, who was the leading jurist of Nazism and whose work influenced Strauss enormously. Schmidt, in his work *The Concept of the Political*, argued that the political sphere is defined by a real ideological game between enemies and friends. The enemy is, or has to be, presented as a mortal threat "not merely to a person, but to the nation and the nation's form of life."[6]

Given our analyses so far, this is all the more interesting. NSC-68 and U.S. strategy during the Cold War exaggerated the Soviet threat for specific political purposes, both domestic and international, and so does the neocon ruling group today. "I doubt that Bush was aware of the intellectual lineage," Derek Gregory says, "but Schmidt's ghost seems to stalk the corridors of Republican power . . . and Bush's strategy depended on techniques of projection, hysteria and exaggeration that would have been familiar to Schmidt and his heirs."[7] We do not know if Nitze and Acheson were familiar with the work of Schmidt. But we do know that Nitze, Acheson, and Wohlstetter invited Richard Perle, a Pentagon guru, and Wolfowitz to work for them, "for expenses," as Nitze put it, when both were still graduate students in the late 1960s.[8] Under the guidance of the veteran masters, the task assigned to Perle and Wolfowitz was to produce a paper about why America should be strengthening its position with regard to its antiballistic missile defense systems. Amid the Vietnam debacle, the inventors of the hub-and-spoke system of American neo-imperialism were encountering problems in convincing Congress and other senior members of the Johnson and Nixon administrations to strengthen their antiballistic missile system before the SALT (Strategic Arms Limitation Talks) negotiations with the Soviets began. Nitze had played a major role in the SALT negotiations, an experience he described vividly in his autobiography. For the record, he was at the time (1967–69) deputy secretary of defense, a position that Wolfowitz did not seem to have lost sight of over the years to come. Wolfowitz had also participated in the so-called Team B, set up in 1976 by George H. W. Bush when he was director of CIA in the Ford administration.[9]

In this context, it is interesting to note that the friend-enemy dichotomy fits in with another Manichean scheme, the religious dichotomy of good and evil. A key constituency of the neocons that gave George W. Bush the presidency for a second term is the new alliance between Christian Fundamentalists and neo-Zionists.[10] Both groups read the human condition in biblical terms and as a choice between good and evil. But precisely how did the enemy-friend ideological scheme operate in favor of U.S. neo-imperialism during the Cold War? Who was the chief enemy in the 1990s, that is, after the collapse of the Soviet bloc? What is the ideological and strategic significance of the post-9/11 theme of the war on terror? How do the neocons use this theme both domestically and internationally? Why and how did it come to dominate the U.S. agenda and what do pro-Israeli neocons have to do with all this? At which points do the neocons and the Fundamentalists cross each other? These are the issues to which we now turn.

"EVIL COMMUNISM" AND "GOOD ISRAEL"

During the Cold War and throughout the capitalist world, the United States portrayed the Soviet Union as an evil force and as a dictatorship. In films, in theaters, in television shows and the news, in mainstream newspapers and the radio, in the education system, the Soviets were "belligerent" and "barbarians," whereas the "free world," guided by America, was a landscape of peaceful coexistence, prosperity, democracy, and civilization. Hollywood dominated the competition game for the global film production and distribution networks in the West. But anti-Nazi/anti-Japanese war films and films about the Holocaust did not lag far behind. The same goes for books, publicity, editorials, news, teaching in primary/secondary schools and universities, and so on. The lesson was learned: To control the present and the future of information, one has to have the instruments to control information about the past.

This is the best way to control people's minds, particularly in the Anglo-Saxon countries where this forty-year-long brainwashing has led the majority of their domestic populations to think of themselves as the guardians and promoters of the most civilized, liberal, and democratic values in the world. It has also led them to think in terms of black and white, friends and enemies—that is, in Manichean terms, something which, as we saw earlier, Kennan deplored. Moreover, it has led them to think of Israel in almost surreal and sacred terms, leveling accusations of anti-Semitism at whoever criticizes the acts of the Israeli state against the Palestinians. How could the victims of the Holocaust commit acts of genocide against the Palestinians similar to those Nazi Germany inflicted on them? From 1973 to 2003, the United States vetoed thirty-four UN resolutions criticizing Israel and also disapproved in the UN General Assembly the equation of post-1967 Zionism with nationalism as both being destructive and regressive movements.

Post-1967 Zionism, as Avi Shlaim so courageously put it, is the continuing occupation of the West Bank and Gaza, the continuing building of settlements, the 736 checkpoints, the construction of the illegal wall in the West Bank, the systematic abuse of Palestinian human rights, and the abandonment of the greatest accolade in Judaism, *rodeph shalom*, seeking of peace.[11] Yet the pattern was set during the Cold War and the layers of consensus in people's subconscious were created during that period. The West, under the leadership of the United States, would be bringing the light to the barbarians, that is, the East Europeans, Asians, Africans, and Arabs. Israel, never mind its illegal occupation of the West Bank and Gaza since 1967 and its state-sponsored terror leveled against the Palestinians, is excused by the Holocaust. Students in the West must study the Holocaust alone, not the plight and the rights of the Palestinians side by side with the Holocaust.

Broadly speaking, these elements of racism and Western superiority always existed in Western civilization: They are not exclusively elements of modern neo-imperialist ideology. As a matter of fact, the ancient Greeks used to say "whoever is not a Greek is a barbarian," justifying their wars—either offensive or defensive—and amassing popular consensus on this "moral" ideological ground. This racist motto was useful in many ways, of which the most important one was to facilitate the formation of alliances against the common "barbarian" army. Over the centuries, all these ideas have traveled inside the heads of our Western ancestors, adopted by the French, the British, and other colonial state elites, only to be transplanted into the operational schemes of war and peace of the new global configurations of power after World War II. "Alexander the Great," Bartle Bull says sarcastically, "wanted to bring the light of Hellenic civilization to new lands. He was the first neo-con."[12] The aggressive, imperial contact of the West with other civilizations in the East and the South created and perpetuated international and ethnic/religious conflict. The West is continuing to do the same today: At least since the French revolution of 1789, the movement of the Enlightenment, and the triumph of science over religious mystique, high-tech imperial and nationalist aggression against other peoples, empires, and civilizations has been the privilege of the West.

Over a period of several centuries, there emerged a Western collective memory concerning "the Eastern." The relationship between the Eastern world and Western powers took a number of different forms, but the keynote of the relationship was set for the East and Europe by the Napoleonic invasion of Egypt in 1789, since the Napoleonic expedition itself provided the first systematic setting for a "scientific" appropriation of the East by the West. By the mid-nineteenth century, European views of the non-Western world had changed drastically.

> The coming of the industrial revolution and the beginnings of European colonialism in Asia had intervened to reshape European minds, and if not to "invent" all history, then at least to invent a false universalism under European initiation and guidance. Then, in the second half of the nineteenth century, not only was world history rewritten wholesale, but "universal" social "science" was (new) born, not just as a European discipline, but as a Eurocentric invention.[13]

In light of this, Samuel Huntington's argument for a clash of civilizations between Islam and the West looks preposterous. Huntington argues that "the underlying problem for the West is not Islamic fundamentalism" but Islam as such. Islam is a "different civilization whose people are convinced of the superiority of their culture and are obsessed with the inferiority of their power. . . . The problem for Islam is not the CIA or the US Department of Defense," Huntington continues. "It is the West, a different civilization whose people are convinced of the universality of their culture and believe that their superior, if declining, power imposes on them the obligation to extend that culture throughout the world."[14] This is quite nonsensical: "Islam and the West" are not a matter of two competing cultural imperialisms, or two "superiority syndromes" in the ideological sphere, but a matter of Western military-economic aggressiveness and the imposition of nation-states on multiconfessional empires. As Mark Mazower put it, many in the West forget that "it was the introduction of the Western conception of the nation-state into the multinational societies of the [Near] East that had led to massacre in the first place."[15] In sum, all imperialisms, modern and premodern, have operated, consciously or not, within the framework of the friend-enemy scheme. A new element in the post-1947 neo-imperial ideological scheme of friend-enemy is the progressive insertion of Zionism and neo-Zionism (post-1967 Zionism) as a fundamental element of America's foreign policy; and this, objectively, was and is against Islam.[16]

But what did the United States make of the friend-enemy scheme, of the "free world versus evil Communism" during the Cold War? What type of political benefits brought it to the hub-and-spoke system of neo-imperial governance? How did the exaggeration of the Soviet threat play out in America's hands? How did the United States manipulate differences among its allies during the Cold War in order to maintain the cohesion of its hub-and-spoke system? We shall make reference to only two examples here from the Cold War period. The first concerns the German zone and the second the Near Eastern theater.

Germany, mainly under the leadership and influence of Willy Brandt in the 1960s and 1970s, had begun taking advantage of the official U.S.-USSR policy of détente (officially announced by President Richard Nixon on July 25, 1969). West Germany launched its own "little détente," the Ostpolitik. As Donald Sassoon remarked, among other things, "Ostpolitik greatly increased the freedom of action of the Federal Republic [of Germany] *vis-à-vis* its allies in the West," creating a solid and forward-looking framework of economic and diplomatic co-operation with the Communist bloc.[17] But this freedom did not go down so well with the Americans, and for their own separate reasons the French and the British. Following a tit-for-tat policy and pursuing a strategy of tension toward the Soviet-led Warsaw Pact (formed in 1955) "by placing Cruise and Pershing missiles on West German soil," the United States destroyed Germany's little détente.[18] The Americans were reminding the

Germans that the main enemy was the Soviet bloc and that all kinds of dealings with it must be done within certain limits and under U.S. and NATO supervision and control. The United States was as much afraid of the creation of a German-Russian axis during the Cold War as it is today.[19]

In the Near East, one of the main troubles for the United States (another was Iran after the Islamic revolution of 1979) was the deteriorating situation between two NATO members since 1952, Greece and Turkey, mainly over Cyprus.[20] Despite the fact that the United States had considered Turkey more strategically important than Greece, something reflected clearly, among other ways, in the ratios of military aid toward the two countries, Turkey had felt betrayed at least twice in the first half of the 1960s. First, it was treated with disregard during the Cuban missile crisis (1962), which threatened to make Turkey (as well as Germany) the main theater of confrontation between the two superpowers. Second, President Lyndon Johnson in 1964 stopped Turkey from intervening in Cyprus on the grounds that the United States might not move to protect Turkey's eastern borders if the Soviets moved to cross them in response to Turkey's military action on nonaligned Cyprus.[21] Under these circumstances, it did not take long for Turkey to begin a rapprochement with the USSR.

Turkish-Soviet cooperation reached its apex in 1967–68, when "the USSR agreed to build a number of industrial plants in Turkey, including a steel mill, an aluminium smelter and an oil refinery."[22] More important, in the 1967 (the Six-Day War) and 1973 (the Yom Kippur War) Arab-Israeli conflicts, Turkey, along with all NATO countries—except Portugal but including Britain, Cyprus, and Greece—refused to assist the Americans and Israel. The United States and Henry Kissinger promptly began reconsidering their policy toward Turkey and Turkey's pivotal importance for U.S. security interests in the Middle East, the Black Sea, and the Caucasus region. During the 1974 Cyprus crisis, Kissinger, both secretary of state at the time and national security advisor (the only American official to date to have held both these key posts simultaneously) gave the green light to Bulent Ecevit, the Turkish premier, to invade and partition the island. By getting a slice of Cyprus, Turkey was brought back into the NATO/pro-Israeli fold. Kissinger's success was enormous: a Greek-Turkish war was avoided, so NATO's southern flank maintained its cohesion; Turkish-Soviet relations were disrupted; and

Israel could again count on Turkey for support if similar emergency situations arose in the future.

"I'M RUNNING OUT OF DEMONS"

As we have seen, throughout the Cold War the United States used the liberal ideology of human rights and democratic values as a political vehicle to accentuate existing ethnic, religious, and politico-economic tensions within the Soviet bloc. This was done selectively: Witness the case of Allende's overthrow (and killing) by Pinochet and the CIA in Chile in September 1973, or the killing of Che Guevara in Bolivia in October 1967 by CIA agents. Moreover, Portugal was a member of NATO during Salazar's and Caetano's dictatorships; Greece's dictatorship (1967–74) was installed by a bunch of incompetent colonels, all of whom were on the CIA payroll; and Turkey's participation in NATO has survived three military coups. U.S. double-standard politics triumphed during the Cold War, but then the end justifies the means: The objective was the breaking-up of the "evil Communist system."

U.S. pro–human rights campaigns may have played a complementary role in the disintegration of the Soviet bloc, but they were not the key reason. As we have analyzed elsewhere, Communism's collapse must be understood in the wider context of an international debt crisis and the consequent inability of the USSR in the 1980s to finance a Star Wars program to match that of the United States.[23] Yet because of Reagan's emphasis on a military race with the USSR at all levels, and also because of neocons' declared admiration for Reagan's administration, many analysts trace the origins of neocons to the 1980s.[24] We have tried to show that this is not the case and that the neo-imperial ideas of neoconservatism in America transcend the origins of neocons themselves.

We have argued that the neocons radicalized the existing strategic framework of the U.S. neo-imperial program, which was first established in the late 1940s and early 1950s under Acheson and Nitze. This program was based on a triple strategic assumption: first, the creation of a visible enemy and the exaggeration of the threat it posed to America and the "free world"; second, the consolidation of a hub-and-spoke system of dependence of the Western bloc upon Washington's decision-making processes; third, the centrality of the dollar in global currency markets. But the collapse of the Soviet bloc damaged this program by depriving the United States of an enemy, loosening the dependence of the spokes on the hub, as the Europeans particularly began moving toward a closer political union, further undermining the power of the dollar by the declared aim of the Europeans to launch their own reserve currency—the euro.

Such was the situation during the Persian Gulf War, on the eve of the Yugoslav crisis, and in the run up to the Maastricht Treaty negotiations (1991), when the French and the Germans pushed harder for a common foreign and security policy. When the United States ousted secular Saddam from Kuwait in 1991—the former regional ally of the United States in the Gulf in the 1980s during the Iran-Iraq war (1980–88)— Colin Powell, at the time chair of the Joint Chiefs of Staff, complained, "I am running out of demons, I'm running out of villains."[25] His doctrine of the United States "deterring forward" via employment of overwhelming high-tech force in order to solve emergency situations and post-Communist types of conflict was in jeopardy because of a lack of clearly definable and justifiable enemies. NATO encountered the same problem: It had to define a new set of friends and enemies and envisage new ideological principles; otherwise it would have to dissolve along with the defunct Warsaw Pact. NATO's "new strategic concept," put forward in November 1991, endorsed in its essence Powell's doctrine and anticipated its own future expansions of 1999 (Hungary, Poland, and the Czech Republic) and 2004 (Bulgaria, Estonia, Latvia, Lithuania, Romania, Slovakia, and Slovenia).

But Clinton cut the Gordian knot. Faithful to the hub-and-spoke doctrine of his great predecessors, Clinton's team of strategists deemed that the post–Cold War system of global actors was composed of four main groups. The first group was the so-called core partners, such as the European states, Japan, and Australia. The second group was composed of transition states, such as former Communist states. The third group consisted of the "rogue states," such as Iraq, Iran, North Korea, and Syria, which reject the ideals of the core, sponsor international terrorism, and are eager to acquire, if they do not have already, weapons of mass destruction in order to damage the United States and its allies, the core. Finally, there is a fourth group, the so-called failed states or regions. This category places huge humanitarian pressures upon the United States and its core allies.[26]

Thus, after a fashion, the new post–Cold War enemies had been defined. These were the rogue states and the failed states. As for the transition states, such as Russia, Ukraine, and the "big Asian mystery," China, they would have to embrace full political democracy, advance civil liberties and human rights, adopt a functioning market economy, endorse antiterrorism covenants, and develop partnership agreements with U.S.-led Western institutions, such as NATO and the World Trade Organization. This is the ideological framework within which Clinton's administration geared America's establishment toward the concept of "humanitarian intervention," its apex being the NATO bombing of Yugoslavia in 1999. By the mid-1990s, following the Rwandan genocide and with the breakdown of order in failed states and regions, such as Somalia and Liberia, there were some 20 million refugees across the world. Anglo-Saxon populations could accept this form of ideology to justify neo-imperial wars, given that the groundwork for creating layers of liberal-moral awareness in people's subconscious was accomplished during the Cold War years by both Republican and Democratic administrations.

Not that "humanitarian intervention" by imperial powers was a new idea. In fact, it has been advocated at least since the Treaty of Versailles (1919) to prevent abuses of state power over ethnic and religious minorities.[27] But what we want to stress here is the fact that the Clinton administration opted to present "humanitarian intervention" as its chief ideological instrument in its effort to achieve power-politics ends at a time when the United States was "running out of demons." Clinton's and NATO's armies intervened "humanely" in Bosnia (1993–95) and Yugoslavia over Kosovo (1999); they failed dismally in Somalia (1992–94) and Haiti (1995); and they did not intervene at all in Rwanda (1993–95) or Burundi (1994–96)—let us brush aside Palestine with millions of refugees since 1948, 1956, 1967, 1973, and 1981–83. The cases of Rwanda and Bosnia are typical of the double standard of the United States. In fact, any comparison in the sheer numbers of deaths betrays at once the power-politics motives of the United States: some 8,000 Muslims were massacred in Srebrenica and Zepa by Serb paramilitaries and nationalists, but over 1 million in Rwanda. Notably, UN Secretary-General Boutros-Boutros Ghali called attention to the disproportionate attention Clinton was paying to the western Balkans at a moment when a humanitarian disaster in Rwanda was imminent. Appalled by the apathy of the United States, he resigned over this issue.

No state apparatus anywhere in the world represents a cohesive and solid body politic without inner contradictions and disintegrating and reorganizing tendencies. Ideological disputes, ethnic and religious problems, gender, cultural, and other social issues, clashes of interest and roles, personal rivalries among politicians and bureaucrats, and rivalries between various governmental branches or political parties cut across all state apparatuses. Class struggles play a significant role in the state's tendencies toward fragmentation and reorganization, but not everything is reducible to those struggles, however broadly defined. America's federated state machine, let alone its fragmented social structure and ethnic/religious contradictions—relatively complex by British, Italian, Japanese, or French standards—is no exception. In fact, the U.S. foreign policy process is the result of three, strictly interlinked processes:

1. The fragmented institutional bargaining process at the federal level, which attempts to articulate the demands of ethnic, political, social, and class interests within the institutional bargaining process
2. The class-national and security interests of the United States, which are spread all over the globe, particularly in Eurasia, key sea passages (e.g., Panama and Suez Canals), Latin America, and space
3. A broad—if possible, universal—political-ideological principle on the basis of which the national-class interests of the American elite can be presented convincingly as the interests of the whole world, while enjoying support at home

The largest defect of Clinton's post–Cold War America was that it lacked the third part. No USSR meant no enemy. No USSR meant more room to maneuver for both the Europeans and the United States, in east-central Europe and in the Near and Middle East. But was it convincing enough for the United States to expand NATO or to topple Saddam on the grounds of "humanitarian intervention"? In sum, the collapse of the USSR created a huge problem in America's domestic and global structures of power based upon the hub-and-spoke system. The political ideology of "humanitarian intervention" could not act as a substitute for the USSR. It was unconvincing to many for a variety of reasons, of which the most important were two: first, because of its partial success in Bosnia and Kosovo and its defeat in Somalia and Haiti; and second, it was obvious to everyone that such a policy was bound to border on double standards. For ten years, from August 1991 (the official dissolution of the

USSR) to August 2001, the neocons pressed hard to further militarize U.S. policy and adopt a strategy of preemption against the designated rogue states. But Clinton's administration felt uncomfortable with the idea, precisely because a solid organizing ideological principle and a clear threat that could cement the cohesion of U.S. power projection were missing.

Toward the end of Clinton's first term, Brzezinski saw this deficiency. He wrote that "America is too democratic at home to be autocratic abroad," a fact that "limits the use of America's power, especially its capacity for military intimidation." The defect precisely is that "the pursuit of power is not a goal that commands popular passion, except in conditions of a sudden threat or challenge to the public's sense of domestic well being." Thus, the much-needed consensus on foreign policy issues would be difficult to obtain, "except in the circumstances of a truly massive and widely perceived direct external threat."[28] This direct external threat did not take long to come. After 9/11, the priorities of neo-imperialist ideology had to be reshuffled.

"WAR ON TERROR," OR GLOBALIZING PALESTINE

As the rhetoric of human rights was subordinated during the Cold War to the broad strategy aimed at the disintegration of the Soviet bloc, so the 1990s rhetoric of "humanitarian intervention" was bound to give way and subordinate itself to the scheme of the "war on terror" after 9/11. "America," George W. Bush stated on January 29, 2002, "is no longer protected by vast oceans—we [Americans] are protected from attack only by vigorous action abroad and increased vigilance at home."[29] We have experienced "vigorous action abroad" with the wars on Afghanistan and Iraq, the former a failed state harboring Osama bin Laden, the latter a rogue state suspected of having, or having the possibility of building, weapons of mass destruction. Indeed, according to the neocons, the worst scenario of all is the existence of terrorists or rogue states possessing weapons of mass destruction.[30] Americans have also experienced "increased vigilance at home" with the Patriot Act and other new bureaucratic structures, such as the foundation of the Department of Homeland Security, whose broad areas of responsibility stimulated intense debate among political elites over limiting its powers "lest it approach those once dreaded security ministries in Eastern Europe."[31] But there are also other activities worth mentioning, such as the so-called Campus Watch, an agency encouraging university students in the United States to monitor "anti-American" and "anti-Israeli" teaching in universities.

As Western states during the Cold War had to adopt laws and enforce their powers at home against the "domestic and international Communist threat," so states today across the globe have to securitize their environments with law enforcement agencies and antiterrorist legislation. This imperative is captured by the statement, "it is important for all countries to adopt a 'zero tolerance' policy for terrorist activity within their borders."[32] After all, "citizens from some 90 countries died in the attacks of 9/11."[33] America is assisting all countries "to develop programs that help [states] to acquire the necessary capabilities to fight terrorism through a variety of means, including improved legislation, technical assistance, new investigative techniques, intelligence sharing, and law enforcement and military training."[34] Accordingly, Britain's Blairite elite strengthened its antiterrorist legislation and law enforcement agencies when in 2004–5, before the London bombings of July 7, 2005, it proposed legalizing the placement of terrorist suspects under house arrest without warning and without giving them the right of a legal defense. Overall, 9/11 was a watershed, not in terms of thwarting the essential friend-enemy matrix of U.S. neo-imperialist ideology, but in terms of replacing the Soviet threat with the new threat of global terrorism. "To maintain the momentum since September 11 and keep the global war on terrorism in the forefront," America's new security doctrine declared, "all departments and agencies of the US Government will promote combating terrorism as a standard agenda item for their bilateral and multilateral discussions."[35]

The neocons, by capitalizing on an event of such symbolic-catastrophic magnitude, could entertain this suitable reshaping of neo-imperialist ideology for post–Cold War America. As Derek Gregory put it, the collapse of the twin towers "conveyed with such visual, visceral power the eruption of spectacular terror in the very heart of metropolitan America."[36] In fact, an event like this is difficult to forget (and American media are working hard to keep it alive), unless corrosive and unpredictable phenomena, such as the torture of prisoners in the Abu Ghraib prison in Iraq, become endemic and then come to the attention of the public. "Remember what we saw on the morning of 9/11," Dick Cheney said again and again.[37] But America's post-9/11 "war on terror" serves much larger political, economic, and strategic objectives. After all, if all terrorists are captured, the United States once again will be running out of demons. We acknowledge that terror, whether state or societal, is real, but America's "war on terror" is manufactured and fictitious. We will also put forward some concrete ideas about what is the best way to deal with terrorism, whether it emanates from state or nonstate actors.

In the document *National Strategy for Combating Terrorism*, we read:

> *We live in an age with tremendous opportunities to foster a world consistent with interests and values embraced by the United States* and freedom-loving people around the world. And we will seize these opportunities.... *By striking constantly and ensuring that terrorists have no place to hide*, we will compress their scope and reduce the capability of terrorist organizations.... We will never forget what we are ultimately fighting for—our fundamental democratic values and way of life. In leading the campaign against terrorism, we are forging new international relationships and redefining existing ones in terms suited to the transnational challenges of the 21st century.... The campaign ahead will be long and arduous. *In this different kind of war, we cannot expect an easy or definitive end to the conflict.*[38]

This quote summarizes some key elements of neo-imperial ideology of the war on terror at its best. First, it tells us that this is an era of "tremendous opportunity" for America, inasmuch as America can present its national values as universal ones and impose them on the globe, also by means of violence. Again, this is not a new ingredient of imperialism: It is an ages-old and enduring ideological principle that conditions the political attempt by a group of people to become dominant either nationally or internationally. To dominate others, one's ideas must become dominant over other people's ideas. The events of 9/11 are presented as an opportunity opening the way for America to achieve just that.

Second, the statement tells us that America must strike constantly, incessantly, and where necessary unilaterally and preemptively. America did indeed. Within four years the United States bombed Belgrade, invaded Afghanistan and Iraq and, as we write these lines, America and/or Israel are preparing the ground to go into Syria and Iran. Libya is not a target anymore because, as *The Economist* conceded, Western oil and gas firms are now active in Libya "after Muammar Qaddafi quit the axis of evil."[39] The Europeans drew a line here, which can be seen from the way

Germany, France, and Russia opposed U.S. preemptive action in Iraq. "This is the first occasion since the end of the Cold War," Tariq Ali writes, "when a disagreement between the inner core of the EU and the United States exploded into a public rift, was seen on television and helped polarized public opinion on both sides of the Atlantic."[40] The neocons believe that if America flexes its muscles, the allies will eventually come along. "Soft-power" strategists, such as Joseph Nye, believe that this is not the right way for America to achieve its global aims because it alienates its allies—soft power being the ability to convince rather than coerce others to do what you want them to do. But America is not listening to Nye. Thus, soft-power ideologues argue, the more Washington (the hub) militarizes its foreign policies under the leadership of the neocons and goes it alone, the more the European capitals (spokes) seek to break free from the hub.[41]

This restless condition of U.S. power reminds us of Leon Trotsky's theory of permanent revolution. As one of the outstanding Marxist revolutionaries of the twentieth century and a leading figure in the Russian Revolution of 1917, Trotsky argued that the Russian Revolution of 1917 must not be confined to Russia. Rather, it had to be strengthened by and considered an integral part of a process of continuous revolutionary struggle in other countries, such as Poland and Germany, if the Bolshevik regime in Russia wanted to survive.[42] Trotsky's views were defeated in the Central Committee of the Bolsheviks, but we recall this issue because there are allegations of intellectual links between Trotskyism and several neocons.[43] If these allegations are correct, then the matrix of Trotsky's political thought is simply (and simplistically) being implemented by way of a neocon war program and an outward radicalization of U.S. coercive apparatuses. But even if the allegations are false, the post-9/11 experience of U.S. neo-imperialism does precisely what Trotsky foretold: To free domestic markets, particularly the oil and gas markets, from state intervention, the capitalist state initiates a constant war, radicalizing the international environment by changing regimes and projecting preemptive force.

This brings us directly to the third neocon proposition based on its "war on terror." It makes abundantly clear that this new war may be infinite: "we cannot expect an easy or definite end to the conflict." How, after all, is it possible to eradicate terrorism altogether? The only logical assumption one can make from this paranoia is that the war on terror will last as long as necessary for America to achieve two very specific political objectives: full-spectrum dominance and imposition of its values of liberal democracy and free-market economy on the globe. This is what globalization is all about: the "end of history" that goes hand in glove with a biblical role for America as "the first and last truly global superpower."[44] But can this new friend-enemy scheme operate along the lines of the Cold War? Can it be America's lasting organizational principle in the conduct of its foreign affairs? And how has it operated so far?

U.S. strategists know very well that modern terror is not territorial, although terrorists do have bases and economic assets on earth. It is not state-bound, although there might be states, or underground state agencies, offering to protect it. Rather, terrorists operate through complex networking activities and by using sophisticated technological means. Although these means can in no way match America's military and technological superiority—hence the term *asymmetrical warfare*—terrorist networks manage quite well. The neocons know all that, but when after 9/11 the Taliban in Afghanistan made an offer to the United States to apprehend Osama bin Laden and oust al-Qaeda from Afghanistan, the Americans refused to cooperate. They also rejected an offer by NATO to support America's first real "war on terror." This is all very curious. The Americans presumably went after the terrorists but what in fact they did was to topple the Taliban regime and establish a military presence in the underbelly of Russian security interests and Chinese interests and east of the rogue state of Iran. They did nothing less and nothing more than that. "A few days before September 11," Bülent Gökay observed, "the US Energy Information Administration documented Afghanistan's strategic 'geographical position as a potential transit route for oil and natural gas exports from Central Asia to the Arabian Sea.'"[45] Moreover, during the campaign in Afghanistan, Pakistan and Turkmenistan discussed the "development of a gas pipeline from Turkmenistan via Afghanistan to the port of Gwadar, now being built with Chinese assistance on the Baluchistan coast."[46] Having said that, one conclusion seems to be inescapable—the "war on terror" is but a manufactured device to advance U.S. security and class interests in Europe and Asia. But there is more to the affair than meets the eye.

Bush and the neocons know that they cannot defeat terrorists as they would defeat a failed state. They cannot eliminate terrorists by using state-political violence and state terror. Besides being counterproductive, state terrorism and the projection of overwhelming military power, however technologically advanced, cannot eliminate the phenomenon of suicide attacks and tribal warfare. Enormous resources in personnel and machinery are now needed to police tribal areas. In a memo to General Dick Myers, Paul Wolfowitz, Doug Feith, and General Pete Pace dated October 16, 2003, Donald Rumsfeld asked: "Today we lack the metrics to know if we are winning or losing the global war on terror. Are we capturing, killing or deterring and dissuading more terrorists every day than the madrassas and the radical clerics are recruiting, training and deploying against us?"[47]

Cruelty and belligerence apart, this is a deeply illusionary question to ask, for people who are determined to kill themselves can kill anybody at any place and any time. More specifically, the Pentagon's neocons forget that suicide bombing is predominantly about life, not death. They brush aside the fact that jihad and Osama bin Laden represent for Middle Eastern people what the Communist revolution and Che Guevara represented for the radical Western youth of the 1960s and 1970s. If neo-imperial (e.g., the United States) or neocolonial (e.g., Israel after 1967) states fight terrorists with state terrorism, then the end result is a vicious circle of violence. Yet we must go further. For instance, the Israeli-Palestinian conflict is not a question of two uncompromising nationalisms/fundamentalisms alone. It is, but it is also something else that goes beyond this simplistic assumption. In fact, it is an unequal relationship between the nationalism of oppressed people—the Palestinians—and the nationalism of the oppressor, the Israeli state. As Isaac Deutscher put it so eloquently back in 1967:

> On the face of it, the Arab-Israeli conflict is only a clash of two rival
> nationalisms, each moving within the vicious circle of its self-righteous
> and inflated ambitions. From the viewpoint of an abstract internationalism
> nothing would be easier than to dismiss both as equally worthless
> and reactionary. However, such a view would ignore the social and
> political realities of the situation. The nationalism of the people in semi-
> colonial or colonial countries, fighting for their independence must not
> be put on the same moral-political level as the nationalism of the
> conquerors and oppressors. The former has its historic justification and
> progressive aspect which the latter has not.... Israel's security lies in
> periodical warfare which every few years must reduce the Arab states to
> impotence.[48]

Neo-imperialism and neo-Zionism appear to be brothers in arms. On May 2, 2002, the U.S. Senate and House of Representatives passed motions stating that the United States and Israel "are now engaged in a common struggle against terrorism." Senator Joseph Lieberman was even more explicit: "Israel has been under siege from a systematic and deliberate campaign of suicide and homicide attacks by terrorists. Their essence is identical to the attacks on our country of 11 September."[49] U.S. forces in Iraq practice the lessons they "had learned from the Israeli Defense Force (IDF) in the occupied territories of Palestine." In order to break the resistance, the United States is "copying the use of Arab informers by the Israeli intelligence services. American troops turned Iraqi towns and villages into simulacra of the West Bank." It was also revealed that "Israeli officers had trained assassination squads at Fort Bragg to replicate the IDF strategy of 'targeted killings.'"[50] The conclusion is painful: Israel has been doing to Palestinians and Israel's immediate periphery what America has been doing to the globe. As neo-Zionist fundamentalism matches the Islamic jihad, so the alliance between Christian Fundamentalists and Zionists at home matches the global jihad abroad. A recent study of Christian Fundamentalism and neo-Zionism by Donald Wagner of Chicago's North Park University tracks the remarkable coming together of these two ideological movements with neoconservatism during the George W. Bush era. "By 2000, a shift had taken place in the Republican Party. It began embracing the doctrines of neoconservative ideologues who advocated US unilateralism and favored military solutions over diplomacy. The more aggressive approach was put into action after Sept. 11, and to no one's surprise, Israel's war against the Palestinians and its other enemies was soon linked to the US 'war on terrorism.'"[51] It is therefore generally accepted that Washington's commitment to Israel's existence is a given, which forms a basic dilemma for Bush's policies on Palestine. But one also has to emphasize that neoconservatism is not synonymous with Jewish opinion, as there are many politically engaged Jews who consider the neocon (and neo-Zionist) view of the world to be rabid nonsense.

The neocons attribute the causes of terrorism to poverty, corruption, religious conflict, and ethnic strife.[52] This makes no sense and "with this definition of terrorism," as Henry C. K. Liu put it, "the war on terrorism cannot be won."[53] The real cause of Islamic terrorism is America's overwhelming projection of power over poor and deprived populations in regions rich in raw materials such as oil and gas that are vital for America's declining economy and insecure financial situation. Another real cause of Islamic terrorism is the appalling situation of the Palestinians and the inability of the so-called international community to force on Israel the implementation of UN Security Council Resolution 242 calling for the withdrawal of Israel from the West Bank and Gaza. The best response to terrorism is a civilian response, a new policy of détente. The best response to al-Qaeda and other fundamentalist terrorist groups is the withdrawal of Anglo-Saxon power from the greater Middle East, the withdrawal of the Israeli army from the West Bank and Gaza, and the foundation of an independent Palestinian state. After that, Islam and the West can explore a new democratic, civilian structure of political and economic cooperation based on mutual respect and understanding. This is another way to turn the reality of Huntington's argument on its head. This is also another way to go beyond the simplistic, false, and dangerous religious dilemma of "good" versus "evil." But both Christian Fundamentalists and neo-Zionists, key Bush constituencies, adamantly refuse to think along these lines.

FUNDAMENTALISTS, NEOCONS, AND NEO-ZIONISTS

At the Cornerstone Church in Texas 5,000 Christian worshippers cheer in support of Israel. "Jerusalem is the eternal capital of the Jewish state. Not since Camp David but since King David," says their leader, Pastor John Hagee. Many high profile Israeli politicians have addressed this congregation, among them former Prime Minister Binyamin Netanyahu.[54]

We earlier identified Stefan Halper and Jonathan Clarke's joint account *America Alone* as well as Anne Norton's *Leo Strauss and the Politics of American Empire* as two very useful monographs. They give invaluable information for locating the intellectual roots of neoconservatives, their connections with the business world and the mass media, their strong affiliation with Israel and particularly the Likud Party, and how they came to dominate America's executive agenda in foreign policy. Here is some of the useful information we gathered from their narratives.

Christian Fundamentalists belong to America's Republican and populist traditions. They split into different factions but are united in their distaste for secularism and liberal social values and in a fondness for thinking of the world in terms of "good" and "evil." A large number also fanatically support Israel, because they believe that the second coming of Christ—the apocalypse—will come only after the rebirth of Israel, which itself will be destroyed. In other words, "these Christians are supporting the Jews in order to abolish them."[55]

Christian Fundamentalists have been in and around the political power centers of America from its earliest days, always representing essentially reactionary politics. In the eighteenth century, they saw themselves as the civilizing shock troops of the European invasion; in the nineteenth century they organized against science and modernity; and in the early twentieth century they appeared as the Christian knights of the Ku Klux Klan. They never represented more than regional organizations, until they came under the influence of neoconservative political ideologues in the 1960s and 1970s, who organized them against the various rights movements of that period. Emboldened by the unexpected success of the Reagan presidency, they increasingly offered themselves in coalitions at the local and state level to try to roll back the hot-button issues of feminism, abortion rights, and affirmative action.

In the early 1990s, Christian Fundamentalists were hammered into a well-funded and closely controlled political constituency by strategists such as Pat Robertson and Jerry Falwell and conservative media commentators such as Rush Limbaugh. This created a powerful identity for them as conservative Republicans armed with a program to stop Clinton's social liberalism, which they fervently believed eroded traditional values of family and authority and would ultimately lead to the disintegration of American society. During this period, Fundamentalists and neocons developed an increasingly friendly relationship (even though the majority of the neocons were, and still are, secular) through contacts between Christian leaders like Gary Bauer, executive director of Christian Legal Society, and members of the Project for the New American Century (PNAC).[56] In 1999, William Bennett, a cosignatory of the PNAC and a Distinguished Fellow at the Heritage Foundation, founded Empower America, which was an attempt to aggregate Christian-social fundamentalists under the broader political project of the PNAC agenda. After 9/11, Christian Fundamentalists, a constituency representing some 14 to 20 percent of the electorate, became a critical element in the policy framework of the neocons. Stefan Halper and Jonathan Clarke explain:

> Robertson cited events from the year 632 as evidence that a permanent jihad against those who were not part of the Islamic tradition was inherent in Islam. He could now link terrorism directly to the demand for greater support for Israel, by claiming that America had been at war for thirty years with fanatical terrorists from the Middle East. . . . Franklin Graham, the son of Billy Graham and head of Samaritan's Purse, a Christian relief organization, spoke [of Iraq] as "a source of terror and deadly terror with biological, nuclear and chemical warfare." Together they found common ground with neo-con figures, such as Daniel Pipes and Michael Ledeen in helping to project an ever more hostile backdrop of commentary toward Arab and Islamic culture in the mainstream TV and print media.[57]

Neocons are generally concentrated on America's East Coast, where the real executive power lies. They know from experience and from German political sociologists and jurists, such as Max Weber and Carl Schmidt, that the real power under capitalism is not vested with the people and their elected parliaments, but with the executive powers of the capitalist state and its coercive apparatus (security and defense). They also know from Schmidt and Strauss that sovereignty is not found in what the Constitution says, but in those that can impose at will a state of emergency. A power such as America aspiring to global supremacy must have this capability.

Neocons (and the neo-Zionists) share Christian Fundamentalist convictions of evil versus good, which became a recurrent theme in the Bush administration after 9/11 ("axis of evil," "evil terror" and so on).[58] Because their philosophical sources are totalitarian and metaphysical, they also believe that the American empire is the last empire in history. Both neocons and neo-Zionists widely read such "next to great" conservatives as Robert Goldwin (special assistant to President Gerald Ford) and Irving Kristol, the father of William Kristol (a signatory of the PNAC and chief of staff for Vice President Dan Quayle in the administration of George H. W. Bush). They are all "great Straussians" and admirers of Albert Wohlstetter.[59] Gary Schmitt, a signatory of PNAC, headed President Reagan's advisory board on foreign intelligence. Abram Shulsky, also a signatory of the PNAC and an analyst with RAND, a Pentagon-financed think tank in Santa Monica,

California, "served as director of strategic arms control at the Department of Defense and has held a number of intelligence positions since."[60] Paul Wolfowitz, another prominent Straussian and admirer of Wohlstetter, who served as deputy secretary of defense in the Bush administration and now is director of the World Bank, together with Shulsky led the Pentagon's Office of Special Projects. Richard Perle, who served in Reagan's administration as assistant secretary of defense for international security and in the G. W. Bush administration as head of the Defense Policy Board, "first came to Washington because of his connections to Albert Wohlstetter."[61]

Like Wolfowitz, Perle harshly attacked the Nixon-Ford policy of détente with the Soviet Union and "helped engineer passage of the 1974 Jackson-Vanik Amendment, which restricted trade benefits for the Soviet Union because of Soviet restrictions on Jewish emigration."[62] As a director of the *Jerusalem Post,* Perle also "sought to use his influence in Israel in a clumsy attempt to sabotage the Camp David peace talks in 2000."[63] Francis Fukuyama, a professor at Johns Hopkins and the celebrated author of *The End of History,* has also served in the Pentagon and is now a member of the Bush administration's Council on Bioethics. Lewis "Scooter" Libby is Vice President Cheney's chief of staff. Zalmay Khalilzad, now U.S. ambassador to Afghanistan, was a student of Wohlstetter. He got a job at RAND after being recommended by Wohlstetter himself.[64] While with RAND, he founded the Center for Middle Eastern Studies. From 1985 to 1989 at the Department of State, Khalilzad served as special adviser to the undersecretary of state for political affairs working on policy issues, advising on the Iran-Iraq war and the Soviet war in Afghanistan. Paula Dobriansky, a signatory of a letter sent to Clinton on January 26, 1998, urging him to attack Iraq in order, among other things, to protect Israel, is undersecretary for global affairs at the State Department. Soon after 9/11, most of these people rushed to Hollywood to create the 9/11 Group, an attempt to bring together producers and screenwriters to try to rehearse imaginary terrorist scenarios. Hollywood has taken this seriously. Films such as *The Siege, Executive Decision,* and *The Peacemaker* were designed to further terrorize the American public on the grounds of a false representation of Islam and the Arab world.

From the early 1990s onward, media mogul Rupert Murdoch "asserted his strong personal and business attachments with Israel, and like many neo-conservatives he has received recognition in the United States for his support of Israel." Back in 1982, Murdoch was voted by the American

Jewish Congress of New York Communications Man of the Year.[65] Murdoch controls Fox Broadcasting Network, Fox Television Stations, and the Fox News Channel, and he has major interests in other U.S. and UK satellite networks. He controls print media, such as the *London Times*, the *New York Post*, and the UK's largest populist daily, *The Sun*. He runs some twenty-five magazines, including the *Weekly Standard*, a flagship neocon publication with William Kristol as editor, and *TV Guide*. Murdoch's powers and influence in the United States and Britain are unquestionable. No British government can be elected without support from his corporate media.

"Shortly after his election in 1997," John Pilger wrote in 2002, "Blair shamelessly appointed a friend, Michael Levy, a wealthy Jewish businessman who had fundraised for New Labour as his 'special envoy' in the Middle East, having first made him Lord Levy. . . . This former chairman of the Jewish Appeal Board and former board member of the Jewish Agency," Pilger continued, "who has both a business and a house in Israel and had a son working for the Israeli justice ministry, was the man assigned by Britain's prime minister to negotiate impartially with Palestinians and Israelis."[66] As soon as Michael Howard was elected leader of the Tory Party in Britain in November 2003, he immediately sought Murdoch's public approval and support. Because Murdoch was in Mexico for a conference at the time, Howard traveled to Mexico. Murdoch made several statements of support for Howard and London papers speculated that Blair might lose the support of *The Sun*. If so, then his reelection was in doubt.[67]

These biographical-intellectual sketches explain some of the links between conservative philosophy, the Reaganite right, the Fundamentalists, conservative think tanks, the media, neocons in the universities, and some pro-Israeli sympathizers in the governments of the United States and Britain. Yet they are incomplete. They fail to analyze in depth the broader historical and structural context within which these phenomena have developed. As we have seen, the key to understanding what has been happening since the end of the Cold War and 9/11 is to look at the worsening conditions of America's economic position and the difficulties the hub-and-spoke system of power has been facing since 1989. Neocons (and neo-Zionists) may or may not be good administrators of these conditions, but they do remain administrators: They have advanced no new policy idea, except for capitalizing on 9/11, putting forward the "war on terror" scheme as a substitute for the war on the USSR.

These sketches, moreover, fail to explain the way in which these groups managed to present their factional interests and ideology as America's interests and ideology. Why have these groups been successful? It is not enough to say along with Barry Buzan that "the well-placed influence of Jewish and Christian lobbies play powerfully into the separated powers structure of American politics, preventing the US from putting pressure on Israel."[68] These analyses say very little about the connections of these people with the oil and defense industries, as well as with global capital and the governments of Britain and Israel in particular. They say little about how class and ethnic interests translate into executive power, cooperation of intelligence agencies, and foreign policy agendas. They say little or nothing about the fact that both neocons and neo-Zionists have grown up within the post-1945 U.S. establishment and, therefore, they can be both Republican and Democrats.

Last but not least, these analyses do not dwell on the issue of national-political identity of the protagonists they describe. Why do most of these protagonists identify with post-1967 Israel? Is it because a big chunk of them are Jews, or is it because they are right-wing authoritarian conservatives, whether Democrats, Republicans, or Jews? But even then, how do they survive and assume top executive positions in the upper echelons of U.S. power apparatuses? Is this in the national and capitalist interests of the United States as a whole? And if so, why so?

So far, our analyses answer only some of those questions. Those remaining unanswered, we concede we cannot address here in detail. However, we can offer some thoughts in the hope that they will lead to further investigation on these interrelated topics. We have suggested that the neocon faction in post-9/11 U.S. politics did nothing more and nothing less than to radicalize further the elements and the guiding principles of the Acheson-Nitze hub-and-spoke scheme. We have also seen how the militarization of America's foreign policy after the Cold War and 9/11 is linked to the declining power of the dollar in global currency markets and the establishment of the euro as well as other negative economic indicators for America. We have argued that Acheson and Nitze, two registered Democrats, emphasized a buildup of America's defenses and technological, military, and nuclear superiority by way of exaggerating the threat of the Soviet Union. Similarly, Richard Perle, a registered Democrat, fought Clinton's "soft" policies in the 1990s and still subscribes to all major tenets of the PNAC. Early in 1996, Perle and other neocons advised the neo-Zionist Israeli prime minister, Binyamin Netanyahu, to abandon the Oslo peace process.[69] More concretely, Perle, Douglas Feith, and David Wurmser drafted a document for Israel's newly elected nationalist prime minister to sabotage talks with Arafat and, instead, opt for an open security pact with Turkey and Jordan in order to "contain, destabilize and roll back some of its most dangerous threats."[70] Moreover, the links of the neocons and neo-Zionists with the business world are as strong as—and even stronger than—those enjoyed by the Truman administration. In the words of George Soros:

> The neo-cons behind the Project for the New American Century advocated greater military spending, and many of them were associated with the defense and oil industries. For instance, Richard Perle, who received no salary as head of the Defense Policy Board, made a lot of money as a corporate consultant. Dick Cheney was president of Halliburton before he became vice president, and Halliburton's lucrative contracts in Iraq are well known. I do not say that the neo-conservative ideology was based on monetary interests— I am no neo-Marxist—but there is an undeniable two-way, reflexive connection.[71]

Indeed, there is no need to be a neo-Marxist to see that. Nor is there a similar need to see that Condoleezza Rice, a former provost at Stanford University, Bush's national security advisor (2001–2004) and now secretary of state, sits on the "boards of several major corporations, including Chevron, which named one of its super-tankers after her."[72] The Bush family itself has links with the Carlyle Group, which specializes in global investments in oil and gas, and UNOCAL. Khalilzad, before he assumed his role in Afghanistan, was a chief consultant for UNOCAL.[73] You do not need to be a Marxist to see and say these things. All you need to have is a critical and moral-democratic way of thinking and contemplating them. Yet you also need a historical horizon and depth of vision to reach certain tentative conclusions about what this means in the present situation. You cannot have the theory of a subject without prior knowledge of its concrete history.

As we saw in an earlier time, Acheson's first failure was his attempt in 1947 to essentially demolish the sovereign authorities of the European nation-state. He failed but passed through the back door what he failed to get through the front: He established NATO, making the Europeans dependent on the United States for security and defense matters, and he pioneered Bretton Woods, making European currencies dependent upon the dollar. Most important, he established the operational framework of neo-imperialist ideology, based upon the dichotomy of "evil Communism" versus the "free world."

What the neocons are trying to do today is to revive Acheson's multiple agenda: in economics, through ideologies of globalization that pulverize the sovereign powers of the nation-state in Europe and around the globe; in politics, through the hub-and-spoke system of global governance; in ideology, by articulating a "war on terror" ("evil terror" versus the "free world"). Structurally, neocons have no new idea; they have an old idea recycled in another form. In other words, they are simply managing economic, political, and ideological schemes from the 1940s. Yet, all these are clever moves because both Communism and the classical post–World War II social democracy of the welfare state have been defeated by the policy drives of Reagan and Thatcher. They are also clever moves because they allow neocons and neo-Zionists to project power into the greater Middle East to topple anti-American regimes, privatize oil and gas industries, and at the same time make Israel, according to their view, safer. In fact, the neo-Zionist/neocon scheme for the refashioning of the greater Middle East is such that everyone's interests and ideologies converge: It suits the Christian Fundamentalists because it leads to the rebirth of Israel; it serves neocons and Anglo-Saxons because they want a global free-market economy with minimal state intervention; it suits big capital at large because it tightens domestic security by adopting a response model to terrorism based on a permanent war model with emergency powers, rather than liberal law enforcement;[74] it strengthens dictatorial/ authoritarian elements inherent in any capitalist state, intensifies further the rate of exploitation, and increases labor discipline; finally, it appeals to neo-Zionists because it propagates "regime change" in Iraq, Iran, and Syria first and a solution to the Arab-Israeli conflict will come later. In total, we argue that what lies behind this neocon ideology is Acheson and Nitze's political-ideological framework. It also should not go unnoticed that Wolfowitz has been a distinguished member of the Paul Nitze School of Advanced International Studies at Johns Hopkins University.

When Josef Joffe, a prominent publicist and the editor of *Die Zeit*, was asked whether it was possible to have a world without Israel, his answer was that the question makes little, if any, sense.[75] According to Joffe, Israel contains Arab nationalism and Islamic irrationality. It prevents rival Arab states from fighting for the piece of land Israel now occupies and, in fact, "the 'root cause' of Palestinian statelessness would have persisted, even in Israel's absence." Israel, Joffe argues, is not an anachronism, and its disappearance from the map would foster inter-Arab enmity. Thus, in Joffe's view, the Arab-Israeli conflict is not really a Muslim-Jewish thing but a Muslim-Muslim story, and "factoring Israel out of the Middle East equation" would hardly produce liberal democracy in the region. Joffe argues, in fact, that Israel is a force of good for the region and the world and he cannot understand how "5 million Jews are solely responsible for the rage of 1 billion or so Muslims."

Joffe's short treatise mentions no Mossad, nor the creation of Hamas by Mossad itself. He makes no reference to Ariel Sharon's statement back in the early 1980s, when he said in front of television cameras that "he would have three Palestinians for breakfast,"[76] nor to his criminal policies and wars. Joffe is not interested in reaching unbiased conclusions on the Palestinian question—such an approach requires a moral and democratic understanding of the situation similar to that taken by Isaac Deutscher some forty years ago: to criticize all nationalisms but, most particularly, the nationalism of the oppressor. The fact that Arab nationalism is not united is not for the reasons Joffe put forward. Israel, Britain, and the United States bear a great responsibility for this because for their imperialism to survive, the Arabs must be kept divided.

The achievement of neo-Zionists, such as Joffe, Perle, and others, is that they have managed to put themselves in a position to administer and even radicalize Acheson's and Nitze's schemes. This achievement is remarkable in many respects because the father of post–World War II American neo-imperialism, Dean Acheson, wanted to avoid precisely the complications Joffe refers to when the Jewish state was created on Arab land. Acheson's advice still beckons.

NOTES

1. S. Baxter, "Back in Texas They Just Know God's on His Side," *The Sunday Times*, February 27, 2005.

2. Anne Norton, *Leo Strauss and the Politics of American Empire* (New Haven, CT: Yale University Press, 2004).

3. Alex Callinicos, *The New Mandarins of American Power* (Cambridge, UK: Polity Press, 2003), 48.

4. Stefan Halper and Jonathan Clarke, *America Alone: The Neo-conservatives and the Global Order* (Cambridge, UK: Cambridge University Press, 2004).

5. We are referring to Ivo H. Daalder and James M. Lindsay, *America Unbound: The Bush Revolution in Foreign Policy* (Washington, DC: Brookings Institution Press, 2003), especially pp. 46–48.

6. Norton, *Leo Strauss*, 39.

7. Derek Gregory, *The Colonial Present* (Oxford, UK: Blackwell, 2004), 49.

8. The precise phrase Nitze used is "exceptionally talented graduate students who agreed to work for expenses"; see Paul H. Nitze, *From Hiroshima to Glasnost: At the Centre of Decision* (London: Weidenfeld and Nicolson, 1989), 295.

9. The task of Team B was "to conduct an analysis parallel to that being done inside the intelligence community, of Soviet strategic defenses, missile accuracies, and strategic objectives," ibid., 350.

10. "The neo-Zionists are Israel's new right," says Ilan Pappe, Israeli historian. "For them values like democracy and liberalism are utterly dispensable. The only value that counts is the Jewish nation. If preserving this nation means another war with the Arabs, so be it. If it means occupying more Arab land, so be it. This is the ideology that assassinated Rabin—it knows no inhabitants." In Graham Usher, "The Dove That Wouldn't Fly," *Al-Ahram Weekly On-line*, no. 376 (May 7–13, 1998).

11. Avi Shlaim, "Is Zionism Today the Real Enemy of the Jews? Yes," *International Herald Tribune*, February 4, 2005, 6. Shlaim's article is published side by side with a pro-Zionist argument developed by Shlomo Ben-Ami. The articles are based on remarks delivered in a debate in London on January 25, 2005, organized by the debating forum Intelligence Squared. The motion was: "Zionism today is the real enemy of the Jews." The other speakers were Jacqueline Rose and Amira Hass, for the motion, and Raphael Israeli, against. After the debate, the audience voted 355 to 320 in favor of the motion, with 40 abstentions.

12. Bartle Bull, "Alexander, the First Neo-Con," *FT Magazine* no. 89 (January 22, 2005): 36–37.

13. A. G. Frank, *ReOrient: Global Economy in the Asian Age* (Berkeley: University of California Press, 1998), 14.

14. Samuel P. Huntington, *The Clash of Civilizations and the Remaking of World Order* (London: Simon and Schuster, 1997), 217–18.

15. Mark Mazower, *The Dark Continent* (London: Penguin, 1998), 61.

16. On the subject of U.S.-Israel relations since 1947–48 see, among others, Samuel W. Lewis, "The United States and Israel: Evolution of an Unwritten Alliance," *Middle East Journal* 53, no. 3 (summer 1999): 364–78.

17. Donald Sassoon, *One Hundred Years of Socialism* (London: Fontana, 1997), 333.

18. Peter Gowan, "The Euro-Atlantic Origins of NATO's Attack on Yugoslavia," in *Masters of the Universe? NATO's Balkan Crusade*, ed. Tariq Ali, 18–19 (London: Verso, 2000).

19. On this issue, see in particular Henry Kissinger, "What Kind of Atlantic Partnership?," *Atlantic Community Quarterly* 7, no. 1 (Spring 1969): 18–38; see also Zbigniew Brzezinski, *The Grand Chessboard* (New York: Basic Books, 1997).

20. Cyprus had been a British colony since 1878, populated by a Greek majority and a Turkish minority. Since 1954, Turkey, mostly incited by Britain rather than on its own initiative, had made clear to Greece that it could not accept *enosis* (union of Cyprus with Greece) or an independent Greek Cypriot state and that the only solution was partition or "double *enosis*." In 1960, following the Greek Cypriot-led guerrilla warfare against the British colonial authorities for independence and *enosis*, Cyprus gained an independent government, which was bound to fail due to the equal governing rights of the two, by now hostile, communities on the island. The Cyprus Constitution was chiefly dictated by the British, the masters of the policy of "divide and rule" and the main culprit for the ethnic hatred that developed between Greeks and Turks on Cyprus at least since 1955, when the guerrilla war began. In 1963–64, as predicted, the Constitution broke down due to a Greek Cypriot drive to eliminate the equal governing rights of the Turkish Cypriots. The result was an intercommunal fight, with the Turkish Cypriots withdrawing from government and settling into militarily protected enclaves.

21. The Greek Cypriot leader, Archbishop Makarios, was one of the founders of the nonaligned movement and maintained good relations with Moscow and the Arabs, particularly with Nasser.

22. Suha Bolukbasi, "Behind the Turkish-Israeli Alliance: A Turkish View," *Journal of Palestine Studies* 29, no. 1 (1989), 26.

23. See Bülent Gökay, *Eastern Europe Since 1970* (Essex: Longman, 2001).

24. See, for example, Halper and Clarke, *America Alone*.

25. Quoted in Gregory, *The Colonial Present*, 314, n. 39.

26. For further analysis on this issue, see Vassilis K. Fouskas, *Zones of Conflict: US Foreign Policy in the Balkans and the Greater Middle East* (London: Pluto Press, 2003), chapter 3.

27. See Mazower, *The Dark Continent*, 51–63.

28. Brzezinski, *The Grand Chessboard*, 35–36, 212 passim.

29. George W. Bush quoted in the document *National Strategy for Combating Terrorism*, (Washington, DC: State Department, February 2003), 15.

30. In a widely publicized interview in *Vanity Fair* (July 2003), Wolfowitz, in his attempt to explain why the United States went to Iraq since no weapons of mass

destruction were there, said that there were "several factors" behind the administration's policy, but "for bureaucratic reasons we settled on one issue, Weapons of
Mass Destruction, because it was the one reason everyone could agree on," quoted in
George Soros, *The Bubble of American Supremacy* (London: Weidenfeld and Nicolson,
2004), 52. Soros, a financier by profession, could see that the war on Iraq is but an
expression of America's economic weakness, not a sign of its strength. Soros is against
America's adventure in Iraq and the neocon policy, but misleadingly supports the
unsustainable campaign of NATO and the United States in Afghanistan.

31. Halper and Clarke, *America Alone*, 3.

32. *National Strategy for Combating Terrorism*, 18.

33. George W. Bush, "The Nature of the Terrorist Threat Today" (address to a
joint session of Congress, September 20, 2001), in *National Strategy for Combating
Terrorism*, 5.

34. Ibid., 20.

35. Ibid., 19.

36. Gregory, *The Colonial Present*, 25.

37. See his speech to the conservative Heritage Foundation on October 10, 2003,
downloadable from http://www.mtholyoke.edu/avad/intrel/iraq/cheney.htm.

38. Emphasis ours. See *National Strategy for Combating Terrorism*, 2, 29.

39. "Energy in Africa: To Libya and Beyond," *The Economist* (February 12, 2005),
68.

40. Tariq Ali, *Bush in Babylon: The Re-colonization of Iraq* (London: Verso, 2003), 165.

41. The "soft-power" argument makes little, if any, sense. During the Clinton
administration, and particularly during the Kosovo campaign, an instance of
Clinton's soft-power achievement, NATO nearly broke into pieces. Moreover, soft
power is an insult to the intelligence of the allies: Can they not figure out what
America hides behind its cajoling tactics?

42. L. Trotsky, *Results and Prospects*, in *The Permanent Revolution* (New York:
Pathfinder Press, 1969), 63.

43. On this interesting theme, see the informed debate between Michael Lind—a
former executive editor of the neoconservative magazine *The National Interest*—and
Alan Wald in http://hnn.us/articles.

44. For a sustained critique of this metaphysical position that we find in almost
every U.S. anti-terrorist manual, including Brzezinski's *The Grand Chessboard*, see
Fouskas, *Zones of Conflict*, chapter 7.

45. Bülent Gökay, "The Most Dangerous Game in the World: Oil, War and US
Global Hegemony," in *September 11 and World Politics*, ed. Gokham Bacik and
Bulent Aras, 175–92 (Istanbul: Fatih University Press, 2004).

46. Gopalaswami Parthasarathy, "War against Terrorism and the Oil and Gas
Dimensions," http://www.rediff.com/news/gp.htm.

47. Donald Rumsfeld, "Subject: Global War on Terrorism," *USA Today*, October 22, 2003, http://www.mtholyoke.edu/acad/intrel/iraq/memo.htm.

48. Isaac Deutscher, interviewed by Alexander Cockburn, Tom Wengraf, and Peter Wollen, "On the Israeli-Arab War," first published in *New Left Review*, 1967 (the interview took place on June 20, 1967), in Tariq Ali, *The Clash of Fundamentalisms: Crusades, Jihads and Modernity* (London: Verso, 2002), 396, 402–403.

49. All quotations from Derek Gregory, *The Colonial Present*, 139.

50. Ibid., 243–44.

51. Donald Wagner, "A Heavenly Match: Bush and the Christian Zionists," *The Daily Star*, October 12, 2003, http://www.informationclearinghouse.info/article4960.htm.

52. *National Strategy for Combating Terrorism*.

53. Henry C. K. Liu, "Occupation Highlights Superpower Limits," *Asia Times*, April 20, 2004, http://www.atimes.com/atimes/Middle_East/FD20Ak01.html.

54. *BBC News*, May 7, 2002, http://news.bbc.co.uk/1/hi/world/middle_east/1969542.stm.

55. See "Meet the New Zionists," *The Guardian*, October 28, 2002, http://www.guardian.co.uk/g2/story. Financier and philanthropist George Soros, a Hungarian Jew, remarks, "Since the apocalypse involved the destruction of Israel, Israel might be better off without friends like this," in his *The Bubble of American Supremacy*, 53.

56. Halper and Clarke, *America Alone*, 198.

57. Ibid., 199.

58. See also Peter J. Boyer, "The Believer: Paul Wolfowitz Defends His War," *New Yorker*, November 1, 2004, 46–57.

59. Norton, *Leo Strauss*, 14ff.

60. Ibid., 15.

61. Daalder and Lindsay, *America Unbound*, 28.

62. Ibid., 29.

63. Callinicos, *The New Mandarins*, 49.

64. Ibid., 185–86.

65. Halper and Clarke, *America Alone*, 186.

66. John Pilger, "Blair's Meeting with Arafat Served to Disguise His Support for Sharon and the Zionist Project," *New Statesman*, January 14, 2002, 17.

67. See Paul Waugh, "Murdoch Praises Howard and Hints Blair May Lose Support of 'The Sun'," *The Independent*, November 15, 2003, 3.

68. Barry Buzan, *The United States and the Great Powers: World Politics in the Twenty-First Century* (Cambridge, UK: Polity, 2004), 179.

69. Halper and Clarke, *America Alone*, 20.

70. Callinicos, *The New Mandarins*, 49.

71. Soros, *The Bubble of American Supremacy*, 180.

72. Daalder and Lindsay, *America Unbound*, 24.

73. See, among others, Parthasarathy, "War against Terrorism," http://www.rediff.com/news/gp.htm. Parthasarathy is a former Indian high commissioner to Pakistan.

74. Richard Falk, "Human Rights: A Descending Spiral," *Zaman Online*, January 17, 2005, http://www.zaman.com.

75. Josef Joffe, "A World Without Israel," *Foreign Policy* (January/February 2005), http://www.foreignpolicy.com.

76. Jonathan Wallace, "Breakfast of Scorpions," *The Ethical Spectacle*, May 2002, http://www.spectacle.org/0502/scorpion.html.

PART II

A DREAM COME TRUE: "NOW WE CAN CLAIM THE WORLD"

CHAPTER 5

The Battle for Caspian Oil

Note to school teachers: Find the Caspian on the map, draw a circle around it, and show it to the children. Twenty years from now, or perhaps even 10, some of them may find themselves deployed there.[1]

In his article "The New Great Game," Paul Starobin compares the current geopolitical and economic dynamics in central Asia and the Transcaucasus to the "Great Game" of the nineteenth century. In that classic case, the imperial rivalry was between the British Empire and Tsarist Russia, but Starobin finds in his analysis that the United States is now the major "imperial" player in the region, achieved primarily at the expense of Russia. Once again it seems that Western interests are pitted against Russian influence, with potential conflict on the horizon.

Over the past ten to fifteen years, the Caspian Sea basin has attracted considerable attention because of its potential as a significant source of oil and natural gas for world markets, and international competition for the control of these critical resources is increasing. Geographically, the Caspian Sea is an enclosed body of water, roughly 700 miles from north to south and 250 miles across, lying directly between the states of central Asia and the Transcaucasus. Its salt water connects to the Black Sea through the Volga and Don rivers, the artificial Volga-Don canal, and the Sea of Azov, a branch of the Black Sea. In 1991, during the last days of the Soviet Union, only two independent states—the Soviet Union and Iran—bordered the Caspian Sea basin. Since then, they have been joined by three new states—Azerbaijan, Kazakhstan, and Turkmenistan.

The Caspian Sea basin itself is located at the center of Eurasia, a region rich in diversity of peoples, nations, and cultures. The new countries of the region appear as blots on the map, pimples on the backs of Russia, Turkey, and Iran. In representations by the Western press, they commonly appear in shabby images of natural disasters, the genocide in Armenia, wild horsemen and smiling centenarians in Georgia, and as foreign and barbarous Muslims in Azerbaijan, the North Caucasus, and Turkmenistan. But this is a historically cramped understanding of the area, whose culture and history predate much of that found in Europe. The positive images that survive exist as romantic memories of the Silk Road merchant routes that connected northern and Eastern Europe with Asia Minor and the Greek colonies thousands of years ago. The Argonauts were the first "foreign tourists," so to speak, visiting the Black Sea coast of the Caspian region, and Prometheus, who brought fire to mankind in defiance of Zeus, was said to have been chained to a cliff in the region.[2]

Thousands of years have passed since then, but people are still attracted to the Caspian Sea basin. In modern times, the attraction has been related to the region's natural resources, especially its vast oil and natural gas reserves. In a much earlier time, before the mid-nineteenth century, the region was one of the best-known oil producers in the world. Before the coming of the Russians, petroleum extraction was very primitive, and for centuries petroleum traders extracted their product with rags and buckets. By the time of the tsarist government in 1871, the modern petroleum industry began to take form with the drilling that occurred in what is now the giant Bibi-Eibat field in Azerbaijan. By the end of the nineteenth century, the area experienced its first contact with Western capital as large foreign oil companies entered the area and two competing families began to dominate the Caspian oil industry. The Nobel brothers arrived first, followed by the French branch of the Rothschilds,[3] and in 1898 Russia became the world's largest oil-producing country, holding onto this distinction until 1902, with more than 50 percent of the world's oil produced in the Caspian region.[4]

With the decline of the tsarist empire, civil war spread throughout the region until the Bolsheviks with the revolutionaries finally seized control in 1921.[5] Under Stalin's first Five-Year Plan in 1927, the Soviet state assumed full responsibility for the production of Caspian basin oil, providing for central planning, determining sites, organizing production, and arranging for oil transport. Oil production quickly recovered from the effects of war and revolution, with 1928 output surpassing the former 1901 peak. The Soviet oil industry continued a period of rapid growth during the following decade, with most of this production coming from the Caspian region.[6]

Caspian oil played a major strategic role during the World Wars I and II, and protecting the Caspian oil fields was always an Allied priority. The German leadership clearly recognized the oil fields' importance to its expansionist ambitions and its form of mechanized warfare. Initially, the Germans sought access to the oil by negotiation, and following the 1939 German-Soviet Pact, Soviet oil from the region accounted for fully one-third of German oil imports. When the German-Soviet rapprochement failed, Hitler invaded the Soviet Union, specifically targeting the oil of the Caspian basin. Arguably, the fierce resistance of the Red Army to the southern thrust of Nazi forces that denied Germany its prized Caspian oil was the major turning point in the war in Europe.

When the Soviet Union dissolved in 1991, the vast oil and gas resources of the Caspian basin were once again open to exploitation by Western corporate interests. A race has now begun among powerful transnational corporate interests to secure control, and with the assistance of the most powerful Western states, policies have been designed to advantage their competition. In the decade since they have entered the region, exploration has confirmed that the Caspian basin contains between 70 and 200 billion barrels of oil, or roughly 10 percent of the world's reserves. It also is thought that the world's largest reservoir of untapped oil and gas is to be found in Kazakhstan, Azerbaijan, and Turkmenistan, the former southern republics of the Soviet Union that make up the greater Caspian basin region. Even though reports of possible and confirmed reserve deposits differ widely, interest in the region continues to accelerate.[7] At stake are billions of dollars in oil and natural gas revenues and the vast geopolitical and military advantages that fall to the power or powers that secure a dominant position in the region.

Two basic questions introduced in chapter 1 now return: Who owns the rich oil and natural gas resources, and who will control the transportation of Caspian oil and gas to world markets? The answers to these questions will strongly influence how the world economy evolves in this century and who will sit at the head of the international order that governs it.

FROM THE OIL AND NATURAL GAS RESOURCES OF EURASIA TO WORLD DOMINATION

Oil has become the pivot upon which the axis of war or peace rests. This is consistent with a historical pattern in which control of precious minerals has directly or indirectly led to war. In the last century alone, oil played a key role in at least ten of the twelve major conflicts. It seems that of all the resources that are critical to modernization in the twentieth century, none is more likely to provoke a major war between states than oil,[8] and as oil reserves decline its importance will only grow in the decades ahead.

Unimpeded access to affordable energy has always been a primary strategic interest of the United States, which is now the only superpower remaining in the post–Cold War world. American dependency on imported petroleum has been growing since 1972, when domestic output reached its maximum level of 11.6 million barrels per day.[9] From that point forward, U.S. oil production went into decline and dependency on foreign sources of oil and gas increased. According to estimates, world oil production will begin to reach its peak between 2004 and 2008, which means that the world is depleting oil reserves at a rate of 6 percent a year. At the same time, demand growth is rising at an annual rate of 2 percent, which means that the world's oil industry would have to find the equivalent of 8 percent a year in newly discovered oil reserves to maintain an orderly oil market.[10] Unfortunately, discoveries are lagging behind, primarily because new large oil deposits of oil are not being found, and even if they were there is a considerable lag time between a discovery and turning the oil into a usable energy product. While conservation and renewable energy are much in the news, the reality is that neither of these factors are likely to make any significant dent in the steadily growing demand for oil products. In this atmosphere, competition for existing proven and prospective reserves is increasing, and the Caspian basin with its vast fields of untapped oil has now become the focus in a new version of the Great Game.

For reasons both of world strategy and control over natural resources, the U.S. administration is determined to secure for itself a dominant role in Eurasia. The immediate task of American power in "volatile Eurasia" has been described as "to ensure that no state or combination of states gains the ability to expel the US or even diminish its decisive role."[11] These stated U.S. policy goals include breaking Russia's monopoly over oil and gas transportation routes, promoting U.S. energy security through diversified supplies, encouraging the construction of multiple pipelines through U.S.-controlled lands, and denying other potential powers dangerous leverage over central Asian oil and natural gas resources.[12] This life-and-death struggle to monopolize energy resources simply recognizes that oil remains the lifeblood of a modern world economy. U.S. status as a superpower requires the control of oil at every stage, from discovery, to pumping, to refining, to transportation, and finally to marketing. The Washington-based American Petroleum Institute, voice of the U.S. oil industry, has identified the Caspian basin as "the area of greatest resource potential outside of the Middle East."[13] In 1998, when he played a central role in the U.S. oil industry, current U.S. Vice President Dick Cheney said of the Caspian basin, "I cannot think of a time when we have had a region emerge as suddenly to become as strategically significant as the Caspian."[14]

At stake in this competition is far more than the fate of the resources of the Caspian basin. Caspian oil is non-OPEC oil, meaning that supplies from this region are less likely to be affected by the price and supply policies applied by the oil-exporting cartel.[15] Flows of large volumes of Caspian oil through non-OPEC lands would erode the power of OPEC (Organization of Oil Exporting Countries), as well as its ability to maintain high oil prices and to use oil as a mode of political blackmail.[16]

PIPELINEISTAN

Getting oil from the Caspian-Caucasus to the world markets is not easy because the Caspian basin is landlocked. When the Soviet Union broke up in 1991, multinational oil companies and governments of the leading world powers wove a tangled web of competing pipelines, with leading roles played by British Petroleum (BP) and Amoco (which merged in 1998), UNOCAL, Texaco, Exxon, and Pennzoil, all of which have already invested more than $30 billion in new production facilities.[17] This fabric of oil transportation represents a "pipeline map" around the oil and natural gas resources of the region that connects the area from the

Balkans in the west to Afghanistan in the east.[18] The debate over which route to use for the Caspian's considerable oil reserves has inspired a high-stakes tug-of-war among the countries of the region. At present the only operational oil export route follows the line Baku-Grozny-Tikhoretsk-Novorossiysk. Oil exports from this route depend on tanker transportation via the Turkish Straits. The main alternative to this Russian pipeline is the U.S.-backed Turkish route that runs from the Caspian Sea to the Mediterranean. The Baku-Tbilisi-Ceyhan (BTC) pipeline to transport crude oil extracted from the Caspian Sea shelf to the Mediterranean Sea basin was inaugurated on May 25, 2005 near Azerbaijan's capital, Baku.[19] Construction of the U.S.-sponsored BTC started in 2001, and its final cost totaled well over the $3 billion originally planned. The BTC stretches 1,760 kilometers, including 440 kilometers through Azerbaijan and 250 kilometers through Georgia. It will take several months to fill the conduit. The pipeline is designed to carry oil extracted from Azerbaijan's sector of the Caspian Sea by an international consortium comprising eleven companies. However, many in the oil industry are concerned about a one-pipeline solution because of tensions in the region and would prefer a multiple-pipeline strategy, including a major route through Iran. With the current strained relations between the United States and Iran, the Iranian route seems uncertain. Yet given commercial realities, any political opening could shift the terms of the pipeline debate very quickly.[20]

FROM THE BALKANS TO AFGHANISTAN

The Balkan states are crucial to all these oil pipeline routes because oil destined for Western Europe must pass through one of them at one point or another.[21] During the 1999 Kosovo war, some critics of NATO's bombing of Yugoslavia alleged that the United States and its allies in the West were seeking to secure a passage for oil from the Caspian Sea. This claim was mocked by British Foreign Secretary Robin Cook, who observed that "there is no oil in Kosovo."[22] Of course, this was true but irrelevant. In fact, the truth is much different. In 1997, BP and the Texas construction giant Halliburton proposed a pipeline that would go from Burgas in Bulgaria through Skopje in Macedonia to Vlorë, a port in

Albania.[23] And on June 2, 1999, the U.S. Trade and Development Agency, which had financed initial feasibility studies, announced that it had awarded a half-million dollar grant to Bulgaria to carry out a feasibility study for the pipeline across the Balkans.[24] It seems that their location makes the Balkans a key regional stepping stone to oil interests in Eurasia.[25]

In the same period, it also was claimed that the main global objective of the U.S.-led NATO operations in Kosovo was to pacify Yugoslavia so that transnational oil corporations could secure the oil transportation route from the Caspian Sea into central Europe.[26] After NATO's bombing campaign ended in March 1999, the United States spent $36.6 million to build Camp Bondsteel in southern Kosovo, the largest American foreign military base constructed since Vietnam. Camp Bondsteel was built by Brown and Root, a division of Halliburton, which was the world's biggest oil services company and at the time was headed by the current U.S. vice president, Dick Cheney. Camp Bondsteel, which was created in the image of small-town America, features a fitness center, movie theaters, bowling alleys, and fast-food restaurants where young soldiers go to relax after a hard day's work. It is now an enormous, self-sufficient city with downtown, midtown, and uptown districts, barracks, command centers, helicopter maintenance buildings, a water treatment plant, a library, a chapel, and the best-equipped hospital in Europe.[27] Camp Bondsteel has now become the linchpin in a military system that controls oil routes to European markets. It is located close to vital oil pipelines and energy corridors that are presently under construction, such as the U.S.-sponsored Trans-Balkan oil pipeline.

Rivalries being played out in the Caspian basin will have a decisive impact in shaping post-Communist Eurasia and in determining how the United States will influence the development of the region.[28] They also will have worldwide and not just regional consequences. For example, expansion of U.S. influence in Eurasia poses a direct and immediate threat to China because, among other factors, the expansion of the Chinese economy directly depends on access to petroleum. Its oil needs are expected to nearly double by 2010, which will force the country to import 40 percent of its requirements, up from 20 percent in 1995.[29] China's increasing demand for oil on the world markets has been a major factor in the increase in oil prices and will be the most important factor in determining future oil pricing. Presently, China is the world's number two oil consumer after the United States, and since 2000 has accounted for 40 percent of the growth in the world's demand for crude oil. Presently, China's proven oil reserves stand at 18 trillion barrels, and oil imports account for one-third of its crude oil consumption.[30] However, in response to a burgeoning demand for energy, the Chinese government has stepped up exploration activities within its own borders, begun diversifying its energy sector to include other than oil resources, actively explored developing new nuclear power facilities, reassessed its use of coal and natural gas, sought the development of renewable energy, promoted energy conservation, and encouraged investments in energy-friendly technologies such as hydrogen-powered fuel cells and coal gasification—all in a concerted effort to support an 8–10 percent rate of growth in its gross domestic production.

China has now become an active player in this new Great Game by making secure access to the oil and gas reserves of the Caspian basin a cornerstone of its economic policy. In 1997, the China National Petroleum Corporation, which employs more than 1.5 million people, acquired the right to develop two potentially lucrative oil fields in Kazakhstan, outbidding U.S. and European oil companies. China's longest pipeline, running 4,200 kilometers from the Tarim Basin of Xinjiang Province to a network of gas and oil pipelines in the major east coast metropolis of Shanghai, came online in August 2004. In October 2004, construction began on a 988 kilometer pipeline from Atasu in northwest Kazakhstan to Alataw Pass in Xinjiang that will carry 10 million tons of oil a year when it is completed in late 2005. Feasibility studies are also underway for the construction of over 3,000 kilometers of gas pipeline from Turkmenistan to Xinjiang, and the Chinese government is also helping to develop oil fields in Uzbekistan and hydroelectric power projects in Kyrgyzstan and Tajikistan.[31]

A number of overlapping power blocs are emerging in the Caspian basin that have a shared interest in the development of its oil and gas resources. Theoretically, oil and gas pipelines to China from Turkmenistan and Kazakhstan could be extended to link into the pipeline networks of both Russia and Iran. This model has been dubbed the Pan Asian Global Energy Bridge, a Eurasian network of pipelines linking energy resources in the Middle East, central Asia, and Russia to the Chinese Pacific coast. China's pipeline network also has the potential to bring about a significant strategic realignment in the region. Currently, China derives 13.6 percent of its imports from Iran. In March 2004, China signed a $100 million deal with Iran to import 10 million tons of liquefied natural gas over a twenty-five-year period in exchange for Chinese investment in Iran's oil and gas exploration. Growing Sino-Iranian relations are undermining U.S. sanctions against Iran, and the Bush administration has sanctioned Chinese companies sixty-two times for violating U.S. or international controls on the transfer of weapons technology to Iran and other states.[32] Russia is China's fifth-largest crude oil supplier, with LuKoil now replacing Yukos as China's main supplier of Russian oil. China expects to import at least 10 million tons of oil from Russia in 2005 and 15 million in 2006. Chinese-Russian energy relations appear to be mirroring political and military relations as well. This growing cooperation between China and Russia seems to have resurrected former Russian Prime Minister Yevgeny Primakov's idea for a strategic triangle between Russia, India, and China. These three states, plus Iran, are bound together by shared interests in the push for a multipolar world and respect for the principles of state sovereignty and nonintervention with regard to their respective separatist movements in Chechnya, Kashmir, and Xinjiang.[33]

At the moment, Russia controls most of the export routes for oil from the Caspian basin. According to the view of Russian Defense Minister Igor Sergeev in November 1999, the West's policy is a challenge to Russia with the aim of weakening Russia's international position and ousting it from strategically important regions.[34] Disputes over oil were at the heart of Russia's earlier decision to go to war against Chechnya in December 1994, because its sole operational pipeline for Caspian oil, the Novorossiysk pipeline, which goes directly through troubled Dagestan and Chechnya, was threatened by Islamic separatist forces in Chechnya.[35] Redirecting the oil around Chechnya would impose major costs if the rebellion persisted, and foreign investors would have been wary of any long-term investments. Russia's concerns about Chechnya also grew with the U.S.-NATO war against Serbia in 1999 and the subsequent NATO occupation of Kosovo, and tensions within Russia escalated as the military campaign in Chechnya began. In this context, the Russian 1999 intervention in Chechnya can be seen as a warning to the United States, NATO, and any rebellious provincials that Russia is still a powerful military force. With Vladimir Putin's accession to power, Russia continues to push an aggressive policy designed to recover Russia's control in central Eurasia. Soon after Putin's election, Russia's National Security Council declared the Caspian basin to be Russia's key foreign policy focus.[36]

The Caspian Sea basin, with its huge reserves of oil and natural gas and its strategic position, is a key arena of rivalry between the United States, major European powers, Russia, Japan, and China. All of the major powers, along with transnational corporations, have been seeking alliances, concessions, and possible pipeline routes in the region. In the midst of this increasing competition, an open conflict between the United States and China seems likely as China's growing reliance on Eurasian oil will ultimately bring it into direct confrontation with the United States as the world's largest energy consumer.[37]

WAR ON TERROR AND BLOOD FOR OIL

The war on terror is being used as an excuse to further U.S. control in the oil-rich Caspian Sea basin. Washington considers its military might as a trump card that can be employed to prevail over its rivals in the struggle for political hegemony and resources.[38] Powerful geopolitical and geo-economic interests are fueling the American war drive, which suggests that the real motive for America's operation in Afghanistan is more related to its interest in the resources of central Asia than to any democratic project.[39] If the Balkans are a major key to the transportation of vast Caspian oil reserves to western markets, Afghanistan is the key to oil transportation to world markets through the Indian Ocean.[40] On September 10, 2001, the day before the attack on the World Trade Center, *Oil and Gas Journal*, an oil industry publication, opined that central Asia represented one of the world's last great frontiers for geological survey and analysis, "offering opportunities for investment in discovery, production, transport and refining of enormous quantities of oil and gas resources. Central Asia is rich in hydrocarbons, with gas being the predominant energy fuel. Turkmenistan and Uzbekistan, especially, are noted for gas resources, while Kazakhstan is the primary oil producer."[41]

The September 11, 2001, attacks on America provided an added incentive for using Afghanistan as a convenient target to remind the world of America's capacity for military destruction. Within a week of the commencement of war in Afghanistan, the Bush administration discussed the shape of a post-Afghan government in reference to developing oil and gas pipelines. On December 15, 2001, the *New York Times* reported that "the State Department is exploring the potential for post-Taliban energy projects in the region, which has more than 6 percent of the world's proven oil reserves and almost 40 percent of its gas reserves."[42] When the war concluded, President Bush appointed a former aide to the American oil company UNOCAL, Afghan-born Zalmay Khalilzad, as special envoy to Afghanistan.[43] The nomination underscores the importance of the economic and financial interests at stake in the U.S. military campaign in Afghanistan. The evidence can be found in Khalilzad's work as an adviser for UNOCAL, a major U.S. oil company. Before his ambassadorial appointment, Khalilzad drew up a risk analysis for a proposed gas pipeline from the former Soviet republic of Turkmenistan across Afghanistan and Pakistan to the Indian Ocean. So many business deals, so much oil and natural gas, all these giant multinational corporations with powerful connections to the Bush administration. This is not a paranoid theory, but simply a convergence of political and economic interests traveling under the rubric of Operation Enduring Freedom.[44] As Zoltan Grossman observed, "it is not a conspiracy; it is just business as usual."[45]

The American interests in Afghanistan have been well documented in *Taliban*, a book by Ahmed Rashid.[46] Rashid, hardly a wide-eyed radical, is the Pakistan, Afghanistan, and central Asia correspondent for the *Far Eastern Economic Review* and the *Daily Telegraph* in London. He argues that the United States was hindered by its own embargo of Iran that began in 1980 and was forced to look for other ways of moving oil from the region to the world markets. Sometime in 1994, as Afghanistan tumbled into disarray in the wake of the civil war that followed the 1989 Soviet withdrawal, a highly secretive and heavily armed group emerged called the Taliban. Its declared purpose was to restore peace, to enforce traditional law, and to defend the Islamic character of Afghanistan. However, Rashid says, the key interest in using Afghanistan as a major oil transit route led the U.S. administration in the early 1990s to support this young rebel movement as it fought to bring stability to war-torn Afghanistan. If these rebels could end the Afghan civil war, then the United States could build a pipeline that neither Russia nor Iran would control.[47]

Rashid argues that U.S. economic interests, driven by oil, have for years taken precedence over any human-rights agenda. It was only after

9/11 that U.S. First Lady Laura Bush emerged overnight as a progressive feminist concerned about the brutal repression of Afghan women under Taliban. In fact, the United States originally financed the Islamic mujahideen upon which the Taliban built its rule as it fought against the pro-Soviet Afghani government of the late 1970s. That war pitted the fundamentalist mujahideen against a government that allowed women access to education and employment. With the fall of this secular government, the Taliban dictatorship was free to support the beating and murder of women by their husbands.[48] In 1998, Zbigniew Brzezinski, President Carter's former National Security Adviser, defended U.S. support for Islamic extremism with the following words:

> It was July 3, 1979 that President Carter signed the first directive for secret aid to the opponents of the pro-Soviet regime in Kabul. And that very day, I wrote a note to the president in which I explained to him in my opinion this aid was going to induce a Soviet military intervention.... That secret operation was an excellent idea. It had the effect of drawing the Russians into the Afghan trap.... We now have the opportunity of giving to the USSR its Vietnam war.... What is more important to the history of the world? The Taliban or the collapse of the Soviet empire? Some stirred-up Moslems or the liberation of Central Europe and the end of the cold war?[49]

The evenual outcome of the present maneuvering in Eurasia and its impact on the global strategic equation is not yet totally clear. However, the increasingly heavy involvement of the U.S. administration, significant regional powers, and transnational corporations in the area underscores the central importance of the oil and natural gas resources of the region and the potential for conflicts over its control. The growth of regional antagonisms will be heightened, not attenuated, as the region is integrated more into the global system of production and trade,[50] and with four nuclear-armed countries—Russia, China, Pakistan, and India[51]—the region presents a very dangerous flashpoint of global significance.[52] As the stakes in this competition and the race for regional control increase, the risk of dangerous clashes moves toward a threatening reality.[53] It is not an exaggeration to say that we face a reconstruction of the geostrategic map, not only of Eurasia but of the world as a whole, in a way not seen since the depth of colonial times.

The United States has been aggressively exploiting the disintegration of the Soviet bloc. It has pursued its interests by attempting to absorb the post-Soviet space into the world capitalist system by forcing it open to investment and control by U.S.-based transnational corporations, in particular to U.S.-based oil and gas interests who have their sights set on the resources of Eurasia. The vast oil and natural gas resources of the Caspian Sea basin are now being divided among major oil multinationals.[54] This is a fuel that is feeding renewed militarism, leading to new wars of conquest by the United States and its allies against local opponents, and threatening ever-greater conflicts between the United States and major regional powers, such as China and Russia. Were any of the United States' adversaries—or a combination of adversaries—to effectively challenge U.S. supremacy in this region, it would call into question the U.S. hegemony in world affairs. This is the key to understanding the development of global politics since the end of the Cold War. The U.S. war against the Taliban in Afghanistan is merely one in a long series of wars of U.S. aggression that have spanned the world and that are now focusing their attention on a new Great Game. When the Nobels came to the Caspian Sea region in the late nineteenth century, they commented that in this part of the world, "oil, blood, and politics were completely intermingled."[55] It seems that not much has changed in the last hundred years.

ENDLESS WAR: MARCHING INTO THE ABYSS

Events since 9/11 are reminiscent of George Orwell's classic political novel *1984*. In *1984*, the enemy, the hate figure, is Emmanuel Goldstein, who is said to control spies and saboteurs. Goldstein is the primal enemy—all crimes, all treacheries, acts of sabotage, heresies, deviations, spring directly out of him. Goldstein is the Osama bin Laden figure in Orwell's novel, an extremely elusive person who is never seen, never captured, but believed by the leadership of Oceania (a fictitious superpower, an amalgamation of North America and Western Europe) to be "still alive and hatching his conspiracies, perhaps somewhere beyond the sea, under the protection of his foreign paymasters." Since Goldstein is never captured, the battle against his crimes, treacheries, and sabotages must never end. As Orwell observed, "The heretic, the enemy of society, will always be there, so that he can be defeated and humiliated over again. . . . Goldstein and his heresies will live forever. Every day, at every moment, they will be defeated, discredited, ridiculed, spat upon—and yet they will always survive."[56]

The war on terror can go on indefinitely because unlike the previous wars—World War I, World War II, or even the Cold War—it involves no clear-cut and measurable criteria of success. *Indefinitely* here is just another word for forever.

NOTES

1. Paul Starobin, "The New Great Game," *National Journal* (March 13, 1999), 666–75, http://www.publications.parliament.uk/pa/cm199899/cmselect/cmfaff/349/349ap21.htm.

2. John McLaurin, *Sketches in Crude Oil* (Harrisburg, 1896), 8; E. W. Owen, *Trek of the Oil Finders: A History of Exploration for Petroleum* (Tulsa: American Association for Petroleum Geologists, 1975), 1.

3. R. W. Tolf, *The Russian Rockefellers: The Saga of the Nobel Family and the Russian Oil Industry* (Stanford, CA: Hoover Institute Press, 1976), 141.

4. Bülent Gökay, "The Background: History and Political Change," in *The Politics of Caspian Oil*, ed. Bülent Gökay, 1–19 (London: Palgrave, 2001).

5. Bülent Gökay, *A Clash of Empires: Turkey between Russian Bolshevism and British Imperialism, 1918–1923* (London: I.B. Tauris, 1997), 73–76.

6. M. I. Goldman, *The Enigma of Soviet Petroleum* (London: George Allen and Unwin, 1980), 21.

7. C. Fenyvesi, "Caspian Sea: US Experts Say Oil Reserves Are Huge," *RFE/RL*, May 5, 1998.

8. T. F. Homer-Dixon, *Environment, Scarcity and Violence* (Princeton, NJ: Princeton University Press, 1999), 138.

9. K. S. Deffeyes, *Hubbert's Peak: The Impending World Oil Shortage* (Princeton, NJ: Princeton University Press, 2001), 2–13.

10. *Oil and Gas Investor* 2, no. 1 (January 2002).

11. Zbigniew Brzezinski, "A Geostrategy for Asia," *Foreign Affairs* (September/October 1997), 50–64.

12. U.S. Energy Secretary Bill Richardson quoted in Stephen Kinzer, "On Piping Out Caspian Oil, U.S. Insists the Cheaper, Shorter Way Isn't Better," *New York Times*, November 8, 1998.

13. Marjorie Cohn, "Cheney's Black Gold," *Chicago Tribune*, August 10, 2000.

14. Quoted in *The Guardian*, October 23, 2001.

15. Bülent Gökay, "Oil, War, Geopolitics and Hegemony," *Conflict and Peace in Mountain Societies*, http://www.mtnforum.org/resources/library/gokab02a.htm.

16. B. Shaffer, "A Caspian Alternative to OPEC," *Wall Street Journal*, July 11, 2001.

17. L. Kleveman, "The New Great Game," *The Guardian*, October 20, 2003.

18. S. Parrott, "Pipeline Superhighway Replaces the Silk Road," *RFE/RL*, November 19, 1997.

19. *Agence France Press*, June 2, 2004.

20. Gökay, "The Background," 1–19.

21. D. Yannopoulos, *Athens News*, September 28, 2001.

22. Robin Cook, interviewed by John Lloyd, *New Statesman*, July 5, 1999, 19.

23. George Monbiot, "A Discreet Deal in the Pipeline," *The Guardian*, February 15, 2001.

24. P. M. Wihbey, "Looking at Balkans Route for Caspian Crude," *United Press International* online, June 23, 1999.

25. *Business Week*, April 19, 1999; E. D. Zemenides, "The Next Balkan War," *National Strategy Reporter* (Fall 1997).

26. B. Schwarz and C. Layne, "The Case against Intervention in Kosovo," *The Nation*, April 19, 1999; P. Gowan, "The Euro-Atlantic Origins of NATO's Attack on Yugoslavia," in *Masters of the Universe*, ed. T. Ali, 3–45 (London: Verso, 2000).

27. The base is so huge that KFOR soldiers who are in active service in the former Yugoslavia joke, "What are the two things that can be seen from space? One is the Great Wall of China, the other is Camp Bondsteel." According to leaked comments to the press, European politicians now believe that the United States used the bombing of Yugoslavia specifically to establish Camp Bondsteel. http://www.realitymacedonia.org.mk/web/news_page.asp?nid=1838.

28. "Race to Unlock Central Asia's Energy Riches," *BBC World News*, December 29, 1997.

29. *Oil and Gas Journal*, January 4, 2002.

30. *Asia Times Online*, March 2, 2005.

31. M. Glenny, "To Hell and Baku," *The Observer*, November 2, 2003.

32. Ibid.

33. *Asia Times Online*, March 2, 2005.

34. Reported in *New York Times*, November 15, 1999.

35. A. Towner, "The Russians, Chechens and the Black Gold," in *The Politics of Caspian Oil*, ed. Bülent Gökay, 199–215 (London: Palgrave, 2001).

36. It has been suggested that there may be a quid pro quo between the U.S. and Russian administrations, with Russians providing intelligence support to American troops in Afghanistan and the United States turning a blind eye to a brutal Russian occupation in Chechnya. J. Rarey, "May God Forgive Them," http://www .watchmanjournal.org/000217.html.

37. Richard Norton-Taylor, "The New Great Game," *The Guardian*, March 5, 2001.

38. P. Beaumont and E. Vulliamy, "Armed to the Teeth," *The Observer*, February 10, 2002; B. Jones, assistant secretary for European and Eurasian affairs, *AMBO-News*, February 11, 2002.

39. S. Yechury, "America, Oil and Afghanistan," *The Hindu*, October 13, 2001; "Control of Central Asia's Oil is the Real Goal," *The Telegraph*, October 25, 2001.

40. "Afghan Pipeline: A New Great Game," *BBC News*, November 4, 1997.

41. *Oil and Gas Journal*, September 10, 2001.

42. *New York Times*, December 15, 2001.

43. The UNOCAL energy corporation had begun its efforts to establish pipelines to transport oil and gas through Afghanistan in October 1995.

44. "West Plans Oil Pipeline via Afghanistan," Kazakh Commercial Television, Almaty, *Financial Times Limited*, December 25, 2001.

45. Zoltan Grossman, "New US Military Bases: Side Effects or Causes of War?," *ZNet*, February 5, 2002, http://www.zmag.org/content/TerrorWar/grossman_new_bases.cfm.

46. Ahmed Rashid, *Taliban: Militant Islam, Oil and Fundamentalism in Central Asia* (London: I. B. Tauris, 2000).

47. AsiaSource, interview with Ahmed Rashid, March 21, 2002, http://www .asiasource.org/news/special_reports/rashid.cfm.

48. J. Cotter, "War and Domestic Violence," *The Red Critique*, no. 6 (September–October 2002), http://www.redcritique.org/SeptOct02/thedictatorshipofcapital.htm.

49. *Le Nouvel Observateur*, Paris, January 15–21, 1998.

50. *Time Magazine*, November 12, 2001; *Observer*, October 7, 2001; *Explorer*, February 2000.

51. M. MacDonald, "India, Pakistan Buy Time, but War Still Lurks," Reuters News Service, January 2, 2002; R. Fisk, "War Disturbs the Most Dangerous Political Tectonic Plate in the World," *Independent*, October 8, 2001.

52. Henry Kissinger, "New World Disorder," *Newsweek*, May 24, 1999. This period witnessed an increasing arms race in the region, including a proliferation of nuclear weapons in states like India, Pakistan, Iran, and Iraq. Tamara Straus, "The New Battlefield," *Albion Monitor*, December 15, 2001, http://www.monitor.net/monitor/0112a/newbattlefield.html.

53. B. Gertz, "India, Pakistan Prepare War," *Washington Times*, December 31, 2001.

54. *New York Times*, March 8, 1992.

55. Bülent Gökay, "Introduction: Oil, War and Geopolitics from Kosovo to Afghanistan," *Journal of Southern Europe and the Balkans* 4, no. 1 (2002): 12.

56. George Orwell, *1984* (Harmondsworth, UK: Penguin, 2000), 14 (first published in 1949).

CHAPTER 6

The U.S./NATO War on Yugoslavia

On the night of 24 March, 1999, NATO forces started their air offensive against Yugoslavia. The bombing of Yugoslavia continued until 10 June—lasting 79 days, with 1,200 aircraft dropping around 20,000 bombs and hundreds of missiles from a height of 15,000 feet. According to NATO estimates made during the campaign, around 5,000 members of the Yugoslav armed forces were killed and hundreds of their tanks and heavy guns were destroyed in Kosovo; in the meantime about 1.4 million Kosovo Albanians were forced from their homes—500,000 were allegedly displaced inside Kosovo, and 850,000 fled to the neighbouring countries; 100,000 Albanian men were reported missing, presumably killed by the Serbs. The picture that emerged after the end of the bombing looked somewhat different: in Kosovo NATO's bombing had destroyed 13 tanks and killed about 400 Serbian soldiers (an equal number had been killed by the Kosovo Liberation Army), throughout Yugoslavia anywhere between 500 and 1,400 civilians were killed by NATO bombs—a "collateral damage" that could be three times higher than the Serbian military casualties; some 2,000 Kosovo Albanians—both KLA fighters and civilians—were killed by Serbian forces after the beginning of the air campaign. NATO's takeover of Kosovo in mid-June changed the refugee statistics as well: half of the 850,000 refugees outside the province returned to Kosovo by the end of June, the expected half a million internally displaced Albanians did not materialise, and about 100,000 Serbian refugees (half of the local Serbian population) fled or were evicted from Kosovo.[1]

During the Cold War, Yugoslavia was looked upon by Western intellectuals and politicians either as an example to avoid, or as a case to copy, or a bit of both.[2] Pro-Soviet Communist parties in the West condemned

Yugoslavia for sliding back to liberalism and capitalism. Anti-Communist liberals criticized the country for not allowing party-political democracy and a fully fledged market economy to flourish. "Third way" groups, parties, and intellectuals were praising the Yugoslav model as an example of democratic socialism, alongside the Italian Communist Party. On the domestic front, there were ethnic nationalist groups, a minority among the Yugoslavs, who wanted greater autonomy and even separation from the Yugoslav federation. Then there were those, either Communists or liberals, who wanted to preserve a Yugoslav state, albeit in a nearly co-federal form. Tito, "a practical ruler concerned with his place in history," as Stevan K. Pavlowitch put it, preferred to shape a country as cofederal as it could be at home and as nonaligned as it could be abroad.[3] With the first, he was trying to keep ethnic balances in check, absorbing some, but not all, ethnic tensions. With the second, he basically was trying to get the best of both worlds, that is, to gain support from both the Soviets and the West.

The breakup of Yugoslavia is usually explained by an eruption of rampant ethnic tensions caused by nationalist hatred that already existed between its ethnic communities, as well as by Serb aggressiveness. The Serbs, under Slobodan Milosevic, wanted to take advantage of the post-Tito era (Tito died in 1980) to create either a greater Serbia or a centralized Yugoslavia dominated by the Serbs. To make a long story short, this argument attributes the collapse of Yugoslavia to domestic agents and actors (nationalistic aggressiveness, Serb nationalism and competing nationalist agendas, and ethnic hatred).[4]

We have long disagreed with this simplistic interpretation. Drawing from the seminal work of Susan Woodward and others, we have argued that Yugoslavia's disintegration can be explained only by looking at the linkages between domestic and external factors.[5] In this context, we have showed that, in the final instance, the external rather than the internal environment was responsible for the collapse of the country and the displacement of so many innocent civilians, either by nationalistic aggression or U.S./NATO bombing.[6]

We rehearse this argument here by bringing it into the broader geopolitical and strategic context of U.S. neo-imperialism after the end of Communism. In particular, we focus on the case of Kosovo, showing the degree to which America's security is bound up with Europe's own, a global relationship that is inserted into the post–World War II hub-and-spoke system of European dependency upon the United States.

WHY DID YUGOSLAVIA BREAK UP?

It is impossible to understand the disintegration of Yugoslavia if we do not take into account the following interrelated factors.

First, the regional disparities in the country, most notably the fact that the area north of the river Sava (Slovenia and Croatia) was (and is) richer and far more integrated into Western markets than the southern zones (Macedonia, Kosovo, Montenegro, and Bosnia-Herzegovina). Serbia roughly constitutes the middle ground.[7] In essence, the Yugoslav Communists were caught between efforts to produce a Yugoslav identity, *Jugoslovenstvo*, and attempts, particularly after 1964, to create a cofederal country conceding equal rights of representation to all nationalities composing Yugoslavia. Ten years later, in 1974, Tito created the most liberal/cofederal Constitution that ever existed in post–World War II Yugoslavia. It should not go unnoticed that separatist trends reinforced by regional economic disparities are not a Balkan or East European phenomenon. Italy experienced a similar phenomenon in the 1980s and 1990s, when the party of the Northern League under Umberto Bossi claimed an independent state in Italy's industrial north due to fiscal pressures from the heavily subsidized south. Although the problem of Italy's underdeveloped south is historical and endemic, the trend toward an independent state in the north has been reversed in the 2000s.

Second, Yugoslavia's uneven economic development continued throughout the post–World War II years, state policies being unable to reverse the trend. In fact, the Republics of Slovenia and Croatia were protesting against subsidizing the poorer regions or republics of the country. The crisis of the Yugoslav state deteriorated due to an international debt crisis in the 1970s and early 1980s. The Yugoslavs borrowed large amounts of money from the IMF in order to finance growth via exports. However, due to the first (1973) and second (1979) oil shocks and the general period of *stagflation* (high inflation accompanied by economic stagnation), the Western economies entered a long period of recession and blocked

Yugoslav exports. Under these circumstances, the Yugoslav authorities were forced to go back to the IMF and the World Bank for further assistance, but, this time around, IMF and World Bank assessors employed conditionality—no more handouts without concrete economic reforms (e.g., liberalization of the banking system, privatization, etc.) and a push for a functional free-market economy, capable of guaranteeing the return of the sums delivered by those international lenders.[8] This, among other things, implied revision of the Constitution. It necessitated centralization of political powers and abolition of the principle of equal representation and cofederalism, which was enabling the constituent republics, particularly after 1974, to enjoy their own political and bureaucratic privileges and fiscal economic powers. When Belgrade, under the Serb nationalist Slobodan Milosevic, began implementing the IMF directives—something that suited Milosevic's plans for dominating Yugoslavia—Slovene and Croatian nationalism became a serious political force. But this was not because Croats and Serbs hated each other. This was primarily because the Croatian and Slovene elites did not want to foot the bill for the IMF-led neoliberal reforms. As Susan Woodward argued, "nationalism became a political force when leaders in the Republics sought popular support as bargaining chips in federal disputes" over Constitutional reform.[9] All in all, "the Yugoslav state was a classic case of a structured inequality among regions, in which ethnic tensions were exacerbated via a neo-liberal modernizing package of economic reforms imposed from outside."[10] Thus, the deeper cause of the breakup of Yugoslavia was the IMF and World Bank intervention, an intervention that exploded as it straddled regional disparities and preexisting ethnic tensions.

Third, the interventionist policy of Germany, Austria, Hungary, and the Vatican, encouraging Croatian and Slovene separatism at a moment when it was certain that this would lead to civil war, also contributed to the violent and chaotic breakup of the country. Slovenia, for example, was printing money in Austria on the basis of a deutsche mark peg since 1984. But the most interesting story is that of the collision between Britain and Germany over the issue of recognition of Slovenia and Croatia as independent states. In the run up to the Maastricht Treaty negotiations (1991), Britain managed to opt out from the clauses regarding the Common Foreign and Security Policy and the social charter (determining the minimum wage and so on).[11] How did it happen? In fact, this was the result of informal bargaining between Germany and

Britain, with Germany agreeing to support British requests to opt out in return for Britain's support for the "German position on the EC's diplomatic recognition of Slovenia and Croatia."[12] This was catastrophic, particularly because the recognition of Croatia was turning a substantial group of Serbs there (13 percent) from being a constituent Yugoslav nation into a persecuted minority in Croatia. This was a decisive trigger for the outbreak of civil war and nationalist atrocities from all sides.

Last but not least, America's demand for an independent Bosnia, despite the fact that no ethnic Bosnian majority existed to back such a demand on the ground, made things even more chaotic, at least until the signing of the Dayton accords in 1995. But the United States entered the Yugoslav theater to stop Germany's influence there, not to protect Bosnian Muslims from Serb nationalist aggression. As Lawrence Eagleburger, deputy secretary of state, put it in 1991, "Germany is getting out ahead of the US" with its Croatian drive.[13] NATO's bombing of Bosnian Serb positions brought Milosevic and the Serbs to the negotiating table at Dayton. In effect, the first out-of-area mission of the United States/NATO occurred in Yugoslavia, mostly in order to keep the Germans down, as the old adage goes. At the same time, it reminded the Europeans that their security is an American affair and not a matter of any rapid reaction force they might contemplate building. The road to NATO's eastward enlargement was paved.

AMERICAN TRICKS

As for Bosnia, so for the Kosovo crisis in 1998–99, the main culprits, according to the majority of analysts, were the Serbs and their nationalist leader, Milosevic, and the tensions between the two hostile communities in Kosovo, the majority Albanians and the minority Serbs. The West bears some responsibility in the sense that it did not intervene earlier to prevent the exacerbation of conflict and sort things out there.[14] This is a mild version of the U.S. rhetoric: The West intervened in Kosovo to stop Milosevic, an evil dictator, from massacring ethnic Albanians.[15] The argument for humanitarian intervention unfolded at its best in the Kosovo crisis. Blair and Clinton, champions of the "third way" postsocialist Left, could sell their publics human rights for neo-imperialism: such was the brainwashing by the Western media that only 5,000 protesters from all over Britain marched in London in the early days of the bombing campaign.

NATO and the United States began an illegal war, as they lacked authorization from the UN Security Council. They also began a war that violated the NATO treaty itself: NATO, presumably, was a defensive pact, so NATO countries could resort to military action only if attacked. After Bosnia, this was a second out-of-area mission along the lines of Powell's doctrine: employment of overwhelming and high-tech military power in order, among other things, to minimize the risk of casualties. But this time around, things were a bit more serious, because NATO also violated the Geneva convention. As NATO was bombing Serb targets from high altitudes, it was at the same time making itself immune to risk, a fact that explicitly violates the Geneva convention protocols. But what is the background to the actual bombing campaign that commenced on March 24, 1999? Let us consider the ethnic politics of Kosovo and Belgrade first:

> For centuries Serbs and Albanians have inhabited Kosovo, and from the nineteenth century it became the centre of competing claims and ethnic strife. For the Serbs, Kosovo is the heartland of the medieval Serbian kingdom where many of the important monuments of the Serbian Orthodox Church are situated. And for the Albanians, Kosovo is the cradle of their struggle for independence, the place where the Prizren League was founded in 1878.
>
> Over the centuries administrative power in Kosovo changed hands many times between Serbs and Albanians, Christians and Muslims. Domination of one ethnic group over another emerged as a defining feature of Serb-Albanian relations in Kosovo, whether during the Ottoman period, the world wars or under communism.
>
> Under Tito and his successors Kosovo was the poorest and most volatile part of the Socialist federal Republic of Yugoslavia. The period of Serbian control and repression under security police chief Alexandar Rankovic (1945–66), was followed by a period of Albanian domination (1967–89). According to the 1974 constitution Kosovo enjoyed a quasi-republican status within Yugoslavia, although it remained formally an autonomous province of Serbia. . . . In the late 1980s the Serbian leadership under Milosevic discarded the rhetoric of communism and embraced the hitherto dissident ideas of Serbian nationalism—in particular the call for the restoration of full Serbian sovereignty over Kosovo. In this way the Serbian communists managed to keep power and prevented the emergence of genuine

opposition to their rule. Kosovo was just a pawn in this power game. . . . In 1989 the autonomy enshrined in the 1974 constitution was severely curtailed, and full Serbian control over Kosovo was re-established.[16]

One important point to remember is that the West was very supportive of Milosevic, as he "appeared to be an economic liberal, who might have greater authority to implement the reform" required by the IMF and the World Bank.[17] As late as March 1998, he was still for the West "the right man to do business with."[18] On February 23, 1998, U.S. special envoy to the Balkans Robert Gelbard called the Albanian KLA (Kosovo Liberation Army) a terrorist group. This gave Milosevic the green light to crack down brutally on the insurgents, thus igniting a more general Albanian uprising and intensifying the cycle of violence. A similar trick was played on Saddam before the Persian Gulf War: the United States declared that it had no vital interest in Kuwait, thus giving the signal to Saddam to take Kuwait. We know what followed and why.

In the case of Yugoslavia, there were some negotiations before the actual bombing began. But they were a mockery of impartiality. What the United States/NATO did there was to employ what we call coercive diplomacy: you either take what we offer you on the table, or you will be bombed. But what was on the table?

In February–March 1999, U.S./NATO and Serb and Kosovo Albanian delegations met at Rambouillet, France. For reasons that we explain in the next section, Secretary of State Madeleine Albright wanted to please the Kosovo Albanians more than the Serbs. In fact, the U.S./NATO delegation went so far as to ask the Serb delegation at Rambouillet to comply with three conditions. The first was that within three years the Kosovars should have a chance to vote for independence (and even possible annexation to Albania). The second was that Serbia should implement liberal reforms and accept free-market economic principles. The third was that NATO forces should be given permission to deploy not only in Kosovo, but anywhere in Yugoslavia. These three conditions were attached to the famous "Appendix B." This is very curious. If the United States/NATO wanted peace and not war, then they should not have asked Serbia to comply with these insulting conditions, particularly the third one. The United States/NATO could have asked the Serbs to either partition the province or to accept a cantonal/federal system with a UN security force overseeing the process. But the United States and Britain wanted war, not peace, and the rest of the NATO powers went along with this, whatever their public or private reservations.[19]

WEST-WEST STRUGGLES, RUSSIA, AND CHINA

America wanted war in order to preserve its primacy in Europe and expand its hub-and-spoke system of neo-imperialism in Asia.

The Anglo-Saxon wars in the Western Balkans were bound up with the contraction of Soviet power and the new expansionist doctrine of the Pentagon in Europe and Asia. The aim was to encircle the immediate security zones of Russia and China, wrapping them up from the Baltic states down to the Caucasus, central Asia, the Persian Gulf, and Southeast Asia. At the same time, the United States attempted to engage both Russia and China: It launched the Partnership for Peace (PfP) project in 1993 and offered Russia a political structure of cooperation through the NATO-Russia joint permanent council. China was cajoled through its WTO membership. The subjects of discussion varied from opening Chinese and Russian markets to Western capital and financial operators, to oil and gas issues, pipeline projects, and bilateral security issues, mostly related to the safe transportation of raw materials to Western markets at stable prices denominated in U.S. dollars.[20]

Similarly, the Franco-German answer to the contraction of Soviet power was a politically and economically strong Europe poised to expand eastward in Asia. In absence of the formidable enemy, the Europeans attempted to break free from the hub-and-spoke system. Toward the late 1980s and early 1990s, the French and the Germans pulled together their projects for the reconstruction of east-central Europe and the Balkans.[21] They envisaged an economic package for the reconstruction of the former Communist countries along the lines of a new Marshall Plan, and the creation of a strategic continental axis between European powers and Russia.[22] Also, they were about to launch their own reserve currency, the euro, and had developed plans for an independent energy policy.[23] But this plan went against any concept of American security and economic interests in Europe and Asia, with the Cold War or without. The United

States replied promptly to the Franco-German strategy and, in the end, the United States prevailed.

NATO's expansion deeper into Asia and the U.S. tactics were detrimental to the European project. First, they deprived Europe of a possible strategic cooperation with Russia, something that was inherent in Mikhail Gorbachev's idea for a "Common European House." Second, they were detrimental to the pan-European design itself, envisaged at Maastricht (1992) and at Amsterdam (1997), which included a rough timetable for the institutional consolidation of Europe's loose political structures, on the grounds of a common social, foreign, defense, and security policy.

On the economic front, the United States advanced an alternative economic design based on the aggressive "shock therapy" theory spearheaded by the work of Harvard University Professor Jeffrey Sachs in 1990–91. If anything, Rambouillet indicated that NATO was acting as a neoliberal/neo-imperialist economic and political agent, not as a security/defense pact to protect NATO lands from a military attack. The Bosnian and Kosovo crises reminded the Europeans that the United States remained in real charge of Europe's affairs. Thus, Europe's eastward enlargement would have to take place under NATO's and the United States's security and defense umbrella. In this context, the United States could define Europe's forms of unification, as well as, and even more important, its forms of division. Clinton hinted America's intentions several times during the 1990s. The Europeans, said Clinton, can have a "separable but not separate defense and security identity from NATO" and that "a strong US-European partnership is what this Kosovo thing is all about."[24]

NATO, A NEW PEACEKEEPER

One, of course, should not fail to note that in official U.S. parlance, phrases such as *strong partnership* are code. In diplomatic language, strong partnership means strong U.S. leadership over Europe. More bluntly, it means U.S. hegemonic leadership of Western Europe, the kind of "strong partnership" that used to exist during the Cold War (and in the Persian Gulf War)."[25] Yet, in many respects, the Kosovo war was, particularly for America, a failure.

In January 1997, Henry Kissinger, by way of commenting on NATO's enlargement prospects and the creation of a number of consultative bodies in the alliance's structures, said:

> The panoply of proposals comes perilously close to making Russia a non-integrated member of NATO.... Such an enhancement of Russia's role deflects the institution from its primary mission of defense and begins the process of turning NATO into a vague pan-European diplomatic forum more akin to the United Nations than to a military alliance.[26]

Kissinger's prediction materialized before, during, and after the Kosovo campaign. The Greek and Italian governments almost openly questioned the American drive to declare war on Yugoslavia over the issue of Kosovo, as it would ignite further Albanian nationalism in Macedonia and create more refugees in Greece proper. Both Italy and Greece have large investments in Albania (some 65 percent of fixed capital investment in Albania is Italian) and Greece also has an ethnic minority in southern Albania. All these issues, coupled with the possible destabilization of the fragile Republic of Macedonia, nearly one-third of whose population is ethnically Albanian, may have turned the southern Balkans into a proper war zone.

As far as Russia was concerned, it opposed NATO's drive precisely because it had read U.S. motives correctly: as a means to relaunch NATO in Eastern Europe against Russian security and economic interests. In fact, one should also mention, as we did in the previous chapter, the strategic position of the Balkans in Western energy security, particularly after the oil reserves of the Caspian Sea region were rediscovered in the early 1990s. Because of the trans-Balkan pipeline project designed to transport oil and gas from the Caspian Sea, which begins in the Bulgarian Black Sea port city of Bourgas, crosses Macedonia, and ends in the Albanian Adriatic port of Durres, U.S. power politics in the Balkans are also related to the new geopolitics of oil and gas. Russia responded to the United States in two ways: It vetoed a war resolution in the UN Security Council and it made the spectacular military move in June 1999 of occupying the Pristina airport in Kosovo well before the arrival of U.S. Marines there.

During the actual bombing campaign, the United States faced enormous difficulties. The French, in particular, objected to the Pentagon's selection of targets and were obstructionists throughout. Wesley Clark, NATO's supreme commander, initially thought that a few days of high-tech bombing from high altitudes would be enough to bring Milosevic to his knees.[27] But the war lasted seventy-eight days, precisely because working with the allies required compromises and protracted discussions. "The Pentagon's after-action report of October 1999," Gabriel Kolko wrote, "conceded that America needed the co-operation of NATO countries, but gaining consensus among 19 democratic nations is not easy."[28] This is another, additional, reason why the neocons after 9/11 refused any NATO help in their drive to take Afghanistan. After Kosovo, a strategic decision was made: NATO, that is, the Europeans, could do the "peacekeeping."[29] The United States would be starting and finishing the wars on its own terms. Yet NATO has to be preserved for precisely the same reason the United States created it: "to restrain Europe's inclinations to create an independent military organization."[30] Ultimately, the United States did not abandon this key Achesonian instrument.

NOTES

1. M. Waller, K. Drezov, and B. Gökay (eds.), *Kosovo: The Politics of Delusion* (London: Frank Cass, 2001), vii.

2. A key introduction to the question of Yugoslavia is Ivo Banac's *The National Question in Yugoslavia: Origins, History, Politics* (Ithaca, NY: Cornell University Press, 1984).

3. See Stevan K. Pavlowitch, *Tito: A Re-assessment* (London: Hurst and Co., 1992), 101.

4. Among others, Christopher Cviic, *Remaking the Balkans* (London: Pinter Publishers and the Royal Institute of International Affairs, 1991).

5. Susan Woodward, *Balkan Tragedy* (Washington, DC: The Brookings Institution, 1995).

6. See Vassilis K. Fouskas, "The Balkans and the Enlargement of NATO: A Sceptical View," *European Security* 10, no. 3 (Autumn 2001).

7. On the issue of regional disparities in Yugoslavia, see the seminal article by Iraj Hashi, "The disintegration of Yugoslavia: Regional disparities and the nationalities question," *Capital and Class* no. 48 (fall 1992): 41–88.

8. See Bülent Gökay, *Eastern Europe Since 1970* (Essex: Longman, 2001), 65–66.

9. Woodward, *Balkan Tragedy*, 380.

10. Vassilis K. Fouskas, *Zones of Conflict: US Foreign Policy in the Balkans and the Greater Middle East* (London: Pluto Press, 2003), 42.

11. See Julian Stern, *Early British Government Responses to the Conflicts in Yugoslavia, 1991–1993*, master's thesis, Birkbeck College, University of London, 2003.

12. See Michael Baun, *An Imperfect Union* (Oxford, UK: Westview Press, 1996), 74–75.

13. Woodward, *Balkan Tragedy*, 196.

14. Tim Judah, *Kosovo: War and Revenge* (New Haven, CT: Yale University Press, 2000).

15. For a propagandistic account that summarizes the pro-U.S. argument at its best, see Sidney Blumenthal, *The Clinton Wars* (London: Penguin, 2003), chapter 14. Blumenthal served as senior advisor to Clinton from August 1997 until January 2001.

16. Waller et al., *Kosovo*, viii.

17. Woodward, *Balkan Tragedy*, 106.

18. Martin Woollacott, "How the Man We Could Do Business with Is Becoming the Man We Must Destroy," *The Guardian*, April 3, 1999, 20.

19. The Rambouillet Text, February 1999, given in Waller et al., *Kosovo*, 157–161.

20. Among others, "Bush-Putin Joint Statement on New US-Russian Energy Dialogue," joint press release, May 24, 2002, http://www.freerepublic.com/focus/news.

21. The best statements in this vein are Peter Gowan's "Neo-liberal Theory and Practice for Eastern Europe," *New Left Review* no. 213 (1995) and "The Dynamics of 'European enlargement,'" *Labour Focus on Eastern Europe* no. 56 (1997). Both texts can be found in his book, *The Global Gamble* (London: Verso, 1999).

22. Interestingly, the development strategy for Eastern Europe launched by German Deutsche Bank President Herrhausen was dropped, following his assassination in fall 1989.

23. Among others, Commission of the European Communities, "Towards a European Strategy for the Security of Energy Supply," COM (2002) 321 final, Brussels, June 26, 2002. This report builds on a series of other similar reports drafted in the 1990s; see B. Gökay, "Oil, War and Geopolitics from Kosovo to Afghanistan," *Journal of Southern Europe and the Balkans* 4, no. 1 (2002): 4–13. See also Keith Fisher, "A Meeting of Blood and Oil: The Balkan Factor in Western Energy Security," *Journal of Southern Europe and the Balkans* 4, no.1 (May 2002).

24. See, among others, Nina Brenjo, *War in the Name of the Kosovars? NATO's Decision to Bomb Yugoslavia*, master's thesis, London Metropolitan University, London, 2004.

25. Peter Gowan, "The Euro-Atlantic Origins of NATO's Attack on Yugoslavia," in *Masters of the Universe: NATO's Balkan Crusade*, ed. Tariq Ali, 8 (London: Verso, 2000).

26. Henry Kissinger, "NATO: Make It Stronger, Make It Larger," *Washington Post*, January 14, 1997, A15.

27. See Wesley K. Clark, *Waging Modern Wars* (New York: PublicAffairs, 2001), 421–34 passim.

28. Gabriel Kolko, "Iraq, the United States, and the End of the European Coalition," *The Spokesman* no. 79 (2003): 12.

29. This issue is explored satisfactorily by Julian Lindley-French in his Chaillot Paper *Terms of Engagement* (no. 52, May 2002), produced by the Paris-based Institute for Security Studies.

30. Gabriel Kolko, *Another Century of War?* (New York: New Press, 2002), 81.

CHAPTER 7

The Greater Middle East Initiative

Broadly speaking, the "greater Middle East" project has been presented as an extension of trade benefits to a wider Middle Eastern area, programs of technology and know-how transfer, WTO involvement, financial incentives and assistance to small businesses and individuals (particularly women), legal aid, encouragement of an independent media initiative, and educational exchange programs. It is believed that this sort of activity will lead to the modernization and democratization of the greater Middle East—which includes such areas as Turkey, Afghanistan, and northeast Africa, but not Iran and Syria—and the eradication of terrorism from the region. The U.S. administration has also earmarked some $500 million to support the project.[1]

When *al-Hayat*, a London-based Arabic newspaper, leaked the first working paper on the U.S. project in February 2004, few European and Arab politicians praised the document. First the French turned a cold shoulder. Then Egypt's president, Hosni Mubarak, denounced it as "delusional," whereas Chris Patten, the EU's foreign affairs commissioner, put it as follows: "We would not want to give the impression we are parachuting our ideas into the region."[2]

This is precisely the kind of reaction the Bush administration wanted to register in the run-up to the G-8 and NATO summits of June 2004. Apart from the fact that the initiative as such was aiming at boosting Bush's electoral tactics, the document that was leaked served to prepare the administration ahead of the summits and endeavor to present a new way to meet French and moderate Arab demands. Now, the Greater Middle East Plan is called the Greater Middle East Initiative (henceforth GMEI), to explain that the eradication of terrorism and the democratic transformation of the region cannot come through political processes imposed from outside.[3]

CONSUMING SECURITY

Before and during any of America's wars, its policymakers have always been at pains as to what to do when it is all over. The reconstruction phase has long proved to be the most difficult part of the use of U.S. power, particularly in its Middle Eastern (e.g., Iran, Iraq), Far Eastern (e.g., Korea, Vietnam), Balkan (e.g., Bosnia, Kosovo), and central Asian (e.g., Afghanistan) adventures. Economic reconstruction is not viewed as a conflict-prevention social strategy, but merely as a postconflict neoliberal strategy of profit maximization. Thus, it is no accident that the first policy measure taken by the Bremer authorities in Baghdad after the fall of Saddam was the privatization of the Iraqi oil industry, the optimum guarantee that petrodollars will keep pumping in and out. This was followed by a number of other privatizations, including that of the health service—an instance of supreme liberal anarchism and a solid indication as to how, in socioeconomic terms, the United States conceives the "democratization" of the greater Middle East.

Moreover, given the situation on the ground in Kabul, Baghdad, and elsewhere, and despite its overwhelming military superiority in the sea, the air, and space, the United States is unable to control radical population movements on the ground, and it is also reluctant to take large numbers of casualties.[4] How could a regular army, be it Israeli or American, stop suicide bombers? In general, no security forces can ever stop somebody from killing others if he or she is determined to kill himself or herself. An American columnist put it as follows: "America's war aims may be compromised by America's reluctance to take casualties."[5]

This said, America's post–Cold War wars are not over. Tensions persist all over the northern Balkans, Eastern Europe, the Caucasus, Cyprus, central Asia, and the Middle East. America is "fixing," rather than "solving," conflicts. In fact, the real battle for Baghdad began seriously only after its fall. Does the United States prefer war and not peace? Does the United States prefer to consume, rather than produce, global and regional security?

We have insisted that, in order to answer these questions, we need to link the U.S. domestic economic crisis with the position of the dollar in global currency markets. Donald Rumsfeld and other hawks in the Pentagon and the White House have often portrayed the postconflict issue of economic reconstruction and reconciliation in the Balkans and the greater Middle East along the lines of the German and Japanese cases after their surrender at the end of World War II. This historical parallel makes no sense. Peter Gowan put it as follows:

> In short, world politics is genuinely at a turning point. Condoleeza Rice says she thinks it is 1947. In terms of US military power she may be right. But where is the credit power, where is the dynamic industrial engine? When you have those things, the military sword can indeed enable you to expand your influence across the globe. But when your military apparatus is harnessed to an enormous foreign debt, a tottering Dollar, a gigantic trade deficit, a ballooning budget deficit, a mountain of consumer debt and corporate bulimia, George W. does not seem all that much like Harry Truman.[6]

In fact, 60 percent of the world's manufacturing production in 1950 came from the United States, but only 25 percent in 1999. Some 21 percent of the world's stock of direct investments in other countries were American in 2001, compared with 47 percent in 1960. During the 1990s, the share of U.S. multinationals in the foreign sales of the world's one hundred multinationals decreased from 30 to 25 percent, but the share of EU-based companies increased from 41 to 46 percent. No U.S. companies dominated major industries in 2002 and the U.S. share of exports of commercial services, the fastest-growing part of the world economy, stood at 24 percent in 2001, while the EU had 23 percent—40 percent if intra-EU exports were counted.[7]

This explains a number of things. It explains why the United States does not do peacekeeping but only "peace enforcement" via swift and narrow engagements (in fact, most peacekeepers around the globe come from European countries and Canada) with a cost as low as possible, albeit highly profitable for the U.S. business-military complex. It also partly explains why U.S. "allies must share the financial burden of NATO alliance missions and other administrative and arms procurement duties."[8]

It explains why the Europeans are asked to provide "after-sales services" in reconstruction and donor initiatives, in the wake of U.S. smart bombing campaigns. This all explains why "American lives are so expensive," mainly because U.S. professional military and other contracted agencies pay large amounts of money for wages and other services to keep their soldiers on dangerous battlegrounds. Last but not least, it explains why the United States does not want peace: A declining economy and currency can only survive by expanding the only strong card it possesses—overwhelming military superiority. Obviously, such an analysis goes beyond a mere acknowledgment of the fact that the United States is reluctant to take casualties because of the resulting furor among the American people, which is also true.

DEMOCRATIZATION VIA MILITARIZATION

GMEI is not new at all. Soon after the Persian Gulf War of January–February 1991, then President Bush had capitalized on America's new strategic positioning in the region to initiate both the Arab-Israeli peace process—culminating in the Oslo Accords of 1993 and 1995 under Clinton—and neoliberal economic reforms in the Middle East. But one can even go back to the years preceding the fall of the Berlin Wall, when, in the late 1970s, the Carter-Brzezinski administration made the promotion of human rights and democracy its main policy drive to deal with Communist and Persian Gulf states. However, U.S.-inspired programs for the transformation of the greater Middle East became available for public consumption only after the collapse of the Soviet Union. The most recent strategy draws heavily from schemes already in place, such as the UN Arab Human Development Reports of 2002 and 2003 and the Middle East Partnership Initiative (MEPI) put forward under the Clinton administration. Significantly though, MEPI and now GMEI "were formulated in Washington with little or no consultation from the region."[9] But most important of all, the current GMEI was first formulated publicly by George W. Bush during a speech at the neoconservative American Enterprise Institute on February 26, 2003. The transformation of the greater Middle East, Bush boasted, would have to pass through Baghdad, because "a new regime in Iraq would serve as a dramatic and inspiring example of freedom for other nations in the region."[10] In other words, U.S. claims to originality and claims that its ideas are not imposed from outside do not stand up. Moreover, the means of achieving the democratic transformation of the region were other than peaceful. Fifty days after Bush's speech, U.S. and UK troops were marching toward Basra and Baghdad. The wish—the democratization/transformation of the region—remains unfulfilled. The real outcome is increasing militarization and prolongation of insecurity among the deprived populace of Mesopotamia and the wider region. But there is more to the affair than meets the eye.

Whatever explanation one puts forward concerning the current situation in the former Ottoman space, it must take into account the importance of Israel in the calculations of Washington. Brzezinski, in one of his latest statements, concedes the key position of Israel in U.S. foreign policy considerations.[11] Although, quite rightly, he is careful not to present America's global interests as identical to those of Israel, he falls short of explaining what lies behind the strong U.S.-Israeli strategic partnership. There is no doubt that America's global war on terror is coordinated with the security needs of Israel. Never before in the history of U.S.-Israel relations have the two states been so close in terms of intelligence sharing, economic and defense ties, and foreign policy orientations.[12] As noted in chapter 4, the impression given is that America's actions in the wider Middle East are meant to turn the whole region and the world into a burning landscape resembling Palestine, that is, deeply asymmetrical low-intensity warfare, with suicide bombers, constant refugee crises, population displacements, and unresolved territorial disputes.

The United States and its "special ally," Israel, agree that an important step in the fight against terrorism will be made if democratization and free-market policies prevail in the region. These policies are bound up with educational programs, particularly for Muslim women, not so much because the allies care about Muslim "sexual repression," but because it is believed that Muslim women's secular education and integration into the labor market would lead to a fall in birth rates. As things stand at present, with the current high birth rates of the Palestinians unaltered, the Israelis would constitute an ethnic minority in the whole area of historic Palestine in less than thirty years.[13] Yet the strategic intent of both Israel and the United States is concentrated on the extent to which anti-U.S./anti-Israeli Middle

Eastern actors—what the United States calls rogue states—have the capacity and the means to make sovereign decisions. Moreover, no state ownership of oil, gas, and other hydrocarbon resources by anti-American and anti-Israeli Arab elites should be allowed, and the EU should remain dependent on the United States as far as energy and monetary arrangements around energy are concerned. With regard to the Palestinian question, the answers we get from Washington's neocons and Tel Aviv are almost identical. It is not a matter of giving first a form of state to the Palestinians and then considering going ahead with the democratization/transformation of the region. Quite the opposite is the truth. Priority should be given to the democratization/transformation of the Middle East by whatever means. A passionate neocon advocate of this strategy put it as follows:

> It is worth remembering that Saddam Hussein's invasion of Kuwait in 1990 came on the heels of the first Palestinian intifada, which also provoked much Arab hostility toward the United States. It was Saddam's defeat that cleared a space for the Madrid Conference and eventually the Oslo peace process. Then as now, defeating Saddam would offer the United States a golden opportunity to show the Arab and Muslim worlds that Arab aspirations are best achieved by working in co-operation with Washington. If an American road to a calmer situation in Palestine does in fact exist, it runs through Baghdad. . . . [But] those who say that [the Arab-Israeli conflict] should be tackled before or instead of Iraq and Al-Qaeda have their strategic priorities backward.[14]

This type of systematization of the Arab-Israeli conflict was almost entirely endorsed by the extreme hard-line regime of Sharon in Israel. At the Conference of Presidents of Major American Jewish Organizations in February 2003, Shaul Mofaz, the Israeli defense minister, said that "after Iraq, the US should generate political, economic and diplomatic pressure on Iran." He added that "Israel regards Iran and Syria as greater threats and it is hoping that once Saddam is dispensed with, the dominoes will start to tumble."[15] It seems that for Israel, as for the United States, Iraq was already a spent case even before it was invaded—which must mean something, at least as far as the search for weapons of mass destruction in Iraq is concerned. Rather, the real point at issue for Israel, as for the United States, was whom to deal with next, and how to make the diplomatic or military case for it successfully.

NATO'S TIME

The Arabs and the Europeans were skeptical about the GMEI from the very beginning. In public, the parties reacted not because of the amount of money promised ($500 million) but the clientelistic way of administering the funds allocated—basically via nongovernmental organizations whose elites had strong contacts in Washington—and the new expanded role for NATO missions in the region and Iraq requested by the United States.[16] In private, however, both Arabs and Europeans reacted because the recent GMEI was considered an insult to their intelligence. It came in the wake of preemptive strikes in the region, whose overt aim was democratization and regime change to prevent Saddam from using his weapons of mass destruction against America and the West. This sort of war, reminiscent of Israel's preemptive action against Syria and Egypt in 1967 (the Six-Day War), was not the right precedent after which an initiative of this kind could flourish in the Middle East. How could the United States ask the French, the Germans, and the Arabs for diplomatic and economic support after the end of a war that they had just opposed? And how could the United States and UK do so at a time when all available evidence showed that their invasion and occupation of Iraq had instigated such fierce resistance that the occupation forces and their puppet government could not handle it? The Arabs in particular saw the whole matter as a deflection from the real center of gravity in the region, that is, the Palestinian issue.[17] Here we focus only on the issue of NATO.

We would like to argue that the real GMEI project of the United States began, at least, with the Persian Gulf War in 1991, that is, in the wake of the collapse of the Soviet Union. Then the United States, on the basis of a new "deter forward" concept elaborated during the Clinton years, used NATO to enhance U.S. power out of its area in two consecutive enlargements in the 1990s and early 2000s. In March 1999, the Czech Republic, Hungary, and Poland became members of NATO as a result of a decision by the North Atlantic Council in July 1997. Four years later (March 2004) seven new countries joined the alliance: Estonia, Latvia, Lithuania, Romania, Bulgaria, Slovakia, and Slovenia. This was the fifth, and the biggest, round of enlargement in NATO's history. Amid these changes, the GMEI was to have been tested in the Balkans through America's drive in Bosnia (1993–95) and NATO's bombing of Yugoslavia

(1999). In other words, the real GMEI embraces roughly the former Ottoman and Soviet spaces in their entirety: from the eastern flanks of Germany and Austria to the marshes of the Nile, the Euphrates, and barren central Asian territories and Saudi deserts.

The former Ottoman space (the Balkans, northeast Africa, the Middle East, and central Asia) represents a new great opportunity zone for the United States that opened up after the collapse of the USSR and its withdrawal from east-central Europe, the Caucasus, and central Asia. U.S. security analysts are now working with a new set of borders and geopolitical realities, and their main concern is how to manage these realities—often very complex and rife with intractable ethnic and religious conflict themselves—placing them under U.S. hegemony and security surveillance. The ultimate goal is to enshrine these states and regions in the hub-and-spoke system. In this context, NATO's strategic potential to facilitate the process of transition of the new republics from independent statehood to subordination to the United States figures prominently.[18]

With the recent incorporation into the alliance of some key Balkan and Baltic states, NATO's eastward European enlargement has reached its limits: there is nowhere further to go for the next five to ten years, because of Russia's strong objections, the pro-Russian posture of Belarus, and the still somewhat ambivalent domestic situation in Ukraine. Yet if, for the time being, there is not enough breathing room in Eastern Europe, there is plenty of it in the Caucasus and Caspian Sea region, in Afghanistan—where NATO took on its first out-of-area mission in August 2003—and Iraq.[19] In other words, there is room for NATO to expand, at least de facto, in the greater Middle East. This all was captured perfectly by Nicholas Burns, a former U.S. ambassador to Greece who is now on the policy team of Condoleezza Rice in the State Department. When he was U.S. permanent representative to NATO, addressing a conference on NATO and the greater Middle East in October 2003, Burns said, "NATO's mandate is still to defend Europe and North America. But we don't believe we can do that by sitting in Western Europe, or Central Europe, or North America. We have to deploy our conceptual attention and our military forces East and South. NATO's future, we believe, is East, and South. It's in the Greater Middle East."[20]

There is nothing to hide here. Bush's GMEI initiative aims at bringing NATO deeper into the Islamic world of former Ottoman and Soviet territories, thus dragging the Europeans into a dangerous voyage with no return ticket available. This is as bad for Europeans as it is for the Americans and the rest of the world.

We have seen that NATO scored no real success in Yugoslavia. What looks good on paper is not always so in practice. NATO's mission in Afghanistan has also been an utter failure, and the United States blames the Europeans for that.[21] In fact, America has never managed to translate military victories into political ones after the official end of hostilities. The most recent cases of Bosnia, Kosovo, Macedonia, Afghanistan, and Iraq speak for themselves. In other words, the more NATO power diffuses and spreads itself around the globe, the more the centrality of the United States weakens in it, and the more the negative repercussions of the split between U.S. military, economic, ideological, and political ends are felt. A NATO presence in Baghdad and other Arab capitals to police a neoliberal economic package and Western oil interests—the Bush-GMEI proposal that France has repeatedly turned down—may well turn out to be the worst American nightmare of all.

We may not be so far from this possibility. In October 2004, General James Jones, NATO's commander and the head of U.S. forces in Europe, argued that NATO is readying three thousand NATO troops to go to Iraq to train the new Iraqi army.[22] Interestingly, France had insisted that only two hundred trainers be sent with a "clear mandate and timetable that would not extend the alliance's role beyond training."[23] Clearly, however, the United States has had no intention of keeping a NATO mission in Iraq on a temporary training ticket, this despite the inability of U.S. forces in Iraq to control the insurgents.

A BITTER TURKISH COFFEE

Strictly speaking, the greater Middle East initiative of the United States does not exist. Or, rather, it existed as a rhetorical and public relations exercise designed to help Bush's performance in the run up to the presidential election of autumn 2004 and to diplomatically rebalance European and Russian objections and fears over the U.S. projection of power in the region. It is a soft—to use Joseph Nye's terminology—and rather cheap ideational instrument to achieve hard aims, such as the democratic/free-market refashioning of the wider Middle East and the consolidation of American military and security forces in the region. But just as this objective was to be undermined in the wake of the fall of Baghdad following U.S. and UK preemptive military action, so it is bound to happen under the United States's recent soft exercise of power.

Somehow, the United States had to compromise, at least provisionally: Afghanistan remains a failed state, the Iraqi resistance brought about huge difficulties, and the Cyprus issue remains unresolved. Turkey, whatever its rationale and unlike the UK, has also proved to be a tough nut to crack, by denying U.S. forces the use of its territory to open a northern front in Iraq. Moreover, as the Israeli experience has clearly shown, forms of violence emanating from the region cannot be handled by the U.S. use of preemptive strikes and regime change, just as Sharon's methods cannot stop Palestinian resistance. Projection of overwhelming power over poor and deprived populations brings results other than those desired by the perpetrators. But it should also be noted that population movements on the ground cannot be easily manipulated or defeated by soft neoliberal economic programs and money delivery through corrupt nongovernmental organizations—the declared case of GMEI—or by straightforward blackmailing and diplomatic pressure—the case of Cyprus with the unsuccessful attempt to impose a UN-inspired plan upon both communities. Thus, the latest version of the GMEI is but a compromising project that stands out and makes sense only in terms of an aggressive strategy that has been developed under the aegis of U.S. policymakers in the wake of the collapse of "really existing socialism." In this context, the real GMEI was begun and tested on the ground with the Persian Gulf War and the crisis in the western Balkans. From this perspective, the U.S. project in the former Ottoman and Soviet spaces, at a basic level, aims at expanding the Cold War Achesonian hub-and-spoke system of alliances and dependencies, thus consolidating a set of economic, political, and security arrangements similar to those established in east-central Europe and the Balkans. But this strategy has been failing dismally after the Cold War, particularly after 9/11. It is this strategy that has cost so many lives in New York, Istanbul, Madrid, Kabul, Basra, Baghdad, London, and elsewhere. It is a strategy that some of us continue to call neo-imperialism, despite the fact that there is not yet any serious effort to put up organized political resistance to this international phenomenon. But there are other forms of resistance, such as the antiglobalization movements and antiwar campaigns, as well as other, very violent reactions to U.S. power politics that we disapprove, and against which the United States and its allies have launched their recent "war on terror." This is a very peculiar type of war—it is a bitter war that nobody can win, a bitter Turkish coffee.

We would like to finish this chapter with Robert Fisk, veteran British journalist of Middle Eastern affairs, writing in Beirut (where he lived for almost thirty years) on the second anniversary of the U.S. invasion of Iraq in 2003:

> I was here on the very last day of the civil war, following the Syrian tanks under shellfire up to Baabda. In conflict, you never believe a war will end. Yet it finished, amid corpses and one last massacre—but it ended, and I was free of fear for the first time in 14 years.
>
> And then I watched it all reborn. The muck along the Corniche below my balcony was cleared and flower beds and new palm trees planted. The Dresden-like ruins were slowly torn down or restored and I could dine out in safety along the old front line in fine Italian restaurants, take coffee by the Roman ruins, buy Belgian chocolates, French shirts, English books. Slowly, my own life, I now realise, was being rebuilt. Not only did I love life—I could expect to enjoy it for years to come.
>
> Until, of course, that Valentine's Day morning on the Corniche just down from my home when the crack of a fearful explosion sent fingers of dark brown smoke sprouting into the sky only a few hundred metres from me. And that was the moment, I think, when the beautiful dream ended, as it did for tens of thousands of Lebanese. And I no longer feel 29.[24]

NOTES

1. See Arab Gateway, "Greater Middle East Partnership: The Al Hayat Text of 13 February 2004," http://www.al-bab.com/arab/docs/international.

2. Among others, "A Creaking Partnership," *The Economist*, June 5, 2004, 23.

3. Apart from being a concession to the Europeans and certain moderate Arab elites, the GMEI also addressed concerns of the anti-Bush/Rumsfeld "democratic" establishment of the United States. See, for example, Zbigniew Brzezinski, *The Choice* (New York: Basic Books, 1997), 225–26.

4. For perceptive speculation on these issues, see Peter Gowan, "The New American Century?," *The Spokesman* 76 (2002): 5–23, and "US : UN," *New Left Review* 24 (November–December 2003): 73–99.

5. Richard Cohen, "Even a Low Risk War Brings Its Own Cost," *International Herald Tribune*, January 9, 2002, 7.

6. Gowan, "The New American Century?," 21.

7. We have drawn this information mainly from Richard B. Du Boff, "US Hegemony: Continuing Decline, Enduring Danger," *Monthly Review* 55, no. 7 (December 2003): 1–2.

8. See, among others, Julian Lindley-French, *Terms of Engagement*, Chaillot Paper 52 (Paris: Institute of Strategic Studies, 2002), 50ff.

9. Farid Senzai, "Bush's Shaky Plans for Change in the Middle East," *The Civility Review* 1 (June 11, 2004): 3.

10. "Birth of a Bush Doctrine?," *The Economist*, March 1, 2003, 44–45.

11. See Brzezinski, *The Choice*, 41ff.

12. For a useful description of U.S.-Israeli relations since 1945, see Samuel W. Lewis, "The United States and Israel: Evolution of an Unwritten Alliance," *Middle East Journal* 3 (summer 1999): 364–78. See also Derek Gregory, *The Colonial Present* (Oxford, UK: Blackwell, 2004). Interestingly, "Israel, with a per capita GDP of over $12,000 receives from the US over $3 billion in bi-lateral assistance each year, while the whole of sub-Saharan Africa, with a per capita GDP of under $500 receives a total of about $165 million," in Fraser Cameron, *US Foreign Policy after the Cold War* (London: Routledge, 2002), 52.

13. One can read the Israeli building of the Wall in the West Bank, not only in terms of a further land grab (the Palestinian argument) or to protect Israeli citizens from Palestinian suicide bombers (the Israeli argument), but also in terms of avoiding unwanted developments in the future. If the Palestinians cease to demand a two-state solution, opting instead for fully fledged political and civil rights as citizens of Israel, the Israelis would have to make a serious effort to convince the world how an ethnic minority (the Jews) can rule over an ethnic majority (the Palestinians). This development is something that the Wall may stop from happening.

14. Michael Scott Doran, "Palestine, Iraq and American strategy," *Foreign Affairs* 1 (January–February 2003): 22, 32.

15. Shaul Mofaz as quoted in James Bennet, "Israel Lays Hopes on US Arms," *International Herald Tribune*, February 25, 2003, 1, 5.

16. As Farid Senzai argued, "The enormous level of outside funding has resulted in elitist groups within the NGO community. Rather than facilitating horizontal networks among groups as is the case with domestically funded groups, the external funding has intensified the division between the 'haves' and the 'have nots,' and centralises resources in the hands of the few that have connections with the West," in "Bush's Shaky Plans," 3.

17. In March 2004, a Jordanian official put it as follows: "This whole initiative of democratic and economic development in the Greater Middle East seems like a way out of dealing with the heart of the matter: unless the US helps resolve the Israeli-Palestinian issue, whatever else it does in the region will backfire and will be perceived as insincere," quoted in Zeyno Baran, "Getting the Greater Middle

East initiative right," *In the National Interest*, March 3, 2004, http://www
.inthenationalinterest.com.

18. For further analysis along the same lines, see Vassilis K. Fouskas, *Zones of Conflict: US Foreign Policy in the Balkans and the Greater Middle East* (London: Pluto Press, 2003), chapters 2 and 3.

19. To all intents and purposes, NATO's first out-of-area command operation is rather a failure. NATO has been running ISAF (International Security Assistance Force) in Afghanistan since August 2003 and security has dramatically worsened throughout the country since then, except perhaps in Kabul where the 6,500 NATO peacekeepers are based.

20. Nicholas Burns, "NATO's Future, We Believe, Is East, and Is South," *The Acronym Institute for Disarmament and Diplomacy*, http://www.acronym.org.uk.

21. Moreover, as an American author from the Carnegie Endowment for International Peace has argued, a collapse of NATO's mission in Afghanistan will damage the EU first and foremost, as it would undermine the EU's credibility in constituting coherent security and defense structures. See Michael Beckley, "NATO's Afghan Failure Will Hurt Europe," *Financial Times*, September 30, 2004, 21.

22. See Judy Dempsey, "NATO Role in Training Iraqi Army Takes Shape," *International Herald Tribune*, October 4, 2004, 1, 4.

23. Ibid., 1.

24. Robert Fisk, "Memories of War, Fear and Friendship in My Home City, Where Time Has Stood Still," *The Independent*, March 19, 2005.

CHAPTER 8

Iraq's Shiites Move to Fill a Power Vacuum

Beyond the Euphrates began for us the land of mirage and danger, the sands where one helplessly sank, and the roads which ended in nothing. The slightest reversal would have resulted in a jolt to our prestige giving rise to all kinds of catastrophe; the problem was not only to conquer but to conquer again and again, perpetually; our forces would be drained of attempt.

Emperor Hadrian, AD 117–38

The recent war in Iraq has produced an unintended consequence—a fearsome Shiite Muslim geopolitical bloc that will dominate political life in the Middle East for many years. As the Baath Party collapsed in wake of the U.S.-led invasion of Iraq, Shiite religious groups and militias stepped into the vacuum, especially in the sacred shrine cities.[1] The speed with which they accomplished this came as a huge surprise to the U.S. leadership, which had assumed that the coalition forces would take that role.[2] What they seemed unprepared to comprehend is that although Iraq is an overwhelmingly Muslim country, it is both religiously and ethnically diverse. The 95 percent of the population that is Muslim is divided unequally between Shiites, who claim 62 percent, and Sunnis, who represent 33 percent of the total. Further, the Sunnis are divided among Arab, Kurdish, and Turkman ethnic groups. Members of other religions make up 5 percent of the population. The very small Christian population, which represents probably no more than 3 percent of the total, is similarly subdivided among Chaldeans, Assyrians, and others. Ethnically the country is 79 percent Arab, 16 percent Kurdish, 3 percent Persian, and 2 percent Turkman.[3]

For centuries before the creation of modern-day Iraq, the Shia and Sunni branches of Islam engaged in a violent competition over the successor to the Prophet Mohammed. Prior to World War I, Shiites lived under Sunni Ottoman rule and bore the burden of the empire's conflicts with Shiite Persian empires. When the British conquered Iraq in 1917, they ruled it as a colony on the model of India. But in 1920, the Shiites joined with Ottoman officials and landlords and a small group of Sunni religious leaders to organize a rebellion against British rule. In response, the British reformed the political organization of Iraq and granted limited local administration. However, the British arrangements vested the majority of power in the Sunni minority. When the Baath Party overthrew the Iraqi monarchy in 1958, they consolidated political control as a chauvinistic and despotic dictatorship where Sunnis ruled and Shiites were ruled with ruthless brutality.[4]

THE CIA AND SADDAM HUSSEIN

The Baath movement was founded by two Syrians in the early 1940s, with an ideology that combined elements of Arab nationalism, anti-imperialism, and socialism. They were fiercely anti-Communist and actively suppressed the Iraqi Communist Party, which at that time was the largest in the Arab world. In 1957, at the age of twenty, Saddam Hussein joined the Baath Party but, as evidence suggests, quickly became an agent of the U.S. Central Intelligence Agency. A military coup in 1958 brought to power Abd al Karim Qassim, and Hussein participated in the 1959 attempt to assassinate him. In the attempt, Qassim was wounded and his driver killed, as was one of the assassins. But Hussein, who was shot in the leg, managed to escape.[5] Writing in the *Star Tribune*, Eric Black concluded, "The Iraqi Baathists and the CIA had a common interest in getting rid of pro-Soviet Qassim, and several authors believe that Saddam was helping the CIA and the Baathists coordinate a coup."[6]

After the failed assassination, Hussein fled Iraq and spent the next four years in Lebanon, Egypt, and Syria, which together represent the only time that he lived outside Iraq prior to his arrest and incarceration by the

United States in Cuba. During this brief exile, the CIA paid for his apartment and put him through a brief training course while he was in Beirut and, according to Richard Sale, the CIA then helped him get to Cairo, where he attended law school and is believed to have made frequent visits to the U.S. embassy there.[7] The Baathists finally overthrew the Qassim government and killed Qassim in 1963, thus paving the way for Hussein's return to Iraq.

Accounts of this regime change demonstrated the important material support that was provided by the CIA: CIA agents monitored the coup through connections with the conspiring army officers, operated an electronic command center in Kuwait to guide the anti-Qassim forces, and supplied the conspirators with lists of people to be killed. As a former senior CIA official observed, "It was a bit like the mysterious killings of Iran's communists just after Ayatollah Khomeini came to power in 1979. All 4,000 of his communists suddenly got killed." Saddam's biographer, Said K. Aburish, the author of *Saddam Hussein: The Politics of Revenge*, confirms this saying, "The relationship between the Americans and the Baath Party at that moment in time was very close indeed." This conclusion is similar to one by Miles Copeland, a veteran CIA operative, who reported in the United Press that the CIA had enjoyed "close ties" with Qassim's ruling Baath Party, just as it had close connections with the intelligence service of Egyptian leader Gamal Abdel Nasser. A recent public statement by Roger Morris, who served on the U.S. National Security Council during the Johnson and Nixon administrations, confirmed this claim, saying that the CIA had chosen the authoritarian and anti-Communist Baath Party "as its instrument."[8]

The successful coup proved to be a bonanza for the politically ambitious young Hussein. When he returned to Iraq, he was immediately assigned to head the Al-Jihaz al-Khas, the clandestine Baathist intelligence organization, where he first earned his reputation for brutality as an interrogator of Communists, many of whom had been identified by the CIA. Credible evidence says that he was involved in the killing of some 4,000 to 5,000 Communists. But Hussein's first taste of power was short-lived. The Baath Party was toppled and Hussein jailed within months of his return. In 1966, Hussein escaped his imprisonment and went underground to help plot the Baath Party's return to power.[9] Splits in the Baath Party gave Hussein an opening, and he quickly rose to become the party's second in command, just behind Ahmed Hassan al-Bakr, a relative and sponsor. When the Baathists again seized power in 1968, Hussein became vice president and head of security services in the new regime, but soon emerged as the real power in the Baathist government. Some writers claim that the CIA played a role in the 1968 coup as well.[10]

According to David Morgan, Saddam Hussein was first recruited by the CIA in 1958 and groomed for power thereafter: "There's no question—it was there in Cairo that [Saddam] and others were first contacted by the Agency."[11] Roger Morris, a former State Department foreign officer, who was on the NSC staff during the Johnson and Nixon administrations, also acknowledges that the CIA was involved in both the 1963 and 1968 coups in Iraq.[12] He notes that in 1968 the CIA encouraged the palace revolt among Baath Party elements led by Ahmed Hassan al-Bakr, and also encouraged him to turn over the reins of power to Hussein in 1979. He observes, "It's a regime that was unquestionably mid-wived by the United States, and the [CIA's] involvement there was really primary." Thus, U.S. intelligence operatives used Hussein as a policy instrument for more than forty years.[13]

The Iraqi Baath regime that came to power in 1968 was based on the army and on the support of bureaucrats and technocrats. But it never represented more than a narrow segment of the Iraqi population. Even in Tikrit, Hussein's hometown, the regime enjoyed the support of only a small number of families, and army support was reflected only in those officers who had graduated from the elite Baghdad Military Academy. The popular core of Baathist support was similarly essentially limited to the Sunni Muslim population of northwestern Iraq, with little or no support to be found among the majority Shia and substantial Kurdish populations.

Notwithstanding this limited political base, the regime found sufficient power within the army and through the revenues from oil to rule with little incentive for change or compromise. Only occasionally did they find it necessary to resort to coalition politics, and this was limited to coopting support from leaders in the Christian community. In the 1960s, Shia ulema formed the Dawa al-Islamiya, or Islamic Cause, to work for an Islamic state and social justice. The more militant Mujahidin, or Muslim Warriors, was founded in 1979.[14] However, until the collapse of Baathism in 2003, the regime was able to reduce this opposition to sporadic episodes of terrorism.[15] When the Shiites have rebelled as a group, as they did in southern Iraq in 1991 following the Gulf War, the regime used brute force, and at other times murdered many Shiite clerics and leaders to forestall rebellions. At each step, Shia resentment and hostility grew and intensified.[16] As a consequence, the Iraqi Shia have come to see themselves as a persecuted and repressed majority.

AFTER SADDAM'S FALL

With the collapse of Hussein's Baath regime in 2003, Iraq's Shiite majority recognized an opportunity to gain dominant power in Iraq for the first time in the modern history of the country. As the second most powerful force in Iraq behind the United States, the Shiites of Iraq are openly resisting foreign intervention and expressing a distrust of the occupation by U.S. and British military forces. This follows a long tradition of a politically active Islamic community. It was Shiite Islam in the eleventh and twelfth centuries that organized and directed a cult of assassins (from which the name derives) whose mission it was to terrify Christians and dissident Muslims during the Crusades. It is said that members of this suicide- assassination cult could find—and kill—anybody in the known world that their leader targeted.

Today, Iraq's 15 million Shiites are extremely protective of the Shiite holy cities in their territory, including Karbala and Najaf, which have been regarded as religious shrines for the last fourteen centuries as the resting place of their two most sacred imams, Ali and Hussein. What we are witnessing in Iraq is a historic reawakening of Iraq's Shia community. The importance of this reawakening is hard to overstate, because it has significant consequences for the whole of the Middle East. Iran, Iraq, and Bahrain have Shiite majorities, and while they are minorities in Lebanon and Syria, they are the politically dominant power groups. The eastern province of Saudi Arabia also has a Shiite majority that is undoubtedly the politically most active group in the kingdom, and there are significant Shiite populations in Afghanistan, Pakistan and India.

The reawakening of Shiite Islam has been underway for several decades. It began in Iran and Lebanon in the 1970s but was restrained in Iraq by the extreme secularism of the Baathist Party. By destroying that regime, the recent war in Iraq has opened the door for a Shiite majority to consolidate its control in the region. They have not been restrained in asserting their interests in the new politics of Iraq, and have faithfully followed religious leaders in taking over neighborhoods in cities across the country, setting up armed militias, organizing public services, and establishing long-banned political parties in a bid to make their presence felt.[17] In a country that is already steeped in religion, Shiite religious leaders have a particularly firm grip on rank-and-file believers. It is clear that the Islamist movements will play a major role in the future of Iraq's politics, particularly among the Shiites, and these movements for the most part will be organized and led by the Shiite clergy.

For occupying U.S. and British forces, the new fear is that the Iraqi Shiites will try to follow the example of their bitterly anti-American fellow Shiites in neighboring Iran. While the Shiites universally resent their violent repression by Hussein's Baathist regime, many are also hostile to the United States because of its support for Israel. Leading Shiite factions, supported by Iran, want U.S. forces to leave Iraq as soon as possible, and some but not all of them want an Iranian-style government dominated by Shiite clerics, a goal strongly opposed by the country's Sunni Arab and Kurdish minorities. While some Shiite groups believe that the clergy should not be involved in politics and favor a more secular form of government,[18] Iraqi experts say current power appears to be gathering among three or four main Shiite religious leaders from highly respected religious families that claim to have descended from the Prophet Mohammed. These leaders come from the al-Sadr family, the al-Khoei family, and the al-Hakim family, with the supreme leadership held by the current senior Shiite cleric in Iraq, the Grand Ayatollah Sayyed Ali al-Sistani.[19]

The most active Shiite religious leader since Hussein's regime collapsed has been Muqtada al-Sadr, a young and relatively inexperienced man who comes from a long line of respected religious authorities. He is the young son of Mohammed Sadeq al-Sadr, a Shiite ayatollah, who with two others was murdered by Saddam's regime in 1999. Pro-U.S. observers say Muqtada al-Sadr is among the most worrying of the ascendant Shiite forces in Iraq, but U.S. scholars know little about him—even his age (reports of which range from twenty-two to thirty)—but fear he may support a form of radical Islam. He has already organized his own militia group, the Jammat-i-Sadr-Than, and at least some of his popularity springs from a lingering devotion to his father. From his base at the Hawza, the supreme institution of Shiite learning, al-Sadr has dispatched his close supporters around the country to try to fill the power vacuum left by the Baath Party. Residents of the predominantly Shiite Baghdad slum once known as Saddam City have renamed it Sadr City, and painted new portraits of Muqtada al-Sadr on the stands from which Saddam Hussein's face once beamed.[20]

The Sadr movement appears to be intolerant and authoritarian, and has a class base in the poverty-stricken neighborhoods brutalized by the Baath Party. Eyewitness accounts of the mob killing on April 10 of an American-backed rival ayatollah, Abd al-Majid al-Khoei, who was flown into Najaf from exile in London, point to the significance of the Sadr movement. Following the attack, members of this movement surrounded the houses of Sistani and Ayatollah Said al-Hakim, nephew of Muhammad Baqir al-Hakim, the leader of the Supreme Council for Islamic Revolution in Iraq (SCIRI), demanding that these two leave Najaf immediately. This attempt at radical change in the Shiite clerical leadership of the shrine city was forestalled when 1,500 Shiite tribesmen came in from the countryside to protect Sistani and al-Hakim. Muqtada views expatriate politicians and clerics now returning to Iraq in the same light, heaping abuse on Ahmad Chalabi and the secular-leaning Iraqi National Congress.[21]

The Sadr movement wants an Islamic republic in Iraq, even if not one exactly like the one Ayatollah Khomeini established in Iran.[22] Press reports from the slums of Baghdad suggest that Muqtada is worshipped there and that most of the armed militia now patrolling the neighborhoods of the renamed Sadr City are his followers. One report said that they had repelled an attempt to infiltrate the city by a rival Shiite militia, the Tehran-based Badr Brigade of SCIRI. Like most other Iraqi Shiite clerics, Muqtada wants the Americans out of Iraq as soon as possible. He says, according to one report, "We refuse occupation. If the Americans become occupiers, yes, we have to go to jihad. The Shiite taught the world jihad, and the Iraqi people gave millions of their sons to Saddam Hussein. If they were to defy the Americans, they would not find it hard to give millions more."[23]

In the mosaic of Iraq's ethno-religious politics, it is often difficult for an outsider to distinguish the subtle patterns and determine who is on which side. With Saddam captured, and the U.S. fighting a faceless enemy in Iraq, it was convenient for the occupiers to create a new demon figure. Muqtada al-Sadr fits this role well.

DECEMBER 2004 ELECTIONS

The police chief, a former army colonel who still wears a uniform with eagles on its epaulets, sat in an official's office, flanked by men in dark suits, all awaiting an audience. Behind the desk, the official leaned back. She adjusted the black *abaya* that covered all but her face. Bushra Zamili, the chief of the Najaf elections commission, is a symbol of change in Iraq. The 35-year-old Shiite Muslim, wearing religious dress, was the official to see on election day in Najaf.[24]

Iraq's main Shiite list swept to victory in the country's historic elections, finally translating the majority community's demographic weight into political power after decades under Sunni rule. The United Iraqi Alliance, backed by powerful Shiite cleric Grand Ayatollah Ali al-Sistani, fell short of 50 percent of the vote, but garnered 48.1 percent of the almost 8.5 million cast. Under the formula created for representation, it will hold 140 out of the National Assembly's 275 seats, an absolute majority in parliament. Ali al-Sistani will have to come to an agreement on the presidential council, which requires a two-thirds majority approval from parliament, but will have a free hand to approve the final composition of the Iraqi cabinet.[25] For Iraq's oppressed Shiites, the victory has been a long time coming. Shiite clerics made abundant reference, in the run-up to the January 30 vote, to elections in 1924, when Shiites widely boycotted the polls and ended up excluding themselves from power for the next eight decades.[26]

The role of Islam within the new Iraq was a considerable source of differences when the interim constitution was drawn up under the U.S.-led occupation.[27] But in a surprise statement, Shiite leader Grand Ayatollah Ali al-Sistani and other top clerics called for Islam to be the sole source of legislation in Iraq's new constitution. "All of the ulema (clergy) and marja, and the majority of the Iraqi people, want the national assembly to make Islam the source of legislation in the permanent constitution and to reject any law that is contrary to Islam."[28] Following the defeat of the Iraqi forces in the Persian Gulf War in the spring of 1991, when Shiites in southern Iraq appeared ready to overthrow the Baathist regime with a grassroots revolt, the George H. W. Bush administration chose to step aside and permit Iraqi troops to regroup and crush the rebels with helicopter gunships. The alternative, as the White House saw it then, might have been the collapse of Saddam's Iraq and the rise of a new Islamic state bordering Iran. Now it seems that fourteen years after that attempt, and twenty-six years after Ayatollah Khomeini outmaneuvered Iran's religious and political establishment, Iraqi Shiites are set on a course to repeat that history, only this time through Western-style elections. Whether they succeed in this format or find other means, the increasingly volatile conditions of post-Saddam Iraq present a difficult choice for the U.S. occupation. As a source of conflict rather than stability, the occupation is under tremendous pressure to withdraw. But with emerging Shiite power, the game has taken a new and ominous turn, with the future increasingly dark and murky.[29]

NOTES

1. The Baath Party or Arab Socialist Party was founded in Syria in the early 1940s by militants of the Ihya al Arabi (Arab revival) movement. The Baath Party took as its rallying cry the reunification and liberation of a single Arab nation with an eternal mission to end Western colonization in the Arab world.

2. Jonathan Eric Lewis, "America Encounters the Shiite," May 8, 2003, http://www.shianews.com/hi/articles/politics/0000368.php.

3. *The Christian Science Monitor*, May 14, 2003.

4. David Hirst, "As Shiites Inherit Iraq, the Arab World Trembles," *Daily Star*, January 27, 2005.

5. "How the CIA Found and Groomed Saddam Hussein," Indo-Asian News Service, April 16, 2003, *Friends of Liberty*, http://www.sianews.com/modules.php?name=News&file=article&sid=856.

6. Eric Black, "A History of Iraq, the Cradle of Western Civilization," *Star Tribune*, February 2, 2003, http://www.startribune.com/stories/1762/3626448.html.

7. Richard Sale, "Exclusive: Saddam Key in Early CIA Plot," *United Press International*, October 4, 2003, http://www.upi.com/view.cfm?StoryID=20030410-070214-6557r.

8. Sean Mac Mathuna, "CIA Coups in Iraq in 1963 & 1968 Helped Put Saddam Hussein in Power," http://www.fantompowa.net/Flame/cia_iraq.htm; David Morgan, "Former U.S. Official Says CIA Aided Iraqi Baathists," http://myweb.tiscali.co.uk/rosebud/CIA%20and%20Baathists.htm; ABS-CBN News, September 13, 2003.

9. "US and British Support for Hussein Regime," *Global Policy Forum*, http://www.globalpolicy.org/security/issues/iraq/history/husseinindex.htm.

10. Mac Mathuna, "CIA Coups in Iraq"; Morgan, "Former U.S. Official"; Joseph E. Mulligan, "The War's Economic Motives Are Obvious," http://www.counter-currents.org/iraq-mulligan543.htm.

11. David Morgan, "Ex-U.S. Official Says CIA Aided Baathists: CIA Offers No Comment on Iraq Coup Allegations," Reuters, April 20, 21, 2003.

12. Roger Morris, "A Tyrant 40 Years in the Making," *New York Times*, March 14, 2003.

13. "Early Days and the CIA," Discovery Channel Online, March 14, 2005, http://dsc.discovery.com/convergence/iraqwar/timeline/timeline.html.

14. From this group emerged the Supreme Council for Islamic Revolution in Iraq, SCIRI, a Shia political party that for decades fought the regime of Saddam Hussein.

15. I. M. Lapidus, *A History of Islamic Societies* (Cambridge, UK: Cambridge University Press, 1990), 656–57.

16. PBS, Online NewsHour: Religion and Politics, April 22, 2003, http://www.pbs.org/newshour/bb/middle_east/jan-june03/religion_04-22.html.

17. CBS News, "Shiite Power in Postwar Iraq," April 24, 2003, http://www.cbsnews.com/stories/2003/04/24/iraq/main550852.shtml.

18. "Shiite Leaders Stress Peaceful Resistance, Garner in Baghdad; Preparation for a Five-Year Rule," Iraq-USA, Politics, April 22, 2003, http://www.arabicnews.com/ansub/Daily/Day/030422/2003042240.html.

19. Tony Karon, "Shiites Emerge as Iraq's Key Players," Time Online Edition, April 23, 2003, http://www.time.com/time/world/article/0,8599,446097,00.html.

20. Philly.com, http://www.philly.com/mld/philly/news/columnists/trudy_rubin/5641986.htm.

21. Ed Finn and Avi Zenilman, "A Guide to Iraq's Shiite Clerics," May 15, 2003, http://slate.msn.com/id/2082980/.

22. *New York Times*, April 29, 2003.

23. Juan Cole, "Shiite Religious Parties Fill Vacuum in Southern Iraq," *Middle East Report Online*, April 22, 2003, http://www.merip.org/mero/mero042203.html.

24. Doug Struck, "Iraq's Shiites Plan a Humble Rise to Power," *Washington Post*, February 2, 2005, A1.

25. BBC News, "Shia Hold Lead in Iraqi Election," February 7, 2005, http://news.bbc.co.uk/2/hi/middle_east/4244029.stm.

26. BBC News, "Press Anxiety over Post-Election Iraq," February 14, 2005, http://news.bbc.co.uk/1/hi/world/middle_east/4263669.stm.

27. ShortNews.com, "Iraq Shiites Call for Islam to Be the Source of Law," February 7, 2005, http://www.shortnews.com/shownews.cfm?id=45949.

28. "Iraq Shiite Leaders Demand Islam Be the Source of Law," *Agence France Presse*, February 6, 2005, quoted in http://www.commondreams.org/headlines05/0206-02.htm.

29. "Shiites, Sunnis Forge Peace as Government Prepares Street War against Insurgency," *USA Today*, May 28, 2005, http://www.usatoday.com/news/world/iraq/2005-05-28-iraq_x.htm?POE=NEWISVA; "Fact Sheet: The Shiites of Iraq," Fox News, April 17, 2003, http://www.foxnews.com/story/0,2933,84406,00.html; Robert Kagan, "Shiites and Stereotypes: Iraq Policy's Critics Could Use Some Discernment," WashingtonPost.com, February 18, 2005, http://www.washingtonpost.com/wp-dyn/articles/A33566-2005Feb17.html.

CHAPTER 9

Ukraine: Regime Change, U.S. Style

The conflict over the 2004 Ukrainian elections between Western-supported candidate Viktor Yushchenko and Russian-supported candidate Viktor Yanukovich was presented by the Western media as a simple struggle between the forces of democracy and authoritarianism. The opposition leader, Yushchenko, was characterized as a liberal reformer and his opponent, Yanukovich, was described as the incarnation of Soviet-style authoritarianism. However, behind the simplicity of this presentation a different narrative was unfolding. In reality, the conflict had nothing to do with democracy versus authoritarianism: Yushchenko essentially represented the modern face of a conservative Ukrainian nationalism that has been progressively revived in the western portions of the country since the declaration of Ukrainian independence in 1990, while Yanukovich was little more than a typical post-Soviet petty capitalist oligarch, of which there are dozens of examples in the region that generally, but not always, enjoy the backing of Western powers.

The so-called reformer Viktor Yushchenko was the political face of a social network that is closely tied to the interests of Western military geostrategists, neoliberal technocrats, Polish irredentists, and Ukrainian conservative forces. The alliance of this constellation of forces with powerful conservative interests in successive U.S. administrations during and after the Cold War is well documented. The "marriage" of Yushchenko with these conservatives is literally reflected in his U.S.-born wife, who is of Ukrainian descent and served on the staff of the Reagan

White House. The general conservative agenda of Yushchenko's supporter base also can be seen in the presence of Bibles and crosses at his rallies, in his rhetorical appeals to purify Ukraine of "filth and corruption," in his populist-nationalist-fundamentalist and seriously authoritarian posturing during his swearing in as the president of Ukraine (with one hand on the Bible), in his insistence that he will crush any move toward regional autonomy by national minorities, and in his defense of anti-Semitic publications and accepted backing by neo-Nazi groups.

Rather than a struggle between democracy and authoritarianism, the 2004 Ukrainian election was much more a typical conflict of geopolitical interests, based on the country's importance as a large agricultural and industrial region, plus its crucial position in an important gas transportation network, its proximity to key oil resources in the Caspian basin, and its general geostrategic location as a country bordering Russia. In this sense, it represents a conflict between Ukraine's pro-American west, supported by money and experts from the EU and the United States, and the pro-Russian east, traditionally linked to Russia by economic and cultural bonds both before and during the Soviet eras. With its geographic location north of the Black Sea, Ukraine not only is close to the oil of the Caspian region, but also stands between it and the key oil-importing states of central and northern Europe.

Zbigniew Brzezinski, U.S. national security advisor under President Carter, noted in his 1997 book, *The Grand Chessboard: American Primacy and Its Geostrategic Imperatives*, that neither the West nor Russia can afford to lose Ukraine to its geostrategic and geoeconomic adversaries. According to Brzezinski, Ukraine is one of the most important geopolitical pivots in Eurasia, and control of Ukraine is critical to the interests of the United States and Europe. For the West, Ukraine offers a potentially lucrative market and a critical transportation route for oil and gas, but as Brzezinski points out, "if Moscow regains control over Ukraine, with its 52 million people and major resources as well as access to the Black Sea, Russia automatically again regains the wherewithal to become a powerful imperial state, spanning Europe and Asia."[1]

It should come as no surprise that Putin's Russia wants to pull Ukraine closer to the Russian sphere of influence. Prior to the election, relations with Russia were improving following the ratification of the 1998 bilateral Treaty of Friendship and Cooperation. Under this treaty, Ukraine committed itself to forego any military alliances for the duration of

Russia's twenty-year lease on the naval base in Sevastopol, and the two sides also signed a series of agreements on the final division and disposition of the former Black Sea fleet. In the years immediately preceding the treaty, Russia increased its influence in Ukraine through various political, economic, and military agreements, and through the operations of the giant Russian natural gas monopoly Gazprom, and the Russian electricity and energy complex UES. In September 2003, Ukraine signed an Agreement on a Common Economic Space with Belarus, Kazakhstan, and Russia, which foresaw closer economic relations between the four signatories, eventually leading to the formation of an economic union.[2]

The U.S. administration, on the other hand, sees Ukraine as part of a framework of energy-rich states in the Eurasian corridor, where the United States has aggressively pursued a militarized foreign policy since the end of the Cold War. The United States's aim is to favorably position itself in Ukraine and absorb it into a U.S. dominated sphere of influence. This has already begun through the organization of five Western-oriented former Soviet states into a regional organization, GUUAM (Georgia, Uzbekistan, Ukraine, Azerbaijan, and Moldova), which has been financed in part by Western/NATO military aid and Anglo-American oil interests. As a founding member of GUUAM, Ukraine has become part of the effort to exclude Russia altogether from the oil and gas resources of the Caspian basin.[3]

COLD WAR–STYLE PROXY CONFRONTATION

The conflict around the Ukrainian elections is very much a Cold War–style proxy confrontation between the U.S.-led Western camp and Russian interests. Behind the camps of the presidential candidates one can clearly identify the interests of the rival Ukrainian elites and the competition among the global imperialist powers. As a result of market reforms and privatization in the 1990s, a highly peculiar social and economic system has emerged in the country. At its center are clan-corporate groups, each of which consists of a complex and informally linked network of several privatized enterprises and financial institutions, along with the lobbying structures that represent their interests in the state bureaucracy. Because of the intermingling that has occurred between the top levels of the clans, state officials, and criminal gangs, a kind of oligarchic-bureaucratic system has emerged that controls power in the primarily political main centers of Ukraine.

The last two to three years have seen a slow but consistent economic recovery in some sectors of Ukrainian industry that are directly connected to the Russian economy. Russia's economic growth itself has been tied since 1999 to high world oil prices and increased oil production. Energy, which underpins the Russian economy and domestic stability, is the key aspect of Russian influence in Ukraine, because Russia provides cheap oil and gas and absorbs a substantial part of the industrial production of eastern and southern Ukraine. In turn, most of the growth in Ukrainian industry has taken place in this same region, which is concentrated in heavy metallurgy and other resource-intensive production. Thus, it is no accident that Ukrainian economic growth coincides with powerful transfers of Russian capital into the country.[4]

Outgoing Ukrainian President Leonid Kuchma tried to follow a middle path between the interests of the United States and Russia. Initially, he sought NATO and EU membership for the country, and went so far as to send 1,500 Ukrainian troops to Iraq. In doing so, Kuchma enjoyed full Western support. During the Clinton years, U.S. officials turned a blind eye to the use of state media and police to secure Kuchma's reelection in 1999 when his main challenger was Petro Symonenko, chair of the Ukrainian Communist Party, with an openly anti-IMF and anti-NATO agenda.[5] However, during this same period, Kuchma also sought to improve relations with Russia, claiming a new era in relations between members of the Commonwealth of Independent States after his return from the CIS summit held in Moscow on March 28, 1997.[6] With great power rivalries heating up in 2004, Ukrainian leaders no longer had the luxury of maintaining this delicate balance of power.

There is clear evidence that both Russia and the West interfered in Ukraine's election process in an effort to further their respective interests. It is quite possible, and even probable, that substantial fraud also occurred in the election on both sides. It should have come as no surprise that the corrupt and authoritarian government of outgoing President Kuchma manipulated the outcome of the first election: it was, after all, part of his pattern. However, there also is strong evidence that the United States, with various members of the Bush administration and various American "prodemocracy" front groups, had a crucial hand in destabilizing the regime before and during the elections. The U.S. government funded and organized the activities of U.S. consultancies, pollsters, and diplomats, and both the United States and the EU openly supported and financed Yushchenko and exploited the growing opposition to Kuchma's authoritarian regime to call for a vote for the opposition.

The U.S. manipulation of the Ukrainian election was greatly assisted by its EU partners. German newspapers contributed a propaganda campaign, with *Sueddeutsche Zeitung* declaring, "Putin wants to keep Ukraine under his thumb. . . . Russia does not want to let the country out from under its influence and is not ready to accept the feelings of a majority of the people."[7] The German business daily *Handelsblatt* concurred, saying Ukraine is of vital interest for Putin, not just because it is an important corridor for transporting energy but also because it gives Moscow clout: "The master of the Kremlin invested himself heavily in the Ukrainian elections and will continue to do so in order to keep control over all the lands between the Donau [River] and the Don [River] firmly in the hands of Moscow. This has less to do with economics than with Putin's political goal of rebuilding a Russian empire. Without Kiev," the paper continues, repeating the Brzezinski line, "Moscow becomes a regional power."[8]

All this can be labeled an operation engineering democracy through the ballot box and civil disobedience. It was first used in Europe in Belgrade in 2000, and in Georgia in 2003. Ten months after the success of the campaign in Belgrade, the same technique was used again, this time in Belarus (2001), but there it failed to create the expected results. Otpor (resistance), the group that overthrew Milosevic, received funds from the U.S. government via the National Endowment for Democracy (NED) and the Agency for International Development.[9] The NED was established by the Reagan Administration in 1983 to do overtly what the CIA previously had done covertly—that is, promote Cold War propaganda and operations through Freedom House, which is now chaired by former CIA director James Woolsey and supported by billionaire George Soros's foundations, whose donations always support NED operations.

Once they were finished in Belgrade, Veterans of Otpor traveled to Georgia to help train the Kmara (enough) movement, to Belarus to support the Zubr movement, and finally to Ukraine to bolster the Pora movement. In each case, the so-called democracy movement was carefully branded with a single-phrase slogan such as "He's Finished" or "High Time" and an uncomplicated logo, designed—like the fist used in Serbia or the ticking clock used in Ukraine—so that it could be easily reproduced on posters and stencil-spray-painted in public places.[10] All this was a sophisticated and brilliantly conceived exercise in Western branding and mass marketing.[11] This U.S. technique, labeled the "postmodern coup," is predatory and reckless, and a clear act of imperial arrogance: the same old story of the good—be it "democracy," "human rights," or "self-determination"—against the bad, or in George Bush's lexicon, the "evildoers," that the United States brings to others.

"REVOLUTION IN CIVILIAN AFFAIRS" AND A POSTMODERN JAMES BOND

The emphasis on the use of new communication technologies to rapidly deploy small groups suggests that what we are seeing is a civilian application of what U.S. military leaders call the Revolution in Military Affairs doctrine, which depends on highly mobile small-group deployments enabled by real-time intelligence and communications.

Speaking at the Secretary's Open Forum at the State Department on June 29, 2004, in a speech titled "Between Hard and Soft Power: The Rise of Civilian-Based Struggle and Democratic Change," Dr. Peter Ackerman, a supporter of the Bush administration's "regime change" objectives, elaborated on the issue involved. He proposed that youth movements, such as those used to bring down Serbia, could also be used to bring down the governments in Iran and North Korea, and could have been used to bring down Iraq, thereby accomplishing all of Bush's objectives without having to rely on military means. He further reported that he has been working with Lawrence Livermore Laboratories, a top U.S. weapons designer, to develop new communications technologies that could be used in other youth movement insurgencies. "There is no question that these technologies are democratizing," he stressed in reference to their potential use in bringing down China. "They enable decentralized activity. They create, if you will, a digital concept of the right of assembly." Dr. Ackerman is the founding chairman of the International Center on Nonviolent Conflicts in Washington, DC, of which former U.S. Air Force officer Jack DuVall is president. Together with former CIA director James Woolsey, DuVall also directs the Arlington Institute of Washington, DC, which was created by former chief of naval operations advisor John L. Peterson in 1989 "to help redefine the concept of national security in much larger, comprehensive terms" by introducing "social value shifts into the traditional national defense equation."[12]

The long history of the CIA argues that the creation and deployment of political coups requires agents on the ground. The main manager for CIA coups on the "street side" has been the Albert Einstein Institution, which was formed in 1983 as an offshoot of Harvard University under the leadership of Dr. Gene Sharp. The institution specializes in "nonviolence as a form of warfare." Dr. Sharp had once been the executive secretary for A. J. Muste, the famous U.S. Trotskyite labor organizer and peacenik. George Soros and the NED, with Colonel Robert Helvey, a former U.S. Army officer with thirty years of experience in Southeast Asia, acting as president, now fund the group.

Colonel Helvey's identity provides important clues to the real purpose of the institution. Initially, he was an officer in the Pentagon's Defense Intelligence Agency and served in Vietnam, and during his army career he was the U.S. defense attaché in Yangon, Myanmar, from 1983 to 1985, when Myanmarese students were clandestinely organized to work with Aung San Suu Kyi and in collaboration with Bo Mya's Karen insurgent group. Later, in the mid-1980s in Hong Kong he moved on to train student leaders from Beijing in the finer points of mass demonstration techniques, and it was these tactics that were subsequently used in the now famous Tiananmen Square confrontation of June 1989. Currently, this group is now believed to be working with the Chinese Falun Gong, teaching them similar civil disobedience techniques. Colonel Helvey theoretically resigned from the army in 1989, but his work with the institution and the George Soros's group began before his retirement. Since 1999, he has served as the case officer supervising youth groups in the Balkans and Eastern Europe, where he and his colleagues created Otpor, Kmara, Pora, and other clones that are replicating themselves in virtually every corner of the former Soviet Union, as well as Africa and South America.[13] The work of the institution appears to be aimed at achieving for the United States through civilian means what had been militarily difficult in the 1980s.

Colonel Helvey is not the only foreign agent working covertly to advance Western interests in the Eastern European region. Geert-Hinrich Ahrens, head of the OSCE's vote-monitoring operation in Ukraine, was

German ambassador to Colombia in the late 1990s when German secret agent Werner Mauss was arrested for working closely with the narco-terrorist ELN, whose bombings were financed by the cocaine trade. Ahrens was also nearby in Albania and Macedonia as the narcotics-smuggling Kosovo Liberation Army (KLA) was being formed with U.S. and German patronage. Similarly, Michael Kozak worked closely with the cocaine-smuggling Contras before he became the U.S. ambassador whose 2001 effort to overthrow Belarus's government failed.[14]

In a December 11, 2000, *Washington Post* article titled "U.S. Advice Guided Milosevic Opposion," Michael Dobbs publicly revealed the networks and methods used in Serbia by the United States to manipulate events there, including the role of Colonel Helvey:

> While the NDI [National Democratic Institute] worked closely with Serbian opposition parties, IRI [International Republican Institute] focused its attention on Otpor, which served as the revolution's ideological and organizational backbone. In March, IRI paid for two dozen Otpor leaders to attend a seminar on nonviolent resistance at the Hilton Hotel in Budapest, a few hundreds yards along the Danube from the NDI-favored Marriott. During the seminar, the Serbian students received training in such matters as how to organize a strike, how to communicate with symbols, how to overcome fear and how to undermine the authority of a dictatorial regime. The principal lecturer was retired U.S. Army Col. Robert Helvey, who has made a study of nonviolent resistance methods around the world, including those used in modern-day Burma and the civil rights struggle in the American South.[15]

As Helvey worked among the Otpor activists, he introduced them to the ideas and theories of Gene Sharp, whom he describes as "the Clausewitz of the nonviolence movement," referring to the renowned Prussian military strategist.[16] But, as Dobbs observed in his article, "Regarded by many as Eastern Europe's last great democratic upheaval, Milosevic's overthrow may also go down in history as the first poll-driven, focus group-tested revolution."

Tim Marshall, a reporter for Britain's Sky TV, published a book in Serbia covering the period 1998–2000, which included the NATO bombing of Yugoslavia in 1999 and the overthrow of Milosevic. Marshall is very proud of his connections with secret services, in particular his associations with the British ones. His book, *Shadowplay*, is a detailed account of their activities, which are presented as the key factors in the political events that he describes. Marshall's primary focus is Milosevic's fall from power and its orchestration from behind the scenes, especially on the role played by British and U.S. intelligence. He openly supported the overthrow of the Milosevic regime and generally supports the U.S. "New World Order," as do many of his colleagues. He carefully documents the role of the main intelligence players, and his account is thick with references to "an M16 officer in Pristina," "sources in Yugoslav Military Intelligence," "a CIA man who was helping to put together the coup," "an officer of the US naval intelligence," and so forth. He quotes secret surveillance reports from the Serbian secret service, knows who the minister of defense desk officer is in London who drew up the strategy for getting rid of Milosevic, knows that the Foreign Secretary's telephone conversations are being listened to, knows which Russian intelligence officers accompanied Russian Prime Minister Yevgeni Primakov to Belgrade during the NATO bombing, knows which rooms are bugged in the British Embassy and where the Yugoslav spies are who listen to diplomats' conversations, knows that a staff member on the U.S. House of Representatives International Relations Committee is, in fact, an officer of U.S. intelligence, seems to know that secret service decisions are often made with very minimal ministerial approval, describes how the CIA physically escorted the KLA delegation from Kosovo to Paris for the prewar talks at Rambouillet where NATO issued the official delegation of Yugoslavia an ultimatum it knew that the delegation could only reject, and refers to very high-level secret negotiations in which people sought to betray one another as Milosevic's power collapsed.[17] All of this detail contributes to the authenticity of what he says and underscores the unnatural character of the public telling of the story.

In the aftermath of the so-called Serbian revolution, after the fall of Milosevic, the NED, Albert Einstein Institution, and other related outfits all contributed to the establishment of self-proclaimed youth groups for democracy throughout the rest of Eastern Europe.[18] Commenting on that expansion in a report on his 2001 trip to Serbia, Albert Einstein staffer Chris Miller wrote:

> Since the ousting of Milosevic, several members of Otpor have met with members of the Belarusian group Zubr (Bison). In following developments in Belarus since early this year, It is clear that Zubr was developed or at least conceptualized, using Otpor as a model. Also, [Albert Einstein's report] From

Dictatorship to Democracy is available in English on the Zubr website at www.zubr-belarus.com Of course, success will not be achieved in Belarus or anywhere else, simply by mimicking the actions taken in Serbia. However the successful Serbian nonviolent struggle was highly influenced and aided by the availability of knowledge and information on strategic nonviolent struggle and both successful and unsuccessful past cases, which is transferable.[19]

The terms of struggle in the Ukraine described here are framed by the Western press in the same polarized language that characterized the Cold War and that currently defines the "war on terrorism." The democratic claims of the United States and its Western allies are entirely hypocritical. After an election condemned by international observers as blatantly fraudulent, Ilham Aliyev was inaugurated as president of the former Soviet republic of Azerbaijan in October 2003. When the opposition launched protests in the streets of Baku, the Azerbaijani capital, authorities responded with a nationwide crackdown in which more than 1,000 people were arrested, including key opposition leaders and election officials. Human Rights Watch documented cases of torture and threats of rape in prison against senior opposition leaders. When U.S. Secretary of Defense Donald Rumsfeld visited Azerbaijan in December 2003, electoral fraud was not even an issue as Rumsfeld congratulated Aliyev on his "victory."[20] More recently, the United States and its Western allies similarly accepted the outcome of the Afghan elections, which were marked by widespread allegations of vote fixing and intimidation, and in which large parts of the country were unable to participate as a consequence of the continuing chaos in war-torn Afghanistan.

As should be evident, the purpose of these "regime changes" is not to promote democracy but to secure U.S. strategic interests. By encouraging an uncompromisingly partisan position and initiating an extensive covert intelligence campaign on behalf of the Yushchenko camp, the United States has increased the danger of a civil war or partition of Ukraine along ethnic and religious lines—between the majority Russian-speaking Orthodox Christian east and the mainly Ukrainian-speaking Catholic west. The United States seems to be narrowly committed to a very anti-Russian agenda in a region that is still suffering from a Cold War hangover. Eventually, this policy will demand 100 percent loyalty to Washington's geostrategic vision for the region and zero tolerance for any cooperation between former Soviet republics and Russia.

To achieve regime change in Ukraine, the CIA ordered that exit polls be presented as definite even before the counting of the votes began, sent thousands of observers, recruited through the intermediary of Eastern European associations, to the country to complain about election fraud, and paid thousands of dollars to opposition members and trained them in street demonstrations. The so-called peaceful people's revolution was conceived as a spectacle for Western television,[21] and in the end, U.S.-sponsored candidate Yushchenko won the election with a small margin.

Ukraine has been democratized. Who is next?

NOTES

1. Zbigniew Brzezinski, "The Grand Chessboard: US Geostrategy for Eurasia," *Foreign Affairs* (November–December 1997), http://hir.harvard.edu/articles/?id=627.

2. Conference Yalta agreement on the Common Economic Space effect on euro-integration prospects of Ukraine, November 20, 2003, Lviv, Ukraine, http://www.ji-magazine.lviv.ua/conf-nov2003/progr-eng.htm.

3. *The GUUAM Group: History and Principles*, November 2000, http://www.guuam.org/general/browse.html.

4. Jérôme Guillet, "Russia, Ukraine, Oil, US Diplomacy—All in One," http://www.cdi.org/russia/johnson/9029-18.cfm.

5. "The Ukrainian Elections—A Dangerous Fairy-Tale," December 2, 2004, http://www.killingtrain.com/archives/000304.html.

6. Roman Woronowycz, "Kuchma Says CIS Summit Heralds New Era in Relations among Members," *The Ukrainian Weekly* 65, no. 14 (April 6, 1997), http://www.ukrweekly.com/Archive/1997/149701.shtml.

7. "Hope in Ukraine, Despair in Iraq," *Spiegel Online*, November 24, 2004, http://service.spiegel.de/cache/international/0,1518,329434,00.html.

8. Ibid.

9. On July 29, 1999, the U.S. Senate held hearings on how to most effectively use the Serbian "opposition" to effect U.S. plans in Yugoslavia. Hearing of the European Affairs Subcommittee of the Senate Foreign Relations Committee, "Prospects for Democracy in Yugoslavia," http://emperors-clothes.com/analysis/hearin.htm.

10. T. Bancroft-Hinchey, "The OTPOR Factor in the Ukraine?," November 23, 2004, Pravda RU, http://english.pravda.ru/mailbox/22/101/399/14629_Ukraine.html.

11. Ian Traynor, "US Campaign Behind the Turmoil in Kiev," *The Guardian*, November 26, 2004.

12. Jonathan Mowat, "Coup d'État in Disguise: Washington's New World Order 'Democratization' Template," February 9, 2005, http://www.globalresearch.ca/articles/MOW502A.html.

13. For the text of the interview with Robert Helvey, who was sent by the International Republican Institute to teach seminars in nonviolent strategy for a group of Otpor students in the spring of 2000, see http://www.pbs.org/weta/dictator/otpor/ownwords/helvey.htm, Belgrade, January 29, 2001.

14. *Sydney Morning Herald*, September 27, 2001.

15. Michael Dobbs, "U.S. Advice Guided Milosevic Opposion," *Washington Post*, December 11, 2000, http://www.washingtonpost.com/ac2/wp-dyn?pagename=article&contentId=A18395-2000Dec3&notFound=true.

16. In Mowat, "Coup d'État in Disguise."

17. J. Laughland, "Techniques of a Coup d'Etat," *Sanders Research*, January 12, 2004, http://www.sandersresearch.com/; Tim Marshall, *Shadowplay* (Belgrade: B92, 2003) in Serbian.

18. A. Gene Sharp, senior scholar-in-residence, Albert Einstein Institution, explains in detail how a nonviolent resistance should be organized; http://www.creativeresistance.ca/toolkit/2002-sept05-from-dictatorship-to-democracy-chapt9.htm.

19. In Mowat, "Coup d'État in Disguise."

20. U.S. Foreign Aid Watch Organization, "Rumsfeld Following the Scent of Oil to Azerbaijan?," December 4, 2003, http://www.foreignaidwatch.org/modules.php?op=modload&name=News&file=index&catid=&topic=16.

21. Thierry Meyssan, "Subversion Ukraine: The Street against the People," http://signs-of-the-times.org/signs/rv-ukraine.htm.

CHAPTER 10

Beasts in Samaritan Clothing

And all of you—whether French and English, Russians and Germans, Italians and Americans—we have seen you all together once before in brotherly accord, united in a great league of nations, helping and guiding each other: it was in China. There too you forgot all quarrels among yourself, there too you made a peace of peoples—for mutual murder and the torch. Ha, how the pigtails fell in rows before your bullets, like a ripe grainfield lashed by the hail! Ha, how the wailing women plunged into the water, their dead in their cold arms, fleeing the tortures of your ardent embraces!

And now they all turned to Martinique, all one heart and one mind again; they help, rescue, dry the tears and curse the havoc-wreaking volcano. Mt. Pelee, great hearted giant, you can laugh; you can look down in loathing at these benevolent murderers, at these weeping carnivores, at these beasts in Samaritan clothing.[1]

The earthquake that produced the December 26, 2004, tsunami in the Indian Ocean occurred because the Burma Microplate slid under the large Sunda Plate. A sudden jarring shift under the sea floor at about 01:00 GMT called a "megathrust" forced the floor of the Indian Ocean to abruptly move about 15 meters toward Indonesia and raised the Indian tectonic plate underneath the neighboring Burma microplate about 10 meters along a length of more than 1,000 kilometers. The two movements sent a wave of water through the full depth of the overlying ocean racing toward the Malay Peninsula, Bangladesh, India, Sri Lanka, and East Africa at an incredible speed of hundreds of miles per hour. The event released a force estimated as nearly equivalent to 200 million tons of TNT beneath the Nicobar and Andaman Islands and the tip of the island of Sumatra called Aceh Province.

With little to disrupt it, the wave swept north and west, unleashing a calamity of biblical proportions.[2] Entire towns were wiped from the map, more than 150,000 people were killed, and millions have been left in urgent need of food and shelter. Almost a third of the dead were children, and hundreds of thousands of people lost everything, with millions more facing a future of polluted drinking water, a lack of sanitation, and no health services.[3] This was an almost unimaginable disaster. It was particularly unimaginable for those in the First World who have never before seen destruction on this scale.

Such disasters have always been with us, but our view of them is strongly influenced by our own social and economic environment. With the current state of scientific and technical development, such disasters represent a terrible menace, not because they cannot be prevented, but because the basic means that exist for warning about them are unevenly and unjustly distributed throughout the world. The ability of the people to minimize damage from natural disasters is closely tied to their ability to respond quickly and effectively when one strikes, which itself relies to a large degree on the resources generally available and the form of social organization in societies in specific countries and places around the world. If a warning system had been in operation in the area of the Indian Ocean, such as the inexpensive and reliable buoy system in the Pacific Ocean, much of the death and destruction that came from this tsunami could have been prevented. These systems are not difficult to install, and tsunami detector buoys have been used by the United States for more than half a century to prevent unnecessary damage and death.[4]

A tsunami buoy system could have been installed in the Indian Ocean, which has seen more than its share of great earthquakes and seismic events over the centuries, including the great Krakatoa eruption in Indonesia in 1883, which produced a tsunami more than 40 meters (120 feet) high that killed an estimated 36,000 people on the surrounding islands.[5] Had such a warning system been installed and in operation, warnings of this quake and tsunami could easily have been transmitted to the people of the area through existing radio and telecommunications systems.

One of the few places in the Indian Ocean that got the message of the quake was Diego Garcia, a speck of an island used principally by the U.S.

Navy to conduct bombing raids on Afghanistan and Iraq and house Camp Justice, one of the secret facilities used for holding and interrogating suspected terrorists in the U.S. war on terror.[6] Just 1,000 miles from India and in the direct path of the tsunami, the Navy was informed of the quake as a consequence of being part of the Pacific warning center's contact list.[7] Attempts were made to contact other concerned parties in the region, but as Charles McCreery of the Pacific Warning Center in Hawaii recounts, "We started thinking about who we could call. We talked to the State Department Operations Center and to the military. We called embassies. We talked to the navy in Sri Lanka, any local government official we could get hold of.... We were fairly careful about who we called. We wanted to call people who could help."[8] The State Department claimed to have notified India, but the Indian government said it received no such warning in the two hours that elapsed between the quake and the tidal wave that hit the Indian coastline in the southern province of Tamil Nadu. Nor did the Sri Lankan government receive a warning.[9] A network of sea-level gauges and deep-sea sensors is linked by satellite to round-the-clock monitoring stations in Hawaii, Alaska, and Japan. In addition, U.S. security and intelligence agencies have many sea-bottom sensors in the Indian Ocean for detecting submarines, nuclear explosions, earthquakes, and tsunamis. These devices and their collecting agencies must have detected the earthquake and the resulting tsunami when it occurred, but nevertheless did not pass on the information to those at risk because it was "classified."

In the aftermath of the tsunami, numerous articles appeared in the media attempting to explain the geological causes of the disaster. While it was useful information, none of it attempted to explain the social and political factors that led to such a horrific loss of life. Although the tsunami resulted from an earthquake near Sumatra, its devastating effects on southern Asia and East Africa were not wholly caused by a natural disaster. In reality, the human cost was primarily due to the widespread poverty that continues to plague these postcolonial countries. The homes that were destroyed and the lives lost were mainly those of the poor, who live close to the sea from which they derive their meager incomes. Their homes were flimsy shanties that could withstand neither floods nor storms of a smaller scale, let alone the monster that was this earthquake and tsunami. The mainstream media commonly describe the "indiscriminate" destruction of the tsunami, but it was discriminating in that the vast majority of deaths were those of the poor. In a system that drives hundreds of thousands of people to live illegally in shacks on beaches because they cannot afford adequate housing even after working long hours, could the results have been otherwise?

A DIVIDED WORLD

While earthquakes and tsunamis are natural disasters, decisions to spend billions of dollars on wars of conquest while ignoring simple measures that can save human lives are not. The devastation caused by the Asian tsunami constitutes a powerful demonstration of the irrational and inhuman nature of the neoliberal system. It was entirely within the bounds of modern technology to prevent the vast majority of the suffering and death occurred, and if the earthquake and tsunami had taken place in the Pacific rather than the Indian Ocean, the results would have been very different. The presence of a high-tech early warning system, developed to protect the shorelines of North America and Japan in particular, would have issued a warning within minutes of an initial tremor; coastal warning systems, such as those in the Hawaiian islands, would have warned those closest to the beach; and the general telecommunications system would have advised the rest. But without such warning systems, the countries bordering the Indian Ocean were left totally unprepared.

Forbes magazine's annual listing of the world's billionaires hit a record 587 last year, nearly half of whom live in the United States. Their collective wealth amounted to $1.9 trillion, more than the combined gross domestic product of the world's 170 poorest countries.[10] A 2003 UN report found that at least 1 billion people live in extreme poverty without the most basic essentials of life, and that their conditions are worsening. This system of extreme inequality is the other tsunami, a worldwide economic tsunami causing 24,000 deaths every day from poverty and debt, which are consequences that follow from the way the world's economy has been structured. "Some 2.8 billion people—two in five—still struggle to survive on less than $2 a day."[11] The UN acknowledges that this an unfair and extremely unhealthy situation, calling on the richest countries in a 1990 Paris conference to implement a program of action to ease the economic burden of the world's poorest nations. More than a decade later, nearly every commitment made in response by the governments of rich Western states has been broken.[12]

A recent report from Oxfam says that 45 million more children will die needlessly by 2015 because rich countries are failing to provide the essential basic resources they had promised in poverty relief. According to an Oxfam report, *Paying the Price,*

> the sums that rich countries invest in global poverty reduction are shamefully small: At an average of $80 per person per year in rich countries, the sum is equivalent to the price of a weekly cup of coffee. What is more, the wealthier these countries have become, the less they have given in aid. Rich countries today give half as much, as a proportion of their income, as they did in the 1960s. In 1960–65, rich countries spent on average 0.48 per cent of their combined national incomes on aid. By 1980–85 they were spending just 0.34 per cent. By 2003, the average had dropped as low as 0.24 per cent.[13]

Jeremy Hobbs, Oxfam's executive director, added, "The world has never been wealthier, yet rich nations are giving less and less. Across the globe, millions of people are being denied the most basic human needs—clean water, food, health care and education. People are dying while leaders delay debt relief and aid."[14]

THE U.S. RESPONSE TO THE ASIAN TSUNAMI

U.S. Secretary of State Condoleezza Rice declared that the tsunami constituted "a wonderful opportunity to show not just the US government but the heart of the American people."[15] Even after twice raising its aid pledge to $350 million, the U.S. contribution to tsunami relief is equivalent to what the United States spends in a day and a half on the war in Iraq.[16] This fact also contrasts sharply with other "aid" the United States has given the region in the form of military and intelligence "assistance." Indonesia in particular has been of long-term interest to U.S. foreign policy, enjoying considerable attention from the CIA and military intelligence agencies. On October 1, 1965, the CIA, working with fascistic Indonesian military officers led by General Suharto, organized a coup that removed the left-nationalist President Sukarno from power. In the aftermath of the coup, military personnel and right-wing death squads slaughtered over half a million members of the Indonesian Communist Party (PKI) and other left-wing groups.[17] In 1990, retired U.S. diplomats and CIA officers, including former ambassador to Indonesia Marshall Green, admitted helping the Indonesian military organize this mass killing, and according to a report published in the *Washington Post* on May 21, 1990, State Department and CIA officials at the U.S. Embassy in Jakarta personally provided the names of thousands of local, regional, and national leaders and activists to the armed forces, which then killed or detained most of those named.[18]

For the next three decades, General Suharto's brutally repressive and U.S.-backed regime kept Indonesia safe for the world capitalist system, which was rewarded with critical CIA support to keep it in power until 1998.[19] During this period, the agency's collaboration with Suharto's two main secret police forces, the BAKIN and KOPKAMTIB, led to the execution of nearly 2 million people,[20] and the destruction was capped by a fiscal tsunami, the worst economic recession since 1963, which devastated the Indonesian economy and caused its currency to collapse in 1998.[21] The country had been under close IMF supervision for ten years before its currency collapse, but the IMF gave no warning that the currency was overvalued. Rather, in response to the crisis, the IMF forced the government to cut public expenditure to restore "financial credibility," and the crisis quickly worsened. In 1998, real Indonesian GDP contracted by an estimated 13.7 percent and inflation reached a staggering 77 percent. While the economy bottomed out in mid-1999, real GDP growth for the year was an anemic 0.3 percent.[22] Many economists later argued that Indonesia needed not economic austerity but expansionary policies, which could have prevented the financial crisis from becoming a deeper social and economic crisis. The IMF ignored this basic argument and also ignored the realities of the country's fragile political and social systems. In the end, the IMF-imposed austerity measures failed to stop the financial panic, and the crisis spread to all sectors of the Indonesian economy.[23]

In reality, many of those who were washed to their deaths in Indonesia on Boxing Day, December, 2004, in Indonesia's Aceh Province, where the earthquake and tsunami caused the greatest casualties, were killed by IMF policies. According to the Asian Development Bank, almost 30 percent of Aceh's population of 4 million were living below the poverty line before the tsunami, even though Aceh is rich in oil and gas. Unemployment was estimated at 40 percent and less than half of the province had access to safe drinking water and electricity.[24] Human rights groups earlier reported that the Indonesian military was responsible for the deaths of more than 20,000 Acehnese between 1989 and 2004, and some 2,000 Acehnese died in 1998 during a special military operation to crush the escalating rebellion.[25] Roughly half the city of Banda Aceh, on the northwestern tip of Sumatra, Indonesia, was reduced to ruins by the double blows of a powerful earthquake and giant tsunami, with more than 166,080 poor Acehnese offically confirmed dead and hundreds of thousands more made homeless.[26]

As reported in the *Jakarta Post*, a month before the tsunami, the British government gave its support to an arms fair in Jakarta, "designed to meet an urgent need for the [Indonesian] armed forces to review its defence capabilities." UK arms companies were among those attending the first-ever arms fair in Indonesia,[27] and a subsidiary of UK-based BAE Systems and Rolls-Royce was among the exhibitors. Rolls-Royce itself manufactures engines for the Hawks, which along with British-supplied Scorpion armored vehicles, machine-guns, and ammunition, were terrorizing and killing people in Aceh right up to the day the tsunami struck.[28]

MEDIA AND GLOBAL HYPOCRISY

High-profile news coverage of the tsunami and its victims aroused the world's sympathy and helped to launch a huge worldwide relief effort. The corporate media hailed the promises of assistance from the United States, Australia, and other wealthy countries, but also exposed the hypocrisy of the Western press. Human-invented disasters, which dwarf the so-called natural ones, have punctuated the history of the last five centuries. One need only remember colonialism, slavery, two world wars, South African apartheid, the Persian Gulf War, the September 11 terrorist attacks and the war in Afghanistan, the invasion of Iraq, HIV/AIDS, genocide in Rwanda, ad infinitum. What then makes a disaster catastrophic, calling for widespread sympathy? Is it one created by us, or by nature? Should our compassion be divisible—that is, immediate, hot, and total when a disaster is wrought by nature, but detached, cold, and unconcerned when one is devised and put into practice by us?

One cannot help but contrast the media's tsunami coverage with what has happened and is happening to Iraqi civilians as a result of the U.S. invasion and occupation. U.S. Defense Secretary Donald Rumsfeld and former U.S. commander in Iraq Tommy Franks both said, "We don't do body counts."[29] As of March 17, 2005, the researchers of the Iraq Body Count have recorded over 18,000 civilian deaths since the beginning of the U.S. invasion, and hundreds of thousands more are now homeless, with serious health risks.[30] Why don't the victims of this war merit the same kind of interest and high-profile media campaign? With over 400,000 deaths of children under five in U.S.-occupied Iraq and Afghanistan, why the sudden grief over a tsunami? Are the Iraqi or Afghani children less dead?

After a helicopter flight into Aceh Province, former U.S. Secretary of State Colin Powell said that he had never seen anything like that devastation in his entire military and government career—"I've been in war, and I've been through a number of hurricanes, tornadoes and other relief operations but I have never seen anything like this. I cannot begin to imagine the horror that went through the families and all of the people who heard this noise coming and then had their lives snuffed out by this wave," he said.[31] What of the horror of the Iraqi families who endured the ceaseless U.S. aerial bombardments and roar of cannon barrages for days before U.S. tanks laid waste to their environment? General Powell could have seen far greater devastation had he taken a low-flying helicopter trip over the Iraqi city of Fallujah after its "pacification" a few months earlier. Such a flight would have given him some idea of what a man-made tsunami left in one of Iraq's main urban cultural centers. Thanks to a tidal wave of fire and steel unleashed by U.S. warplanes, artillery, and tanks, the fabled city of mosques now lies in ruins.

In 1953, an American commanding general in Korea portrayed the total destruction of the Toksan dam as "perhaps the most spectacular [strike] of the war" and "immediately scheduled two more dams for destruction."[32] Five more dams lay in ruins after the attack was concluded, which together "supplied water for the irrigation system of an area that produced three-quarters of North Korea's rice." U.S. Air Force records joyously announced that this was a premeditated consequence. "To the average Oriental," said one report, "an empty rice bowl symbolizes starvation."[33]

Let us do what we can for the victims of the tsunami. But no matter how much we weep for them, no matter what donations we spare, the offerings will not spare us from history's judgment, if not God's.[34]

NOTES

1. Rosa Luxemburg, after a volcanic eruption in May, 1902, at the port of St. Pierre; first published on May 15, 1902, in *Leipziger Volkszeitung*. Online version, 1999, at marxists.org.

2. Editorial, *Nature*, January 5, 2005; Catherine Marquis-Homeyer, "Asian Quake and Massive Tsunami Shake the Earth," January 10, 2005, http://www.thecurrentonline.com/news/2005/01/10/Opinions/Asian.Quake.And.Massive.Tsunami.Shake.The.Earth-831452.shtml.

3. telegraph.co.uk, "Casualty Figures by Nation," January 28, 2005, http://news.telegraph.co.uk/news/main.jhtml?xml=/news/2005/01/04/utoll2.xml.

4. K. Chang, "In Past Tsunamis, Tantalizing Clues to Future Ones," *New York Times*, January 4, 2005, http://query.nytimes.com/gst/abstract.html?res=30814FA395D0C778CDDA80894DD404482.

5. G. Pararas-Carayannis, "The Tsunami Page," http://www.drgeorgepc.com/Vocano1883Krakatoa.html. The explosion is regarded as the greatest natural disaster in recorded human history, dropping ash in New York City and producing sympathetic tsunamis that washed ashore on the western coasts of North and South America and were in evidence as far away as the English Channel.

6. "Diego Garcia 'Camp Justice' 7°20'S 72°25'E," http://www.globalsecurity.org/military/facility/diego-garcia.htm.

7. *New York Times*, December 28, 2004.

8. Jan TenBruggencate, "Ewa Center Tried in Vain to Help," December 29, 2004, http://the.honoluluadvertiser.com/article/20.

9. Patrick Martin, "Bush's Response to South Asia Disaster: Indifference Compounded by Political Incompetence," *World Socialist Web Site*, December 30, 2004, http://www.wsws.org/articles/2004/dec2004/bush-d30.shtml.

10. Forbes.com, "Special Report: The World's Richest People," February 26, 2004, http://www.forbes.com/2004/02/25/bill04land.html.

11. "State of World Population Report 2004, the Cairo Consensus at 10: Population, Reproductive Health and the Global Effort to End Poverty," http://www.unfpa.org/swp/swpmain.htm.

12. Emily Smith, "Poverty Fight Needs $100bn in Aid," July 8, 2003, http://edition.cnn.com/2003/BUSINESS/07/08/un.human/.

13. Oxfam, *Paying the Price*, http://www.oxfam.org.uk/what_we_do/issues/debt_aid/mdgs_price.htm.

14. Ibid.

15. Joe Vialls, "Did New York Orchestrate the Asian Tsunami?," January 5, 2005, http://www.vialls.com/subliminalsuggestion/tsunami.html.

16. The War in Iraq Cost the United States: $157,604,489,109, March 7, 2005, http://costofwar.com/.

17. Before the coup, the PKI, nominally backed by Sukarno, was a legal and formidable organization and was the third largest Communist Party in the world. It claimed 3 million members, and through affiliated organizations—such as labor and youth groups—it had the support of 17 million others.

18. In "US Officials Provided Indonesian Military with Death Lists," the Editorial Board of the WSWS, May 20, 1998, http://www.wsws.org/news/1998/may1998/coup-m20.shtml.

19. Ralph McGehee, "The Indonesian Massacres and the CIA," *Covert Action Quarterly* (Fall 1990), http://www.thirdworldtraveler.com/CIA/McGehee_CIA_Indo.html. Ralph McGehee worked for the CIA from 1952 until 1977 and now writes about intelligence matters.

20. Ronald Hilton, "Indonesia: Suharto," 2004, http://wais.stanford.edu/ztopics/week020105/indonesia_050201_suharto.htm.

21. World Trade Organization, "Indonesia: December 1998," http://www.wto.org/english/tratop_e/tpr_e/tp94_e.htm.

22. Wikipedia, "Economy of Indonesia," http://www.answers.com/topic/economy-of-indonesia.

23. Choike.org, "IMF Management of the Financial Crises," http://www.choike.org/nuevo_eng/informes/1730.html; International Monetary Fund, "The IMF's Response to the Asian Crisis," January 1999, http://www.imf.org/external/np/exr/facts/asia.htm.

24. Asian Development Bank, http://www.adb.org.

25. Borgna Brunner, "The Year of Living Dangerously: Indonesia after Suharto," June 7, 1999, http://www.infoplease.com/spot/indonesia1.html.

26. *Asia News*, "Indian Ocean Tsunami Death Toll Approaches Quarter Million," January 19, 2005, http://asia.news.designerz.com/indian-ocean-tsunami-death-toll-approaches-quarter-million.html?d20050119.

27. In A. Wood, "UK Arms Companies Market into Indonesian War Zones," Indymedia UK, November 24, 2004, http://www.indymedia.org.uk/en/2004/11/301913.html.

28. John Pilger, "The Other Tsunami," *New Statesman*, January 10, 2005.

29. Derrick Z. Jackson, "The Tsunami Victims That We Don't Count," *Boston Globe*, January 7, 2005, http://www.boston.com/news/globe/editorial_opinion/oped/articles/2005/01/07/the_tsunami_victims_that_we_dont_count?mode=PF.

30. The Iraq Body Count Database, June 17, 2005, http://www.iraqbodycount .net/database/.

31. "Powell Shock at Aceh Destruction," January 5, 2005, http://news.bbc.co.uk/ 2/hi/asia-pacific/4147853.stm; Jonathan Miller, "Anguish in Aceh," Channel 4, January 5, 2005, http://www.channel4.com/news/2005/01/week_1/05_aceh.html.

32. In May 1953, wave upon wave of American fighter-bombers destroyed and emptied the 2,300-foot Toksan dam, an earth-and-stone reservoir in North Korea. Floodwaters from the dam surged and washed out bridges and roads and swept away railway lines. The massive flash flood destroyed hundreds of buildings and devastated rice field after rice field.

33. Renato Redentor Constantino, "Tsunami Hypocrisy and War," January 13, 2005, http://www.lewrockwell.com/engelhardt/engelhardt35.html.

34. Jackson, "The Tsunami Victims That We Don't Count."

Conclusion: An Overview of the New American Imperialism

In conclusion, we would like to reemphasize several of the arguments made throughout the book, including the following points.

First: The key point that distinguishes this new American imperialism from all other imperialisms and colonialisms is that first and foremost, the British and the French, but also the Germans, Italians, and Dutch, never elaborated a truly global and all-encompassing expansionist strategy. Their main political concern was to carve up the world between themselves and reclaim the parts of it that they disputed.

Political and military operations before World War II were carried out by the traditional methods of competing alliances and blocs. Admittedly, this was bound to lead to interimperialist wars and, finally, to the collapse of the imperialist system itself. However, soon after World War II, and despite Winston Churchill's efforts to revive Britain's old-fashioned colonial scheme, U.S. strategists organized a new imperialism, based on a hub-and-spoke system of global governance. This new imperialism was envisioned as quasi expansive, suggesting that it would never contract. The United States was to be the hub in this system, with all other capitalist powers making up the spokes, and the system would spin according to the orders of the hub.

In the early years of the Cold War, Western Europe and Japan became spokes, but a balance of power was kept in the Middle East to placate the

Arabs and support the British. We traced the paternity of this scheme to then U.S. Secretary of State Dean Acheson and Paul Nitze. The scheme was put into practice in the late 1940s, using NATO and the framework of NSC-68 as a foundation. This new imperialism was intended to absorb tensions among the world's senior powers, organizing them around advanced political, military, and ideological technologies and directing them according to U.S. class and bureaucratic interests. From the 1960s onward, it became apparent that the United States was deviating from this Achesonian model with regard to the U.S. "special relationship" with Israel–a fact that complicated relations between the United States and the oil-rich Gulf States. Strains also appeared in the inner workings of the system as Western Europe and Japan developed their own strong economies, and the global economic order established at Bretton Woods in 1944 began to break down.

Second: The hub-and-spoke approach to U.S. global governance was politically as well as economically useful. Starting with Bretton Woods, the United States successfully created a global monetary order based on a central role for the dollar. However, under pressure from the strong economies of Western Europe and Japan, and efforts by the Europeans in the late 1960s and early 1970s to create their own reserve currency, this system collapsed in 1971. The United States responded to the crisis by severing the dollar from gold and allowing its value to float all other currencies. The effect of this shift was to force the international economy to adopt the dollar as the world's standard currency.

Drawing lessons from the first (1973) and second (1979) oil crises, and after the collapse of the Soviet system, in the late 1990s the Europeans finally managed to produce their own reserve currency to challenge the weakening dollar and the declining U.S. economy. These developments were linked to neoliberal policies of deregulation and financial liberalization that had been spearheaded in the 1980s by Anglo-American conservatives such as Margaret Thatcher and Ronald Reagan. These neoliberal policies had delinked finance and banking from industrial capital and state control, and left monetary and financial movements to be managed by private operators who determined monetary values according to market speculation. Today, a battle between the euro and the dollar is transforming the world of international economics and the world of global politics, particularly in Eurasia and its crucial subregions in the greater Middle East. As we have tried to show, the U.S. war in Iraq was more a consequence of the euro-dollar competition in oil markets than the result of any particular desire by the United States to acquire the second largest oil reserves in the world. What this suggests is that U.S. imperialism in this period is driven less by conquest and more by the need for economic control.

Third: The world has changed dramatically since the fall of the Berlin Wall in November 1989, but the United States continues to employ the same neo-imperial hub-and-spoke system and the same instruments to achieve its strategic aims and political ends. The United States uses NATO and other international organizations to engage strategic zones or states to acquire more spokes to spin around its hub. It similarly uses the IMF to force developing countries to become more dependent on the U.S. Treasury. And it uses the WTO to open up global markets to U.S. products, while carefully protecting the U.S. market from foreign competition. Because of its economic weakness and vulnerability vis-à-vis Europe and Southeast Asia, the United States has become overtly aggressive and militaristic. Since at least September 11, 2001, the neoconservatives in the Pentagon and the White House have been radicalizing the Achesonian neo-imperial system, not by restructuring it but by introducing an ideological dimension, which we summarize below. In reality, the United States did not adopt a new political strategy after 1989, or for that matter after 9/11; rather, a closer look shows that the decisions shaping the U.S. military campaigns in Afghanistan and Iraq demonstrate a remarkable continuity with those made before 9/11. We argue that the Bush administration is attempting to increase its military control in the central Eurasian region to achieve energy security and global geopolitical goals.

Fourth: The decline of U.S. economic power and the relative retreat of its dominant position in the world economic system have promoted a drift in U.S. foreign policy that favors military action. Believing that it can still reshape the world solely through overt force has led to an increased need for American troops to be stationed in remote corners of the globe, something that Andre Gunder Frank calls "U.S. imperial political military blowback." Thus, the so-called war on terror has facilitated U.S. military penetration into new areas from which it previously was absent. This imposes huge political and economic costs to support U.S. military personnel, who are now deployed in at least 135 countries, or 70 percent of all the UN member countries.

Once upon a time, you could trace a country's imperial reach by counting its colonies. However, in the neo-imperial version, colonies

have become military bases from which imperial interests can be pro-
jected and protected. U.S. military power is now dominant and its limitations are minimal: never in world history has the military supremacy of
a single power been so great. This reflects the reorganization of U.S.
military and security strategies during the 1990s through what has been
labeled the revolution in military affairs (RMA). The full consequence of
the changes made under the RMA may not be known until the distant
future, but the U.S. military is making the most of the new technology
that it is introducing, and energetically exploiting and experimenting
with it in the most extensive global military campaign since the end of
the Cold War. The final result of the RMA will forever change the way
the United States conducts operations and will set the tone for many
of the world's other armies. The political aspect of the RMA is that it is
being used to contain U.S. domestic opposition to U.S. foreign policy by
reducing U.S. casualties. Yet the changes associated with the RMA do
not automatically provide a safer world for the United States: As U.S.
military forces become less vulnerable, U.S. adversaries are likely to increase attacks against U.S. political targets, including U.S. civilians.

Fifth: The U.S. intelligence establishment, once dominated by covert
CIA operations, is now conducted largely through the high-tech monitoring networks created by the National Security Agency and National
Reconnaissance Office. However, most U.S. citizens either remain unaware of these agencies, or, if they know of them, assume that their
activities are far more benign than those of the CIA. Both approaches
miss the significance of how these agencies currently operate. The relentless development of ever more sophisticated spy technologies is intended to ensure that every U.S. military engagement can be turned into
a "turkey shoot," similar to that of the Iraqis who were slaughtered on the
road to Basra during the Persian Gulf War in 1991. Following the trauma
of the war in Vietnam, the political perception has been that the U.S.
public will accept military interventions only where U.S. casualties are
limited. In practice, military planning now includes choices that allow for
potentially no casualties for "our side," and spy satellites, drones, motion
sensors, and smart bombs have all become the familiar high-tech weapons
of choice to be used against real and potential enemies.

Sixth: Since ancient times, the political game has been defined by the
relationship between "enemies" and "friends." If the Democratic Party
disappeared from American politics and no other competitor with the

Republicans emerged, the Republicans would find themselves in an awkward predicament: They would have to rule as despots and dictators—but then, for how long? To maintain a fig leaf of democratic respectability, they would have to create another competitor to replace the Democrats. Having "enemies" is suitable and functional: It creates a gloss of antagonism and competition, whether or not it creates any real debate and contest over specific issues. It keeps the rivals sharp and saves them from inertia, and generally keeps things rolling.

What applies in domestic politics also applies in international politics. The Soviet Union and the United States were two global "enemies," each with their own bloc of "friends." The Cold War was functional, particularly for the United States: As we saw, each time the United States wanted to rally its European allies, it was enough to create tension between itself and the Soviet Union. But this opportunity disappeared with the collapse of the Soviet Union. Colin Powell's cry "I'm running out of demons" is more than telling in this respect: who is the enemy that the United States would have to recall to advance its expansionist strategy by pulling together its friends? Throughout the 1990s, the United States made various experiments, mostly concerning the idea of promoting free-market democracy, pluralism, and human rights across the globe via NATO, the IMF, and the transformation of GATT into WTO. This idea came straight from the Cold War experience of the United States in Europe. But whereas during the Cold War it was used mainly to destabilize the Soviet system, in the 1990s it was used for expansionist purposes and power politics. Given the economic power of the Europeans and their claim to present themselves as independent actors in international affairs, the U.S. projection of power via the rhetoric of "human rights" no longer persuades. In a way, the attack on September 11, 2001, should have made Powell and other neoconservatives very happy. The "demon" they were looking for finally emerged: Islamic terrorism. From September 11 onward, both U.S. domestic and international politics could reshape themselves according to the new reality of the Pentagon's "war on terror." As in the Cold War, every U.S. ally would have to change its domestic security and international priorities according to the scheme of this new evil: terrorism could now be substituted for Communism with the same effect.

Seventh: We have looked at the intellectual origins of neoconservatism and its links to business, the media, and the state of Israel. It would be wrong to say that what is happening today is a "Jewish conspiracy." Rather, we believe that what is happening is a long and protracted political and ideological process whose guiding principles were first inserted into the Truman Doctrine and continued to the end of the Cold War. During this period, U.S.-Israel ties were reinforced after successful Israeli military operations, particularly following the spectacular Israeli victory against the Arabs in 1967. The powerful neo-Zionist constituency in America staunchly supported those ambitious and competitive Jewish members of the neocon clique, and the Pentagon and White House simply hijacked some of those individuals after 9/11. There is no conspiracy in this because Israel did not mastermind the guiding principles of U.S. grand neo-imperial strategy, as Israel did not exist at the time of their creation.

It might be said that the appearance of the Wolfowitz-Libby document in 1992 launched the argument for a replacement of the "evil Communism versus the free world" scheme. This is true, but their new "war on terror" scheme remains solidly within the structural context of the Achesonian policy of exaggerating the threat coming from the enemy. For a variety of economic, political, and ideological reasons, we have argued that this neoconservative strategy will have a short life. The United States could keep its current military predominance for decades, but its direct and indirect costs impose a heavy long-term burden on the United States for which it has no answer. If anything, the costs and burden are currently marginalized in the rhetoric of the U.S. administration. It is too early to tell. History is still in the making, but there are some useful indicators that a hard-line imperial grand strategy as now pursued by the Bush neoconservatives runs the risk of repeating an old history, which shows that powerful states tend to trigger self-encirclement by their own overestimation of their power.

Eighth: All our case studies prove the hypocritical character of U.S. foreign policy and the illusionary vision of U.S. intellectuals. Hypocritical because U.S. policymakers use moral principles to deceive the people, advancing through back-door power politics goals that are against the American people themselves (just think of the tax burden on every American citizen for each U.S. war venture abroad). Illusionary because most neoconservative intellectuals have a millenarian belief that their empire is unchallenged at every level—culturally, militarily, politically, and economically—and therefore will last forever. Brzezinski's thesis in the closing lines of *The Grand Chessboard* is that "America is the first and last truly global superpower," although he conditions that statement with a number of things that America has to do to guarantee its eternal supremacy. This is both ahistorical and metaphysical. As our case studies have demonstrated, the tensions and contradictions created by U.S. global management after the end of the Cold War have been greater than its policies could resolve. With the advancement of the neoconservatives to power after 9/11, these tensions and contradictions have become even more pronounced and difficult to handle. Full-spectrum dominance, after all, is a strategy employed by the weak and the decadent, not by the strong and the secure.

Ninth: So many covert U.S. military and intelligence operations and campaigns, so many business deals, so much oil and natural gas, and all these giant multinational corporations with such powerful connections to the Bush administration. This is not a paranoid theory, but simply a convergence of political and economic interests traveling under the rubrics of "war on terror," "Operation Enduring Freedom," "axis of evil," and "bringing democracy to former Communist states." Our argument is not based on the image of a few evil people conspiring in secret against the people for their evil aims—a conspiracy theory is a narrative that blames societal or individual problems on a scapegoat. However, diverging from conspiracy theory does not ignore the fact that indeed there are real conspiracies, criminal or otherwise. In particular, the U.S. political landscape is littered with examples of illegal political, corporate, and government conspiracies such as Watergate, the Iran-Contra scandal, and the systematic looting of the savings and loan industry. Having said that, we generally consider the belief in conspiracy theories a pointless diversion of focus and waste of energy. While real conspiracies have existed throughout history, history itself is not a conspiracy. Conspiracy theories presume that people acting as people do, including planning, plotting, cheating, deceiving, and pursuing power, cause events. Thus, conspiracy theories obscure the impersonal forces, like geopolitical factors, market economics, globalization, social evolution, and other such abstract explanations of human events. Accepting a conspiracy theory then becomes a convenient way to dismiss the facts and give in to fear, and in that sense conspiracy theories can be a comfortable substitute for the more difficult truth. They provide answers, but they are false answers. The neoconservative demagogues want to create a world in their image, but that does not constitute a conspiracy; it is just the way the system currently works and they are taking advantage of structural opportunities.

Tenth: From the collapse of former Yugoslavia through the various post-Yugoslav wars, various political and economic crises, U.S./NATO interventions in other parts of the former Soviet bloc, and the recent U.S. wars in Afghanistan and Iraq, though all these wars and conflicts had regional contexts, they all have collectively been the response of the United States to the problems created by the collapse of the Soviet Union. All have connections to the larger contests between the United States and its European allies over the division of resources and the political and military control of Eurasia, undertaken by the United States to stem its economic decline. These interventions have let the United States gain a strong foothold in the key lands of Eurasia, and turned this strategic landmass into an American sphere of influence. The vast oil and natural gas reserves of Eurasia are the fuel that is feeding this powerful drive, which may then lead to new U.S. military operations against local opponents as well as major regional powers, such as China and Russia. Were any of its adversaries, or a combination of adversaries, to effectively challenge this emerging U.S.-led security system in the region, it would call into question the dominant role of the United States in the post–Cold War era. For the present U.S. administration, the most effective way to secure its position is through use of its mighty military machine, and this is the key to understanding the development of global politics since the end of the Cold War.

Bibliographic Essay

As we give full details about our sources in the endnotes, we have decided to present in this short essay our comments on some key sources—quoted in the text or not—that we consider to be relevant for any critical understanding of the present phase of U.S. neo-imperialism in Eurasia. This can be no more than an illustration of the immense range of material available for the study of U.S. neo-imperialism.

Apart from the classic works of J. A. Hobson, Rudolf Hilferding, and V. I. Lenin on the subject of international finance and classic colonialism and imperialism, students should consult Wolfgang J. Mommsen's *Theories of Imperialism* (Chicago: University of Chicago Press, 1980). Mommsen's work offers a comprehensive introduction to the subject of critical approaches to imperialism. Undoubtedly, if one wishes to go deeper into the subject, one should look at the internationalization of capital and labor and the issue of globalization, starting from Karl Marx's own *Capital*. The third book of *Capital* is extremely relevant to the discussion on globalization today. In this context, A. G. Frank's *Re-Orient: Global Economy in the Asian Age* (Berkeley: University of California Press, 1998), is a book that deserves to be read alongside the classic works of Marx, Engels, Lenin, and Mao. We also find Nicos Poulantzas's work *Classes in Contemporary Capitalism* (various French editions since 1974—in English available from Verso/New Left Books) still relevant, particularly in understanding the complex articulation and antagonisms between various forms of capital at national and international levels. In their essay "Global Capitalism and American Empire" (*Socialist Register* 2004; London: Merlin Press, 2003), Leo Panitch and Sam Gindin use Poulantzas's work extensively. This issue of *Socialist Register* is dedicated to U.S. neo-imperialism and the essays are really comprehensive.

David Harvey's work *The New Imperialism* (Oxford, UK: Oxford University Press, 2003) is an attempt to relaunch the relevance of Hannah Arendt's and Rosa Luxembourg's theories on imperialism. A geographer by profession, Harvey's work is remarkable. Although somewhat opaque, particularly its section on "accumulation by dispossession," it makes fascinating reading. Another geographer, Derek Gregory, wrote *The Colonial Present* (Oxford, UK: Blackwell, 2004), which we have used several times in this work. It is the most scholarly, detailed, unbiased, and courageous account of America's and Israel's policies in Palestine, Afghanistan, and Iraq. A must-read.

We are both influenced by the work of Peter Gowan. He is Britain's foremost neo-Marxist, analyzing concretely, comprehensively, and critically post-1945 international political economy and international relations. We owe to Gowan the insight that U.S. neo-imperialism is essentially Achesonian/Nitzean in nature. We set to work and our findings do indeed confirm Gowan's acumen. His prize-winning *The Global Gamble* (London: Verso, 1999) is a classic text and a must-read for all those interested in reaching an understanding of America's neo-imperial strategies in Europe and Asia. In this context, we should also not fail to mention Michael Hudson's work *Super Imperialism* (London: Pluto, 2003). His analyses of the IMF and the World Bank should be read hand in hand with Gowan's analyses of the strategies these two institutions employed in the course of post–World War II history. From this perspective, the picture is completed only with reference to Donald Sassoon's monumental *One Hundred Years of Socialism* (London: Fontana, 1997). Sassoon narrates the political history of the parties of the Left in Western Europe since 1945 by placing them in the policy context of their changing international and national environments. We also highly recommend Frances Fox Piven, *The War at Home: The Domestic Costs of Bush's Militarism* (New York: New Press, 2004), as well as Cornel West's superb *Democracy Matters: Winning the Fight against Imperialism* (New York: Penguin, 2004).

Immanuel Wallestrein's *The Decline of American Power: The US in a Chaotic World* (New York: New Press, 2003) and Emmanuel Todd's *After the Empire* (New York: Columbia University Press, 2003) are two books that explain vividly how and why U.S. imperialism and U.S. society are in a deep crisis. We are in total agreement with their analyses on these two issues and we have tried to explain that U.S. projection of power is but an expression of U.S. weakness, not strength. In this context, one should read the superb account by Rahul Mahajan, *Full Spectrum Dominance: US Power in Iraq and Beyond* (New York: Seven Stories Press, 2003).

Our idea of post-1967 Zionism, what we call neo-Zionism, draws from the revisionist works of Benny Morris, *Righteous Victims: A History of Zionist-Arab Conflict 1881–2001* (New York: Vintage, 2001) and Avi Shlaim, *The Iron Wall: Islam and the Arab World* (New York: Norton, 2001). To understand the way neo-Zionism operates in the United States, one must start with a work by Stefan Halper and Jonathan Clarke, *America Alone: The Neo-Conservatives and the Global Order* (Cambridge, UK: Cambridge University Press, 2004). This is a work with some important inaccuracies. For example, both authors believe that U.S. Cold War strategy was guided by Kennan's idea of containment. The authors declare themselves to be conservatives—nothing wrong with that—yet their analyses are very close (if not identical) to those of Joseph Nye on soft power and Zbigniew Brzezinski in his last book, *The Choice*. Yet we recommend *America Alone* as a starter on the influence of neo-Zionism in the United States, simply because both authors are frank and speak their minds. In fact, their information on the neocons and their connections with the business and media worlds are invaluable. Undoubtedly, one should also visit the Web site of the Project for the New American Century (www.newamericancentury.org). A superb Web site providing reports and meticulous maps of the Israeli-Palestinian situation on the ground is www.fmep.org, the Web site of the Foundation for Middle East Peace.

The best-ever book on the history of Iraq is Hanna Batatu's insuperable *The Old Social Classes and the Revolutionary Movements of Iraq* (Princeton, NJ: Princeton University Press, 1978). Tariq Ali's useful but not at all original *Bush in Babylon* (London: Verso, 2003) draws almost entirely from Batatu. A highly readable essay on Iraq and U.S. imperialism was written by the group Research Unit for Political Economy, *Behind the Invasion of Iraq* (New York: Monthly Review Press, 2003). A very informative book on central Asia, edited by Alexei Vasiliev, is *Central Asia: Political and Economic Challenges in the Post-Soviet Era* (London: Saqi Books, 2001). On Iran, the energy resources of the Caspian Sea region, and the competition between OPEC and non-OPEC oil, we recommend the volume edited by Al Mohammadi and Anoushiravan Ehteshami, *Iran and Eurasia* (Ithaca, NY: Ithaca Press, 2000), and that edited by the Emirates Center for Strategic Studies and Research (ECSSR), *Caspian Energy Resources* (Abu Dhabi: ECSSR, 2000). We also recommend Lutz Kleveman, *The New*

Great Game: Blood and Oil in Central Asia (London: Atlantic Books, 2003). Bernard Mommer's *Global Oil and the Nation-State* (Oxford, UK: Oxford Institute for Energy Studies, 2002) is a must for a comprehensive understanding of the issue of "royalties" and state sovereignty over oil and gas, as well as the U.S. strategy of globalization with respect to these key issues. An overview on the foreign policies of the Middle Eastern states is given by Raymond Hinnebusch and Anoushiravan Ehteshami (eds.), *The Foreign Policies of Middle East States* (London: I.B. Tauris, 2004). On Turkey and Eurasia, the following two monographs by Bulent Aras are more than valuable: *The New Geo-politics of Eurasia and Turkey's Position* (London: Frank Cass, 2002) and *Turkey and the Greater Middle East* (Istanbul: Tasam, 2004). See also Bulent Aras (ed.), *War in the Gardens of Babylon: The Middle East after the Iraqi War* (Istanbul: Tasam, 2004). On Afghanistan, see Michael Griffin, *Reaping the Whirlwind* (London: Pluto, 2001).

There is very little on Britain's follow-the-elephant imperialism. Mark Curtis's *Web of Deceit: Britain's Real Role in the World* (New York: Vintage, 2003) is a courageous attempt in that direction and we highly recommend it. On NATO and Yugoslavia, apart from the seminal work by Susan Woodward, *Balkan Tragedy* (Washington, DC: Brookings Institution, 1995), we recommend the essays edited by Tariq Ali, *Masters of the Universe?* (London: Verso, 2001). For general informative accounts on NATO, see S. Victor Papacosma et al. (eds.), *NATO after Fifty Years* (Lanham, MD: SR Books, 2001) and Ted Galen Carpenter (ed.), *NATO Enters the 21st Century* (London: Frank Cass, 2001).

Most of the books published on the issue of terrorism and America's "war on terror" are either propagandistic or fail to grasp the real problems facing late modern societies, particularly after 9/11. A good collection of essays is edited by Craig Calhoun, Paul Price, and Ashley Timmer, *Understanding September 11* (New York: New Press, 2002). We also recommend David Ray Griffin, *The New Pearl Harbor* (New York: Arris Books, 2004), and Noam Chomsky, *Power and Terror* (New York: Seven Stories Press, 2003). Bülent Gökay and R. B. J. Walker's (eds.) *11 September 2001 War, Terror and Judgement* (London: Frank Cass, 2003) gathers together scholars from Europe, North America, and Asia to offer a series of thoughtful and illuminating analyses of the post-9/11 world. See also Arundhati Roy, *War Talk* (Cambridge, MA: South End Press, 2003). Perceptive essays on 9/11 can also be found in Gokhan Bacik and Bulent Aras (eds.), *September 11 and World Politics* (Istanbul: Fatih University Press, 2004).

Index

About the Authors

VASSILIS K. FOUSKAS is a Senior Lecturer in International Relations at Stirling University. He is the founding editor of the *Journal of Southern Europe and the Balkans* and the author of *Zones of Conflict: U.S. Foreign Policy in the Balkans and Greater Middle East* (2003) and *Italy, Europe, and the Left* (1998).

BÜLENT GÖKAY is a Senior Lecturer in International Relations at Keele University. He is the editor of the Eurasian Studies Network and the author of *The Politics of Caspian Oil* (2001) and co-editor of *Kosovo: Politics of Delusion* (2001) and *11 September 2001: War, Terror, and Judgement* (2003).